The Visual FoxPro©
Report Writer: Pushing it to
the Limit and Beyond

By Cathy Pountney

Hentzenwerke Publishing

Published by:
Hentzenwerke Publishing
980 East Circle Drive
Whitefish Bay WI 53217 USA

Hentzenwerke Publishing books are available through booksellers and directly from the
publisher. Contact Hentzenwerke Publishing at:
414.332.9876
414.332.9463 (fax)
www.hentzenwerke.com
books@hentzenwerke.com

The Visual FoxPro Report Writer: Pushing it to the Limit and Beyond
    By Cathy Pountney
    Technical Editor: Dave Aring
    Copy Editor: Farion Grove

ISBN: 1-930919-25-5

Manufactured in the United States of America.

This book is dedicated to a very special person—my Mom.
When I was in the tenth grade, I had a heart-to-heart discussion
with my Mom about what I wanted to be when I grew up. I was torn between
an Accountant (because I loved number crunching) and an Engineer
(because I loved math and my drafting class). Mom steered me to
something I had never considered—computers.
Thanks, Mom. I owe my entire career to you!

Our Contract with You, The Reader

In which we, the folks who make up Hentzenwerke Publishing, describe what you, the reader, can expect from this book and from us.

Hi there!

I've been writing professionally (in other words, eventually getting a paycheck for my scribbles) since 1974, and writing about software development since 1992. As an author, I've worked with a half-dozen different publishers and corresponded with thousands of readers over the years. As a software developer and all-around geek, I've also acquired a library of more than 100 computer and software-related books.

Thus, when I donned the publisher's cap almost five years ago to produce the *1997 Developer's Guide,* I had some pretty good ideas of what I liked (and didn't like) from publishers, what readers liked and didn't like, and what I, as a reader, liked and didn't like.

Now, with our new titles for 2002, we're entering our fifth season. (For those who are keeping track, the '97 DevGuide was our first, albeit abbreviated, season, the batch of six "Essentials" for Visual FoxPro 6.0 in 1999 was our second, and, in keeping with the sports analogy, the books we published in 2000 and 2001 comprised our third and fourth.)

John Wooden, the famed UCLA basketball coach, posited that teams aren't consistent; they're always getting better—or worse. We'd like to get better…

One of my goals for this season is to build a closer relationship with you, the reader. In order for us to do this, you've got to know what you should expect from us.

- You have the right to expect that your order will be processed quickly and correctly, and that your book will be delivered to you in new condition.

- You have the right to expect that the content of your book is technically accurate and up-to-date, that the explanations are clear, and that the layout is easy to read and follow without a lot of fluff or nonsense.

- You have the right to expect access to source code, errata, FAQs, and other information that's relevant to the book via our Web site.

- You have the right to expect an electronic version of your printed book to be available via our Web site.

- You have the right to expect that, if you report errors to us, your report will be responded to promptly, and that the appropriate notice will be included in the errata and/or FAQs for the book.

Naturally, there are some limits that we bump up against. There are humans involved, and they make mistakes. A book of 500 pages contains, on average, 150,000 words and several megabytes of source code. It's not possible to edit and re-edit multiple times to catch every last misspelling and typo, nor is it possible to test the source code on every permutation of development environment and operating system—and still price the book affordably.

Once printed, bindings break, ink gets smeared, signatures get missed during binding. On the delivery side, Web sites go down, packages get lost in the mail.

Nonetheless, we'll make our best effort to correct these problems—once you let us know about them.

In return, when you have a question or run into a problem, we ask that you first consult the errata and/or FAQs for your book on our Web site. If you don't find the answer there, please e-mail us at **books@hentzenwerke.com** with as much information and detail as possible, including 1) the steps to reproduce the problem, 2) what happened, and 3) what you expected to happen, together with 4) any other relevant information.

I'd like to stress that we need you to communicate questions and problems clearly. For example…

- "Your downloads don't work" isn't enough information for us to help you. "I get a 404 error when I click on the **Download Source Code** link on **http://www.hentzenwerke.com/book/downloads.html**" is something we can help you with.

- "The code in Chapter 10 caused an error" again isn't enough information. "I performed the following steps to run the source code program DisplayTest.PRG in Chapter 10, and I received an error that said 'Variable m.liCounter not found'" is something we can help you with.

We'll do our best to get back to you within a couple of days, either with an answer or at least an acknowledgement that we've received your inquiry and that we're working on it.

On behalf of the authors, technical editors, copy editors, layout artists, graphical artists, indexers, and all the other folks who have worked to put this book in your hands, I'd like to thank you for purchasing this book, and I hope that it will prove to be a valuable addition to your technical library. Please let us know what you think about this book—we're looking forward to hearing from you.

As Groucho Marx once observed, "Outside of a dog, a book is a man's best friend. Inside of a dog, it's too dark to read."

Whil Hentzen
Hentzenwerke Publishing
March 2002

List of Chapters

Table of Contents

Chapter 4: The Data Source   51

Chapter 5: Report Objects   65

Chapter 6: Adding Pizzazz to the Objects 101

Acknowledgements

Boy, I don't even know where to begin with doling out the *thanks*. There are so many people who have helped me along the way that it's hard to thank each and every one of them.

My first *thanks* has to go to Whil Hentzen for giving me the opportunity to write this book. I have always felt passionately about creating reports and this book has given me the opportunity to express that passion as well as teach others how to use the Visual FoxPro Report Writer. I also have to thank Whil for giving me the opportunity to present a Report Writer session at WhilFest 2001. The positive feedback I received from those who attended my sessions just proved to me how eager and willing people are to learn, if given the chance.

My next *thanks* goes to my Technical Editor, Dave Aring. Dave kept me in line and didn't let me get lazy with my writing. He made sure my explanations were clear and accurate. Sometimes I thought he went a little overboard with his suggestions, but after sleeping on them, I usually realized he was right. I also want to thank Dave for all his work on the graphics for this book. He went above and beyond the call of duty!

The Microsoft Visual FoxPro team also deserves a big *thanks* for creating such an awesome product. I recently had the opportunity to spend six months in Redmond working on the Fox Team as a contractor and it was one of the best experiences I've ever had. I gained a lot of respect for everyone on the team. Ricardo Wenger has put together a great team of dedicated individuals who are very passionate about what they do. They truly want to create the best possible product for the Fox Community. I want to thank each and every person on the Fox team for creating a great product and for letting me be a part of it for six months. I really miss you guys!

Speaking of the Fox Community, if you've never gone to a conference or hung out in an online forum such as the Universal Thread, you don't know what you're missing. The entire Fox Community is so willing to help that it'd be a shame to not accept the help. I can't believe it took me 10 years to find out about it. Thanks to everyone in the Fox Community.

Many of the following people have directly helped me with my career and FoxPro knowledge in one way or another. Others have helped me indirectly by offering utilities or providing advice on the Universal Thread. Some have even inspired me by asking questions to which I didn't know the answer, but it motivated me to figure out the answer just for the sake of knowing. There are so many people to thank that I'm sure I'm forgetting to mention somebody, for which I apologize in advance. In any event, here's the long-winded list of names: Rick Bean, Sergey Berezniker, Craig Berntson, Chick Bornheim, Frank Camp, Steve Dingle, Jim Duffy, Markus Egger, Hank Fay, Bob Grommes, John Henn, Ramon F. Jaquez, Carl Karsten, John Koziol, Christof Lange, Andrew MacNeill, Mark McCasland, Larry Miller, Nadya Nosonovsky, Mike Potjer, Ed Rauh, Edhy Rijo, Ted Roche, Steve Sawyer, Rick Schummer, Bob Stone, Rick Strahl, and Hilmar Zonneveld.

Finally, a very special *thanks* goes to Mike Levy. I met Mike at the Chicago O'Hare airport while waiting for my connecting flight to the 1999 DevCon in Palm Springs. Even though I had been programming in FoxPro for 10 years, this was the first conference I had ever attended. I was shy and nervous and had no idea what to expect. I anticipated spending all my non-session hours in my hotel room working on a project. I certainly didn't realize that there was such an awesome Fox Community that gathered at every waking moment. Mike took me under his wing and made it a point to introduce me to as many people as possible. I met so many people that my head was spinning by the end of the conference (and not because of the tequila). By the end of the conference, I realized that the Fox Community was like no other and I felt honored to be a part of it. Needless to say, though, I didn't get any work done on my project. Nonetheless, I am indebted to Mike for opening the door to the Fox Community and will always consider him a very special friend (and an awesome pool player too).

—Cathy Pountney

About the Author

Cathy Pountney is the President of Frontier Software Solutions, Inc., which she founded in 1989. In her 20 years of developing software, she's written applications for a variety of businesses and different vertical markets. When she started her company 13 years ago, she began using Fox products and has since developed a strong passion for the "Fox." Recently, she even had the privilege of working as a contractor onsite in Redmond with the Microsoft Fox Team for six wonderful months. In January 2002, Cathy accepted a full-time position with Optimal Solutions, Inc., where, among other things, she works on the *School Finance 2k* application, which is written completely in Visual FoxPro 7.0 and implemented in numerous school systems throughout Michigan.

In addition to developing software, Cathy has authored several articles for *FoxTalk* and *The Information Systems Consultant.* She also co-authored *Inside FoxPro 2.5 for DOS* many years ago. Cathy is the co-founder of the Grand Rapids Area FoxPro User Group and actively participates on the Universal Thread. She has spoken at several FoxPro user groups across the U.S., at the 2001 Great Lakes Great Database Workshop, and is scheduled to speak at the first Essential Fox Conference in April 2002.

You can contact Cathy at cathy@frontier2000.com, view her Web site at www.frontier2000.com, and view Optimal's Web site at www.optimalinternet.com.

How to Download the Files

Hentzenwerke Publishing generally provides two sets of files to accompany its books. The first is the source code referenced throughout the text. Note that some books do not have source code; in those cases, a placeholder file is provided in lieu of the source code in order to alert you of the fact. The second is the e-book version (or versions) of the book. Depending on the book, we provide e-books in either the compiled HTML Help (.CHM) format, Adobe Acrobat (.PDF) format, or both. Here's how to get them.

Both the source code and e-book file(s) are available for download from the Hentzenwerke Web site. In order to obtain them, follow these instructions:

1. Point your Web browser to **http://www.hentzenwerke.com**.

2. Look for the link that says "Download."

3. A page describing the download process will appear. This page has two sections:

   - **Section 1:** If you were issued a username/password directly from Hentzenwerke Publishing, you can enter them into this page.

   - **Section 2:** If you did not receive a username/password from Hentzenwerke Publishing, don't worry! Just enter your e-mail alias and look for the question about your book. Note that you'll need your physical book when you answer the question.

4. A page that lists the hyperlinks for the appropriate downloads will appear.

Note that the e-book file(s) are covered by the same copyright laws as the printed book. Reproduction and/or distribution of these files is against the law.

If you have questions or problems, the fastest way to get a response is to e-mail us at **books@hentzenwerke.com**.

Chapter 1
Introduction

Reports are key to a successful software application. It could even be argued that both commercial and custom applications can be judged by how well they generate output. After all, it doesn't matter how efficiently the users can enter data, how much information the system can store, or how many complicated calculations the system can process if there's no way to see the final outcome of all that work.

All too often, developers look down on the task of creating reports. In some shops, it's even considered a low-end task that's given to junior developers. I passionately disagree with this philosophy for several reasons.

Reports can be very high-profile and very important to the success of a company. The executives of a company rely on the reports created by your application to make decisions. If the reports you create are difficult to understand—or worse, inaccurate—bad decisions could be made. These bad decisions could even lead to the downfall of the company.

Reports can be internal or external to a company. In other words, some reports are only used within the company. However, in many other situations, reports are used outside of the company and highly affect the business and sales. For example, a report can be a sales proposal for an insurance company. Another example is a financial report given to a company's accountants or auditors. And another example is a 50-page report showing the results of an inspection, for which the client charges big bucks. If these reports do not look professional and are not accurate, the sales and repeat business of that company could be greatly impacted. So considering how important these reports are, do you really want to put a junior programmer on something this important?

Here's another reason why you should consider reports a top priority in any application you develop. Many times, the executives don't use your application on a day-to-day basis. They rely on their staff to do that. The only interaction the executives have with your application is the printed reports that are handed to them on a daily, weekly, and monthly basis. Therefore, the executive's opinion about the software is heavily weighed by what he or she sees. I don't know about you, but that's certainly enough to motivate me to provide top-quality reports in all the applications I develop—especially because the executives are the ones signing my check!

Overview of chapters

Throughout this book you'll see two terms that need a little clarification up front—the Report Designer and the Report Writer. The *Report Designer* is the tool used to create reports from within Visual FoxPro. The *Report Writer* is the Visual FoxPro engine that runs the reports you've created. These two terms are used quite often, so be sure you understand the difference between them.

Wizards

The next chapter, Chapter 2, "The Report Wizard," is dedicated to explaining the Report Wizards. By working through the quick and easy wizards, you'll have a chance to learn about some of the features of Visual FoxPro reports without having to get into the nitty-gritty. It's a great place to start so you're not overwhelmed all at once.

The Report Wizard supplied with Visual FoxPro consists of two separate options: a One-to-Many Report Wizard and a Single-Table Report Wizard. In addition to the Report Wizard, there's also a Label Wizard to assist you in creating labels.

The Report Designer

Chapters 3-8 are dedicated to teaching you how to create reports with the Visual FoxPro Report Designer. You'll start with Chapter 3, "Learning the Basics." This chapter gets you started using the Report Designer. From there, you move on to Chapter 4, "The Data Source," which explains where the data comes from and all the different options you have in making it available for use in the report.

Next, you move on to Chapter 5, "Report Objects," which is the *meat and potatoes* of creating a report. This chapter explains how to put things on the report and move them around. The next chapter, Chapter 6, "Adding Pizzazz to the Objects," explains how to spiff up all the things you put on the report in the previous chapter. This chapter is where you learn how to add finesse to the report.

The next two chapters—Chapter 7, "Data Grouping," and Chapter 8, "Report Variables"—take you deeper into the Report Designer and teach you how to build the complex reports needed to solve many reporting issues of today's applications.

The "after life"

After you've learned *how* to create reports, Chapter 9, "Running Reports," shows you how to run the reports. This chapter also discusses distributing reports with your application and how to give end users the ability to modify reports.

By the time you reach Chapter 10, "Solutions to Real-World Problems," you'll know just about everything there is to know about the Report Writer. This chapter shows you how to pull together all the things you've learned so you can solve some real-world reporting problems. This is one of those chapters you'll read and say to yourself, "Aha!"

The next chapter, Chapter 11, "Hacking the FRX," dives into the inner workings of Visual FoxPro reports. By learning how it works behind the scenes, you gain the advantage of being able to manually manipulate reports into submission with brute force. Sometimes life is not fair and you have to play hardball. By the time you're done with this chapter, you'll know how to take the gloves off and rumble.

The Label Designer

Labels are nothing more than reports—on tiny paper. All you have to do is tell Visual FoxPro what size the label is, and from there, it's practically the same as designing a report. Chapter 12, "Labels," walks you through creating labels and points out the few differences between reports and labels.

The "other world"

The final chapter, Chapter 13, "Beyond the VFP Report Writer," is dedicated to exposing you to several different third-party tools and utilities. Some of them work with the Visual FoxPro Report Writer, and some of them are used in place of the Visual FoxPro Report Writer. The idea behind this chapter is to make you aware of other options so you can make the best decision possible for all your reporting needs.

Parts of a report

Visual FoxPro reports are *driven* by a single table or cursor. For each record in the table or cursor, one Detail band is generated on the report. You must have at least one record in the table or cursor for the report to print. If no records exist in the table or cursor, no report is printed.

 Reports consist of several different parts, called *bands*. Some reports only contain a few bands, and other, more complex reports contain all the possible bands. **Figure 1** and **Figure 2** show a sample report with all the possible bands of a Visual FoxPro report. This report, BANDS.FRX, is included in the source code available with this book. The following list explains what those bands are and when they're printed.

- **Title band:** The Title band is printed once, and only once, at the beginning of the report. It can appear on its own page, or other bands may immediately follow the Title band. The Title band is an optional band you can add to a report.

- **Page Header band:** The Page Header band appears at the top of each and every page. This band is mandatory; however, you don't have to put anything in it, and you can define it with a zero height.

- **Column Header band:** The Column Header band appears at the top of each and every column set. A *column set* may consist of several columns of data for an individual record, and some reports may have *multiple column sets,* such as 2-up mailing labels. This band is automatically added to a report when the report is defined as having multiple column sets. For reports with a single column set, this band does not appear.

- **Group Header band:** The Group Header band is added to a report whenever you define a Data Grouping. It prints once at the beginning of a new Data Grouping, and optionally, can be defined to repeat when the Data Group overflows to another page. In an overflow situation, the Page Header band prints first, followed by the Column Header band (if applicable), and then the Group Header band is printed. For each Data Group defined on a report, one Group Header band is created. Therefore, it's possible to have multiple Group Header bands.

- **Detail band:** The Detail band is printed once for each record in the table that drives the report. You can, however, run a report with the summary option, which suppresses the Detail band altogether.

- **Group Footer band:** The Group Footer band is added to a report whenever you define a Data Grouping. It prints once following the last Detail band of a particular

Data Grouping. For each Data Group defined on a report, one Group Footer band is created. Therefore, it's possible to have multiple Group Footer bands.

- **Column Footer band:** The Column Footer band appears at the bottom of each and every column set. This band is automatically added to a report when the report is defined as having multiple column sets. For reports having a single column set, this band does not appear.

- **Page Footer band:** The Page Footer band appears at the bottom of each and every page. This band is mandatory; however, you don't have to put anything in it, and you can define it with a zero height.

- **Summary band:** The Summary band prints only once after the final Detail band and after any final Group Footer bands. Notice that the Summary band prints before the Column Footer and Page Footer bands. You can also indicate that you'd rather have the Summary band print on its own page after all other bands, in which case no Page Header or Page Footer band prints with the Summary band.

General information

This book is based on Visual FoxPro 7.0, prior to the release of Service Pack 1. However, the Report Writer hasn't changed much over the years. In fact, there's really not a whole lot of difference between today's Report Writer and the legacy FoxPro 2.x Report Writer. Much of what you'll learn in this book can be applied to older versions of the Report Writer.

Throughout this book, you'll see the following icons used to point out special notes, tips, and bug alerts.

This icon is used to point out information specific to FoxPro 2.x. It may be a simple note telling you a feature didn't exist in FoxPro 2.x, or it may be a tip on how to simulate a missing feature. I also use this icon to point out any major differences between the 2.x version and the current version that might trip you up when following along.

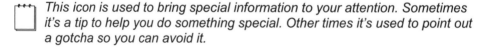

This icon is used to bring special information to your attention. Sometimes it's a tip to help you do something special. Other times it's used to point out a gotcha so you can avoid it.

Bug Alert!

This icon is used to point out bugs that exist in the Visual FoxPro Report Writer so you can work around them.

Tasmanian Traders

100 Main Street
Anytown, MI 99999
(800) 555-1234

} Title band

[Customer List by Country]   } Page Header band

Company Name	Company Name
Argentina } Group Header band	**Brazil** (continued)
Cactus Comidas para llevar	Ricardo Adocicados
Océano Atlántico Ltda.	Tradiçao Hipermercados
Rancho grande	Wellington Importadora
3 customers in Argentina } Group Footer band	*9 customers in Brazil*
Austria	**Canada**
Ernst Handel	Bottom-Dollar Markets
Piccolo und mehr	Laughing Bacchus Wine Cellars
2 customers in Austria	Mère Paillarde
	3 customers in Canada
Belgium	
Maison Dewey	**Denmark**
Suprêmes délices	Simons bistro
2 customers in Belgium	Vaffeljernet
	2 customers in Denmark
Brazil	
Comércio Mineiro	**Finland**
Familia Arquibaldo } Detail band	Wartian Herkku
Gourmet Lanchonetes } Detail band	Wilman Kala
Hanari Carnes } Detail band	*2 customers in Finland*
Que Delícia	
Queen Cozinha	

03/15/2002	Page Footer band	**Page** 1

Figure 1. *The first page of this report shows all but the Summary band.*

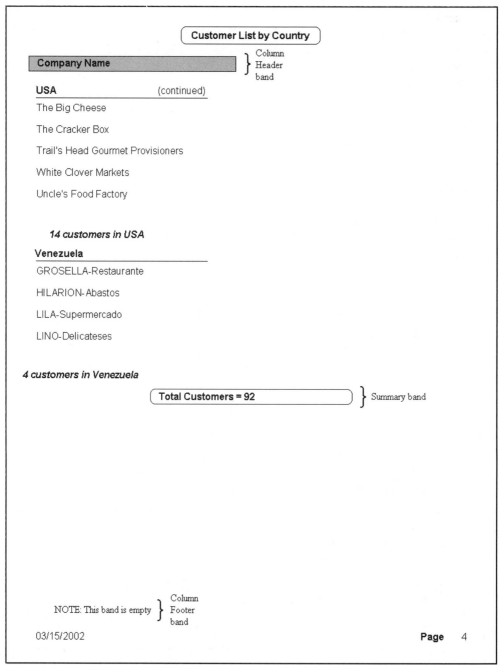

Figure 2. *The last page of this report shows the Summary band. Also notice that no Title band prints on this page.*

Toolbars

Several toolbars are used in the Report Designer. Many of them are specific to a particular chapter and are discussed when appropriate. However, there's one general toolbar, the Report Designer toolbar, which can be used to access many options and other toolbars used within the VFP Report Designer.

You can display the Report Designer toolbar (shown in **Figure 3**) using one of two methods. The first method is to select View | Toolbars... from the main VFP Menu bar. This invokes the Toolbars dialog, from which you can select the Report Designer option and then select the OK button. The second method is to right-click on an unused portion of any *docked* toolbar and then select Report Designer.

Figure 3. *Use the Report Designer toolbar to access many options and toolbars used within the VFP Report Designer.*

The Report Designer toolbar consists of the following five buttons, from left to right.

- **Data Grouping:** This button is used to invoke the same Data Grouping dialog that can also be invoked by selecting Report | Data Grouping... from the main VFP Menu bar. This dialog is discussed in greater detail in Chapter 7, "Data Grouping."

- **Data Environment:** This button is used to invoke the same Data Environment that can also be invoked by selecting View | Data Environment... from the main VFP Menu bar. The Data Environment is discussed in greater detail in Chapter 4, "The Data Source."

- **Report Controls Toolbar:** This button is used to toggle the same Report Controls toolbar that can also be toggled by selecting View | Report Controls Toolbar from the main VFP Menu bar. The Report Controls toolbar is discussed in greater detail in Chapter 5, "Report Objects."

- **Color Palette Toolbar:** This button is used to toggle the same Color Palette toolbar that can also be toggled by selecting View | Color Palette Toolbar from the main VFP Menu bar. The Color Palette toolbar is discussed in greater detail in Chapter 6, "Adding Pizzazz to the Objects."

- **Layout Toolbar:** This button is used to toggle the same Layout toolbar that can also be toggled by selecting View | Layout Toolbar from the main VFP Menu bar. The Layout toolbar is discussed in greater detail in Chapter 6, "Adding Pizzazz to the Objects."

Enjoy!

I hope you enjoy this book and learn tons of new things. My goal in writing this book is to teach you how to get the most out of the Visual FoxPro Report Writer so you can create awesome reports for all your applications. I can't stress enough how important reports are to the usefulness and image of a final application.

Chapter 2
The Report Wizard

Visual FoxPro provides several different wizards to help you create tables, forms, queries, and so on. The great news for you is that an excellent Report Wizard is also included in the product… at no extra charge! The wizard helps you create reports driven from a single table as well as reports created from a parent-child set of tables. This chapter walks you through the basic steps of using the Report Wizard to create your first few reports.

The Report Wizard supplied with Visual FoxPro consists of two separate options: a One-to-Many Report Wizard and a Single-Table Report Wizard. These tools assist you in creating simple reports inside of VFP. You can use the wizard to create reports that are meant to be run as-is, or you can use the wizard to create a report that you later edit with the VFP Report Designer to add more features or complex options.

Starting the Report Wizard

The first step in using the Report Wizard is choosing which type of report you want to create. Select Tools | Wizards | Report from the main VFP Menu bar to display the dialog shown in **Figure 1**.

Figure 1. *Use the Wizard Selection dialog to choose whether you want to create a one-to-many report or a single-file report.*

You can create two different types of reports with the Report Wizard. The first type is a One-To-Many report. This type of report is driven from a parent-child set of tables. For example, a Customer table (the parent) and an Invoice table (the child) are used to create a report showing each customer and all the applicable invoices for each customer. The second type of report is much simpler and is created from a single table. For example, a simple customer listing of names and addresses created from the Customer table would qualify as this type of report.

Because the first option on the Wizard Selection dialog, One-to-Many Report Wizard, is the more complex of the two, I'll describe that second. First, I'll show you how to create a single-file report. I'll have you skip several of the dialogs along the way to keep this first report as simple as possible. Once you get the hang of how the wizard works, I'll go back and walk you through all of the dialogs and options in the single-file Report Wizard. At that point, you'll be ready to tackle a one-to-many report.

Creating a single-file report

Select "Report Wizard" from the Wizard Selection dialog and select OK to display the Report Wizard dialog shown in **Figure 2**.

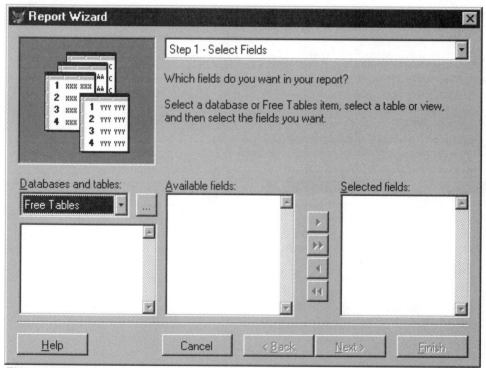

Figure 2. The Report Wizard dialog is your starting point for creating single-table reports.

Creating a single-table report with the wizard is a six-step process. The Back and Next buttons at the bottom of this dialog allow you to navigate through the six different steps. The Finish button jumps straight to the sixth step regardless of which step you're on and lets you finish the report. You can also navigate to a specific step by selecting that step from the drop-down combo box at the top of the dialog. The Cancel button exits the wizard and returns you to the VFP Command Window.

Selecting fields

Step 1 of the wizard is to identify which table drives this report and which fields in that table should appear on the report. If you don't have a database open, "Free Tables" appears by itself in the "Databases and tables" drop-down combo box on the left of the dialog. If you happen to have any databases open, they appear in the drop-down combo box along with "Free Tables."

Select the ellipse button (...) and find the Customer table in the TasTrade sample data (included with VFP or with the downloads for this book). This selects the TasTrade database and shows the tables within the database in the list box. It also shows the available fields for the Customer table as shown in **Figure 3**.

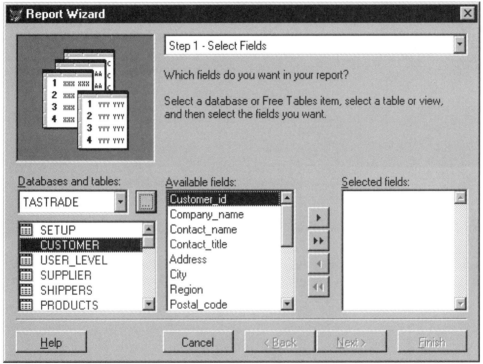

Figure 3. The tables in the selected database are shown along with the available fields in the selected table.

Select the Customer_id, Company_name, and Phone fields from the list of available fields. Select a field by double-clicking the field or highlighting the field and selecting the button with the right-arrow on it. The order in which the items are listed in the "Selected fields" list determines the order in which the items appear on the report. To change the order of the selected fields, click and drag the appropriate Mover command button up or down through the list.

Finishing the report

Once you have the fields selected for the report, select the Finish button to jump straight to the last step of the wizard (see **Figure 4**).

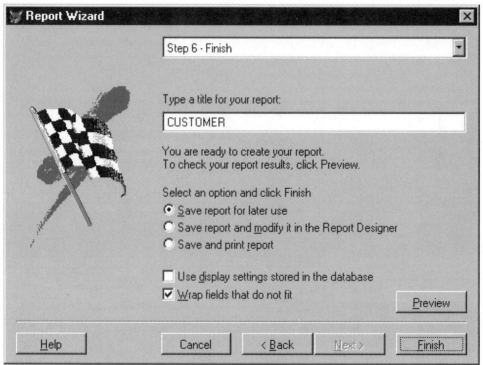

Figure 4. Finishing the report is quick and easy.

Notice that the name of the table, CUSTOMER, is already entered for you as the title that appears at the top of the report. You can accept this or change it to whatever you'd like. For this sample, enter "Customer Phone List" (without the quotes) as the title. Next, select the "Save and print report" option and select the Finish button to bring up the Save As dialog. Select a directory and enter a file name for this report (I called mine CustPhone). The wizard generates the report metadata, saves it to a report file, and then prints the report. Page 1 of the four-page report is shown in **Figure 5**. Wasn't that simple? In just a matter of a few minutes, you created your first report.

Customer Phone List
03/15/2002

Customer ID	Company Name	Phone
ALFKI	Alfreds Futterkiste	030-0074321
ANATR	Ana Trujillo Emparedados y helados	(5) 555-4729
ANTON	Antonio Moreno Taquería	(5) 555-3932
AROUT	Around the Horn	(71) 555-7788
BERGS	Berglunds snabbköp	0921-12 34 65
BLAUS	Blauer See Delikatessen	0621-08460
BLONP	Blondel père et fils	88.60.15.31
BOLID	Bólido Comidas preparadas	(91) 555 22 82
BONAP	Bon app'	91.24.45.40
BOTTM	Bottom-Dollar Markets	(604) 555-4729
BSBEV	B's Beverages	(71) 555-1212
CACTU	Cactus Comidas para llevar	(1) 135-5555
CENTC	Centro comercial Moctezuma	(5) 555-3392
CHOPS	Chop-suey Chinese	0452-076545
COMMI	Comércio Mineiro	(11) 555-7647
CONSH	Consolidated Holdings	(71) 555-2282
DRACD	Drachenblut Delikatessen	0241-039123
DUMON	Du monde entier	40.67.88.88
EASTC	Eastern Connection	(71) 555-0297
ERNSH	Ernst Handel	7675-3425
FAMIA	Familia Arquibaldo	(11) 555-9857
FISSA	FISSA Fabrica Inter. Salchichas S.A.	(91) 555 94 44
FOLIG	Folies gourmandes	20.16.10.16
FOLKO	Folk och fä HB	0695-34 67 21

Page 1

***Figure 5**. This simple report was created with the Visual FoxPro Report Wizard in just a few minutes.*

The rest of the Report Wizard

By now you're probably dying to know what all those skipped steps are and what other features the Report Wizard offers you. Well, hang on... you're about to find out!

Step 2—Group Records

The second step of the wizard is called "Group Records." It allows you to tell the wizard to group the records. The wizard automatically takes care of sorting the records by adding an index to the table based on the groups you've defined. Therefore, you *must* have exclusive use of the table at the time you're creating the report. If you don't, you'll receive an error message that varies depending on whether the table is a free table or belongs to a database container. Free tables generate an "Unable to open table exclusive" error message. Contained tables generate the error message "The DBC containing the selected table was previously opened non-exclusively and the field(s) you chose for sorting are not in an existing index tag. Please select field(s) which already have an index tag or exit the wizard and reopen the DBC exclusively."

> *I want to reemphasize what I just said. The Report Wizard may add a new index to your table based on the selected grouping. Months later when you look at your tables and database and are scratching your head because you don't remember creating a particular index—the answer may be that* you didn't... *the* Report Wizard *did!*

You may define up to three different levels of grouping with the wizard. You may also indicate special summary options such as subtotals for each group.

To follow along with this example, use the wizard to start a new single-table report. In Step 1, select the Customer table and select the following fields: Country, Customer_id, Max_order_amt, Min_order_amt, and Sales_region. Select the Next button to display the Step 2 dialog shown in **Figure 6**.

Select the Country field from the first drop-down combo box. This tells the wizard to sort and group the records based on the country. If you want additional levels of grouping, select the fields in the second and third drop-down combo boxes in a similar fashion. For example, you may want to see data grouped by Country, then State within each Country, then City within each State.

For this example, you're grouping the records based on the entire contents of the Country field, but this isn't the only choice you have available. The wizard also allows you to group the records based on the first letter, the first two letters, and up to the first five letters of the field. This may be done by selecting the Grouping options... button, which displays the dialog shown in **Figure 7**. An example of when you would use this option is a customer phone list. Similar to a phone book, you would group the records by the first letter of the name so you see a slight break in the report for each letter of the alphabet.

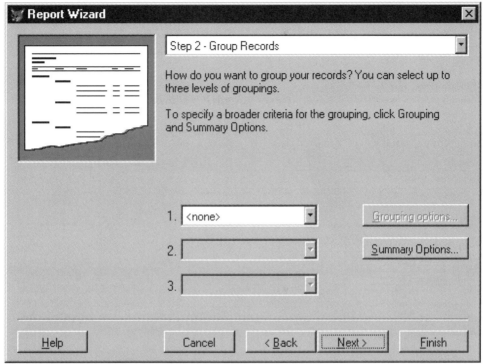

Figure 6. *Step 2 of the Report Wizard allows you to choose up to three different levels of grouping as well as special summary options.*

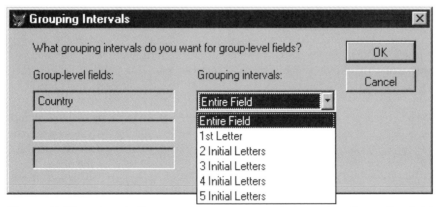

Figure 7. *The wizard allows you to group records based on the entire field or just the first character, the second character, on up to the fifth character of the field.*

Now that you have the records grouped by country, it's time to put some special summary options on the report. Select the Summary Options… button to display the Summary Options dialog. **Figure 8** shows the Summary Options dialog with all the necessary options selected to create the report shown in **Figure 9**.

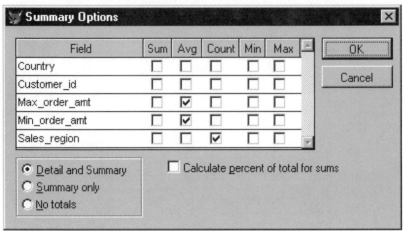

Figure 8. The Summary Options dialog allows you to add special calculations to the report as well as choose how much information to print on the report.

For each field on the report, you may choose up to five different calculations.

- **Sum:** Checking this box provides a subtotal of this field for each group and a grand total of all the records at the end of the report. In addition to the sum, you may check the "Calculate percent of total for sums" check box. This tells the wizard to add an additional figure for each group subtotal. This figure is the percentage of the overall total that is represented by this group.

- **Avg:** Checking this box provides an average of this field for each group and an overall average of all the records at the end of the report.

- **Count:** Checking this box provides a count of the records in each group and a total count of all the records at the end of the report.

- **Min:** Checking this box provides the lowest value of this field for each group as well as the overall lowest value at the end of the report.

- **Max:** Checking this box provides the highest value of this field for each group as well as the overall highest value at the end of the report.

CUSTOMER

03/16/2002

Country	Customer Id	Max Order Amt	Min Order Amt	Sales Region
Argentina				
	CACTU	5,800.00	0.00	
	OCEAN	2,500.00	900.00	
	RANCH	5,700.00	2,900.00	
Count for Argentina:				3
Average for Argentina:		4,666.66	1,266.66	
Austria				
	ERNSH	122,900.00	0.00	
	PICCO	29,100.00	400.00	
Count for Austria:				2
Average for Austria:		76,000.00	200.00	

group subtotals (Argentina: 3)
group subtotals (Austria: 2)

Venezuela				
	GROSR	3,600.00	1,000.00	
	HILAA	28,780.00	0.00	
	LILAS	22,300.00	4,800.00	
	LINOD	21,700.00	4,600.00	
Count for Venezuela:				4
Average for Venezuela:		19,095.00	2,600.00	
Total Count:				92
Average:		18,153.33	2,099.45	

group subtotals (Venezuela: 4)
report totals (92)

Figure 9. This report was created with the wizard using groups and summary options.

In addition to choosing calculations, you may also choose which lines appear on the report.

- **Detail and Summary:** This option prints the group description on a line by itself, followed by a line for each detail record, followed by a summary line for the special calculations chosen. If no calculations are chosen, a blank line is still printed after the details and before the start of the next group.

- **Summary only:** In my opinion, there's a bug with how this option works. The title indicates that only the summary line for each group prints. However, that's not always the case. If you've selected any fields other than the grouped fields, the output you get from this option is exactly the same as the output from the "No totals" option. If you've only selected grouped fields, you get a summary version, but no special calculations appear. This option is *probably* meant to work in conjunction with the SUMMARY clause of the REPORT FORM command, which is discussed later in Chapter 9, "Running Reports."

- **No totals:** This option is similar to the "Detail and Summary" option, with the exception that no summary line is printed after the end of a group. This means that if you've chosen any special calculations, you should not choose this option because it suppresses those calculations.

 Bug Alert! *In my opinion, there's a bug with how the "Summary only" option works, but officially, I don't know whether Microsoft considers this to be a* bug *or a* feature.

Step 3—Choose Report Style

Step 3 is a simple step that allows you to choose which layout you want. The wizard gives you five different choices: Executive, Ledger, Presentation, Banded, and Casual. **Figures 10-14** show examples of the same report created with each of the different styles.

Customer - Executive
11/19/2001

Customer Id	Company Name	Phone
ALFKI	Alfreds Futterkiste	030-0074321
ANATR	Ana Trujillo Emparedados y helados	(5) 555-4729
ANTON	Antonio Moreno Taquería	(5) 555-3932
AROUT	Around the Horn	(71) 555-7788
BERGS	Berglunds snabbköp	0921-12 34 65
BLAUS	Blauer See Delikatessen	0621-08460

Figure 10. The Executive style uses a simple Arial font and keeps the report neat and clean.

Customer - Ledger
11/19/2001

Customer Id	Company Name	Phone
ALFKI	Alfreds Futterkiste	030-0074321
ANATR	Ana Trujillo Emparedados y helados	(5) 555-4729
ANTON	Antonio Moreno Taquería	(5) 555-3932
AROUT	Around the Horn	(71) 555-7788
BERGS	Berglunds snabbköp	0921-12 34 65
BLAUS	Blauer See Delikatessen	0621-08460
BLONP	Blondel père et fils	88.60.15.31
BOLID	Bólido Comidas preparadas	(91) 555 22 82
BONAP	Bon app'	91.24.45.40
BOTTM	Bottom-Dollar Markets	(604) 555-4729

Figure 11. The Ledger style uses a smaller font and uses horizontal lines between each row and vertical lines between each column.

Customer - Presentation
11/19/2001

Customer Id	Company Name	Phone
ALFKI	Alfreds Futterkiste	030-0074321
ANATR	Ana Trujillo Emparedados y helados	(5) 555-4729
ANTON	Antonio Moreno Taquería	(5) 555-3932
AROUT	Around the Horn	(71) 555-7788
BERGS	Berglunds snabbköp	0921-12 34 65
BLAUS	Blauer See Delikatessen	0621-08460
BLONP	Blondel père et fils	88.60.15.31
BOLID	Bólido Comidas preparadas	(91) 555 22 82

Figure 12. The Presentation style is similar to the Executive style, but it uses a smaller font.

Customer - Banded		
11/19/2001		
Customer Id	Company Name	Phone
ALFKI	Alfreds Futterkiste	030-0074321
ANATR	Ana Trujillo Emparedados y helados	(5) 555-4729
ANTON	Antonio Moreno Taquería	(5) 555-3932
AROUT	Around the Horn	(71) 555-7788
BERGS	Berglunds snabbköp	0921-12 34 65
BLAUS	Blauer See Delikatessen	0621-08460
BLONP	Blondel père et fils	88.60.15.31

Figure 13. The Banded style uses shading on alternate lines to give the effect of greenbar paper.

Customer - Casual		
11/19/2001		
Customer Id	Company Name	Phone
ALFKI	Alfreds Futterkiste	030-0074321
ANATR	Ana Trujillo Emparedados y helados	(5) 555-4729
ANTON	Antonio Moreno Taquería	(5) 555-3932
AROUT	Around the Horn	(71) 555-7788
BERGS	Berglunds snabbköp	0921-12 34 65
BLAUS	Blauer See Delikatessen	0621-08460
BLONP	Blondel père et fils	88.60.15.31
BOLID	Bólido Comidas preparadas	(91) 555 22 82

Figure 14. The Casual style is much less formal and uses the Comic Sans MS font.

> *In addition to the five built-in styles, you can also define your own custom styles for the Report Wizard to use. See Chapter 10, "Solutions to Real-World Problems," for more information on how to do this.*

Step 4—Define Report Layout

In Step 4, there are three different options available in the Define Report Layout dialog as shown in **Figure 15**. The first option is the number of columns. The second option is the field layout, and the third option is the orientation.

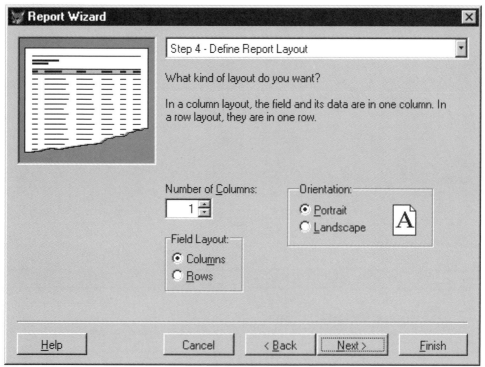

Figure 15. *The Define Report Layout dialog allows you to indicate the number of columns, the field layout, and the orientation.*

The number of columns is somewhat misleading. It is *not* the actual number of columns on the report. That's determined by the number of fields you selected to display on the report. This option refers to the *sets of columns* on the report. In essence, it's similar to printing labels where the labels are 2-up or 3-up on the paper. Selecting a number other than 1 tells the wizard to print the data 2-up or 3-up or whatever number you give it. **Figure 16** shows an example of a customer listing that has two columns.

> *Note: The columns option is not available if you've chosen any groups in Step 2.*

The field layout option allows you to indicate whether you want each field as a separate column (which is the default) or whether you want each field on its own row. All the examples shown in this chapter so far have been created with the Columns option. **Figure 17** shows an example created with the Rows option.

Customers (2-up)
03/16/2002

Company Name	Company Name
Alfreds Futterkiste	Folies gourmandes
Ana Trujillo Emparedados y helados	Folk och fä HB
Antonio Moreno Taquería	France restauration
Around the Horn	Franchi S.p.A.
B's Beverages	Frankenversand
Berglunds snabbköp	Furia Bacalhau e Frutos do Mar
Blauer See Delikatessen	GROSELLA-Restaurante
Blondel père et fils	Galería del gastrónomo
Bon app'	Godos Cocina Típica
Bottom-Dollar Markets	Gourmet Lanchonetes
Bólido Comidas preparadas	Great Lakes Food Market
Cactus Comidas para llevar	HILARION-Abastos
Centro comercial Moctezuma	Hanari Carnes
Chop-suey Chinese	Hungry Coyote Import Store
Comércio Mineiro	Hungry Owl All-Night Grocers
Consolidated Holdings	Island Trading
Die Wandernde Kuh	Königlich Essen
Drachenblut Delikatessen	LILA-Supermercado
Du monde entier	LINO-Delicateses
Eastern Connection	La corne d'abondance
Ernst Handel	La maison d'Asie
FISSA Fabrica Inter. Salchichas S.A.	Laughing Bacchus Wine Cellars
Familia Arquibaldo	Lazy K Kountry Store

Page 1

Figure 16. *This customer listing was created with the wizard by selecting two columns in the Design Report Layout step.*

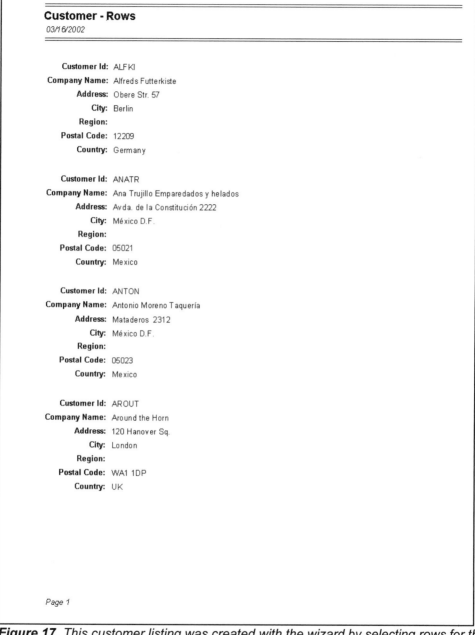

Customer - Rows
03/16/2002

Customer Id: ALFKI
Company Name: Alfreds Futterkiste
Address: Obere Str. 57
City: Berlin
Region:
Postal Code: 12209
Country: Germany

Customer Id: ANATR
Company Name: Ana Trujillo Emparedados y helados
Address: Avda. de la Constitución 2222
City: México D.F.
Region:
Postal Code: 05021
Country: Mexico

Customer Id: ANTON
Company Name: Antonio Moreno Taquería
Address: Mataderos 2312
City: México D.F.
Region:
Postal Code: 05023
Country: Mexico

Customer Id: AROUT
Company Name: Around the Horn
Address: 120 Hanover Sq.
City: London
Region:
Postal Code: WA1 1DP
Country: UK

Page 1

Figure 17. *This customer listing was created with the wizard by selecting rows for the Field Layout option in the Design Report Layout step.*

The orientation option allows you to choose whether you want the report printed in portrait mode or landscape mode. Portrait mode (up and down) means the shorter edge of the paper is on top and the longer edge of the paper is on the side. Landscape mode (side-to-side) means the longer edge of the paper is on the top and the shorter edge of the paper is on the side.

Step 5—Sort Records

The fifth step is where you tell the wizard how you want the records sorted (see **Figure 18**). By default, the records appear on the report in the order they were entered into the table. Most of the time, this isn't how you want to view them. Usually, you want the report sorted by at least one field. For example, you might want a customer list sorted by the customer name or the customer ID.

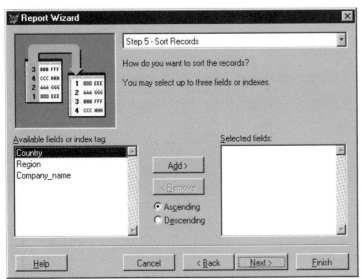

Figure 18. Step 5 of the Report Wizard allows you to indicate how you want the records sorted.

More than one field may be used for sorting, as shown in **Figure 19**. In this example, the report is first sorted by Country and then by Region within each Country. Note that the position of the columns is irrelevant to the sorting order. I just chose to put the columns in the same order as the fields I selected for sorting. You may choose up to three fields to sort by.

This report has the items sorted in ascending order, but you could have just as easily selected descending from the dialog. For example, you may want to print a report of accounting transactions and sort them by date in descending order. This allows you to see the most recent transactions first.

Keep in mind that if you've selected any groups in Step 2 (Group Records), the records are automatically sorted by the groups. Therefore, you don't have to enter those fields again here. However, you may select some additional fields for sorting within the groups. For example, in Figure 9, the records are grouped by Country, and within each country the records are sorted by Customer ID. When I created this report with the wizard, I only selected the

Customer ID field in Step 5 because I knew the grouping options would take care of sorting the records by Country.

Customer (sorting)
03/16/2002

Country	Region	Company Name
Argentina		Cactus Comidas para llevar
Argentina		Océano Atlántico Ltda.
Argentina		Rancho grande
Austria		Ernst Handel
Austria		Piccolo und mehr
Belgium		Maison Dewey
Belgium		Suprêmes délices
Brazil	RJ	Hanari Carnes
Brazil	RJ	Que Delícia
Brazil	RJ	Ricardo Adocicados
Brazil	SP	Comércio Mineiro
Brazil	SP	Família Arquibaldo
Brazil	SP	Gourmet Lanchonetes
Brazil	SP	Queen Cozinha
Brazil	SP	Tradiçao Hipermercados
Brazil	SP	Wellington Importadora
Canada	BC	Bottom-Dollar Markets
Canada	BC	Laughing Bacchus Wine Cellars
Canada	Québec	Mère Paillarde
Denmark		Simons bistro
Denmark		Vaffeljernet
Finland		Wartian Herkku
Finland		Wilman Kala
France		Blondel père et fils

Page 1

Figure 19. *This customer list shows an example of sorting by two fields: Country and Region.*

Step 6—Finish

Whew... the final step! This is it. A few more questions and you're done with this wizard.

The first thing I want to point out on this dialog (see **Figure 20**) is the Preview button in the lower right corner. Clicking this button displays the report on the screen. This allows you to look it over and make sure it's exactly what you want before you finalize the report. If it's not exactly what you want, you can go back through any of the previous steps and change the information. You can keep doing this over and over again until you press the Finish button.

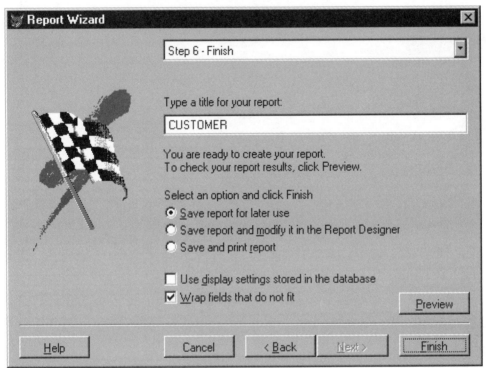

Figure 20. The final step in the wizard allows you to set a few miscellaneous options and save the report.

When previewing the report, the Print Preview toolbar (see **Figure 21**) appears on the screen as a separate window or on a toolbar docked somewhere on the screen, depending on how it was last used in VFP. This toolbar allows you to navigate through the report, change the size of the display, and print the report to the printer using the following buttons.

Figure 21. The Print Preview toolbar can appear as a window by itself or within a toolbar docked somewhere on the screen.

- **First Page:** This option displays the first page of the report on the screen. If you're already on the first page, this option is disabled.

- **Previous Page:** This option displays the previous page of the report on the screen. If you're already on the first page, this option is disabled.

- **Go to Page:** This option displays the dialog shown in **Figure 22**. Enter the page number you wish to jump to and select OK. If you enter a page number greater than the number of pages on the report, the last page is displayed. Selecting Cancel from this dialog returns to the preview and does not move to a different page.

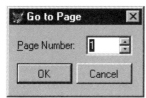

Figure 22. The Go to Page dialog allows you to jump to any page in the report.

- **Next Page:** This option displays the next page of the report on the screen. If you're already on the last page, this option is disabled.

- **Last Page:** This option displays the last page of the report on the screen. If you're already on the last page, this option is disabled.

- **Zoom:** This option allows you to choose how big or small the report should be on the screen (see **Figure 23**). You may choose 100%, 75%, 50%, 25%, 10%, or Zoom. Zoom shrinks the report so the entire page displays on the screen.

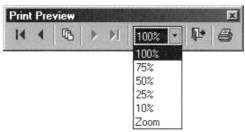

Figure 23. The Zoom drop-down combo box allows you to select the size of the report displayed on the screen.

- **Close Preview:** This option clears the report from the screen and closes the Print Preview dialog.

- **Print Report:** This option sends the report to the default printer, and then closes the Print Preview.

As discussed earlier in this chapter, the text box at the top of the Finish dialog lets you enter a title for the report. By default, the wizard enters the name of the table that drives this report. You can accept the default or enter your own title.

There are three different options available for saving the report.

- **Save report for later use:** This option allows you to save the report to disk. Once the report is saved, it is a normal VFP report and may be edited or run at will.

- **Save report and modify it in the Report Designer:** This option saves the report and then brings up the Visual FoxPro Report Designer. Once you're in the Report Designer, you may edit the report like any other VFP report.

- **Save and print report:** This option saves the report and then prints a copy to the printer.

The last two check boxes on the Finish dialog are miscellaneous settings. The first, "Use display settings stored in the database," controls how each field or heading is displayed. If this box is checked, the wizard uses all format, input mask, and caption settings that have been defined for the fields in the table in the database. If this box is not checked, no formatting is used and the caption matches the field names.

The second check box, "Wrap fields that do not fit," determines what the wizard does with fields that don't fit on the report. If you have selected too many columns for the width of the page, the wizard drops the extra fields off the report if this box is not checked. If it is checked, the wizard wraps those extra fields on the next line and continues in this manner until all fields fit on the report.

The final word

This is it! You've mastered all six steps and you're ready to finish the report. Select the Finish button and you're done. The report is saved, and depending on which save option you chose, it may print or the Report Designer may be invoked for further editing. Nevertheless, you're done with this report.

I want to stress that once a wizard report is saved, it is like any other VFP report. There is nothing special about the report when it has been generated with the wizard. From this point forward, it is a regular report and you may edit or run the report like any other VFP report.

Now that you're an expert with the single-table wizard, it's time to tackle the One-to-Many Report Wizard. Hang on... here we go!

The One-to-Many Report Wizard

So what *is* a one-to-many report? Well, it's really quite simple. It means the report is driven by two tables, a parent table and a child table. For each record in the parent table (the *one* in one-to-many) there may be one or more (*many*) records in the child table. A report on customer orders is the example I'm going to use to demonstrate how the One-to-Many Report Wizard works.

The Orders table contains one record for every order. Each record contains basic information about the order such as Order Number, Order Date, and Customer ID. The Order

Line Items table contains one record for each line on the order and contains fields such as Order Number, Line Number, Part Number, Quantity, and Unit Price.

Just as with the Single-Table Report Wizard, the One-to-Many Report Wizard uses a six-step process to generate the report. However, not all of the steps are the same. The first step in the Single-Table Report Wizard is to select the table. In the One-to-Many Report Wizard, this step is broken out into three different steps: Select the parent table, select the child table, and select the relation.

Step 1 is shown in **Figure 24**. Select which table is the parent table. Then use the arrow buttons to select the fields you want to appear on the report.

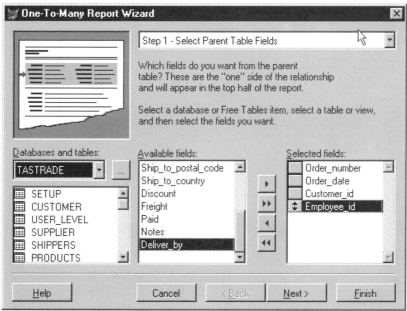

Figure 24. *Step 1 allows you to select the parent table and which fields in that table you want displayed on the report.*

Once you've selected the parent table, you're ready to go on to Step 2 and select the child table (see **Figure 25**). Select the table you want used as the child and use the arrow buttons to select which fields you want displayed on the report.

Now that you've told the One-to-Many Report Wizard which table is the parent table and which table is the child table, you have to tell it how the two tables are related. This is done in Step 3 (see **Figure 26**). The parent table appears on the left side of the dialog and the child table appears on the right side of the dialog. The wizard makes an attempt to find a matching field in each table and displays that as the default. In this example, the wizard was able to determine that the order_id field exists in both tables so it uses that on both sides of the relation. If this wasn't the situation, you could use the drop-down combo boxes on either side to choose the fields that link the two tables together.

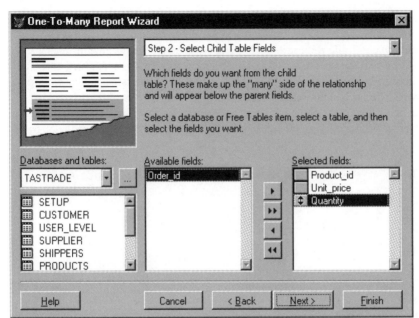

Figure 25. Step 2 allows you to select the child table and which fields in that table you want displayed on the report.

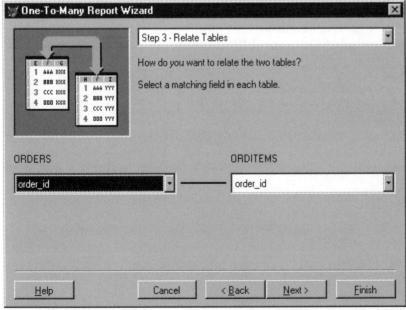

Figure 26. Step 3 is where you tell the wizard how the parent and child tables are related.

Step 4 of the One-to-Many Report Wizard is where you select how you want the records sorted. For the most part, this is the same as Step 5 in the single-table wizard, so I won't bother repeating it all here. Refer to "Step 5—Sort Records" earlier in this chapter for more information. The only difference to keep in mind is that with this dialog, in addition to the list of fields to choose from, the list also includes *indexes* of the parent table. The fields are listed first, followed by a horizontal line, and then followed by the indexes. Each index is identified with an asterisk (*) after the name to distinguish it from a field. To follow along with the Order example I'm creating, select the order_number* index from the list for sorting this report.

Bug Alert! *There's a bug in the One-to-Many Report Wizard that sometimes causes the sort order to be set improperly. It seems to occur when the table has a descending index, which you select as the sort order. The wizard incorrectly sorts the data in ascending order.*

Step 5 (see **Figure 27**) is used to choose the report layout. In essence, this is a combination of three different steps in the Single-Table Report Wizard: Step 2—Group Records, Step 3— – Choose Report Style, and Step 4—Define Report Layout. First, you select the style (see Figures 10-14 earlier in this chapter for examples). Next, you select the orientation. Lastly, you may optionally choose some summary options (see "Step 2— Group Records" previously described in this chapter for more information about the summary options).

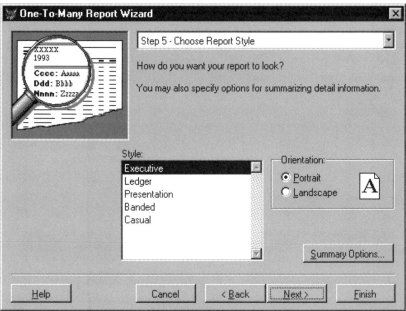

Figure 27. Step 5 of the One-to-Many Report Wizard is a combination of several steps of the Single-Table Report Wizard. It combines options for style, layout, and grouping.

The last step, Step 6—Finish, is the same as in the Single-Table Report Wizard. Use this step to preview the report, set a few miscellaneous options, and finally to save the report. **Figure 28** shows the first page of the 314-page Order report generated with the One-to-Many Report Wizard.

Orders
03/16/2002

Order Id: 1
Order Date: 05/09/1992
Customer Id: BSBEV
Employee Id: 5

Product Id	Unit Price	Quantity
10	31.00	5.000

Order Id: 2
Order Date: 05/12/1992
Customer Id: CACTU
Employee Id: 10

Product Id	Unit Price	Quantity
40	18.40	998.000
59	38.55	24.000
64	33.25	10.000

Order Id: 3
Order Date: 05/13/1992
Customer Id: FOLKO
Employee Id: 6

Product Id	Unit Price	Quantity
31	8.00	15.000
39	12.60	19.000
71	15.00	15.000

Figure 28. This Orders report was created with the One-to-Many Report Wizard.

Bug Alert!   *There's a bug in the One-to-Many Report Wizard that can create blank child records in the child table. It occurs when a parent record has no matching child records and at least one field from the child table is printed in the Detail band. The workaround for this bug involves changing the Print When logic and is described in more detail in Microsoft's KB Article Q137413.*

Conclusion

The Report Wizard supplied with Visual FoxPro is a great way to get started with creating reports. It introduces you to many aspects of reports while keeping the user interface very simple. And the Preview button on the final step really helps you take a peek at the report before you commit to saving it. This gives you the opportunity to go back and make changes over and over again until you're pleased with the results.

The other important thing to remember about reports created with the wizard is that once the report is saved, it is a regular VFP report. There's nothing different that distinguishes the report as one created by a wizard as opposed to one created with the Report Designer. Once you've saved it, you may use the native VFP Report Designer to edit and tweak the report as many times as you wish. Frequently, it may be a real time-saver to create the report with the wizard and then use the Report Designer to tweak it as necessary.

The bottom line—the report wizard is a great tool for creating simple reports or for creating a starting point for more complex reports.

Chapter 3
Learning the Basics

This chapter shows you how to get started by revealing several different ways to invoke the Visual FoxPro Report Designer. It also shows you how to set up the page and the Report Designer environment, and how to add and remove various bands. Finally, this chapter shows you how to preview and run your report from within the VFP Report Designer.

Invoking the VFP Report Designer can be done a number of different ways. If you're the type of person who prefers using menus, you can create a new report or modify an existing report through the main VFP Menu bar. If you're the type of person who prefers to do things through the Command Window, you're in luck too. You can create new reports and modify existing reports through the use of commands in the VFP Command Window.

Invoking the Report Designer via the Menu

To create a new report, select File | New… from the main VFP Menu bar. This invokes the New dialog shown in **Figure 1**. First, select the Report option button and click the New file button. This invokes the Report Designer with a new blank report (see **Figure 2**).

Figure 1. *The New dialog is invoked by selecting File | New… from the main VFP Menu bar.*

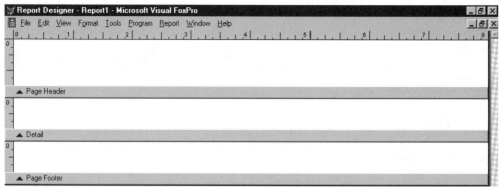

Figure 2. *This is how the Report Designer appears when you've just created a new blank report.*

To open the Report Designer and modify an *existing* report, select File | Open… from the main VFP Menu bar. This displays a standard Open dialog. Navigate to the directory that contains your report and make sure Report is in the Files of type drop-down combo box. Find the report you want to modify, select it, and click the OK button. This invokes the Report Designer with the selected report opened and ready for editing.

Invoking the Report Designer via the Command Window

For those who prefer to use the Command Window (present company included), you can create new reports and edit existing reports very easily. The CREATE REPORT command has two flavors. The first allows you to create a blank report. The second option allows you to create a *Quick Report*, which is based on a table with some fields and information automatically added. The MODIFY REPORT command allows you to edit an existing report.

Create a blank report

The following command is the simplest way to create a blank report:

```
CREATE REPORT
```

This creates the same unnamed blank report shown in Figure 2. If you prefer to name the new report as it's created, use either of the following commands:

```
*-- Create a new blank report called "MyReport"
CREATE REPORT MyReport

*-- Create a new blank report, prompting for a name
*-- (This allows you to navigate to the desired directory and enter a name)
CREATE REPORT ?
```

If you choose a name that already exists and you have SET SAFETY ON, you're prompted with a dialog that asks whether you want to overwrite the current one. If you don't have SET SAFETY ON, the existing report of the same name is opened so you can modify it.

Modify an existing report

Modifying an existing report through the Command Window is very simple, as shown in the following code samples:

```
*-- Modify a report called "MyReport"
MODIFY REPORT MyReport

*-- Prompt for the name of the report to modify
MODIFY REPORT ?
```

Either of these commands invokes the Report Designer with the specified report loaded and ready for editing. Just like the CREATE REPORT command, the MODIFY REPORT command also has more optional clauses available that are geared more for invoking the Report Designer within an application. These, too, will be discussed later in Chapter 9, "Running Reports."

If no report exists by the name you've chosen, a new one is created just as if you had used the CREATE REPORT command and not the MODIFY REPORT command.

Create a Quick Report

A Quick Report is a special way to get started on the report. It creates a new report that contains some fields you indicate. This means that your starting point is a little more advanced than a blank report. Using the Customer table in the TasTrade samples, the following command creates the report shown in **Figure 3**:

```
CREATE REPORT reports\MyReport ;
  FROM data\customer ;
  FIELDS customer_id, company_name, phone
```

The Quick Report version of the CREATE REPORT command only creates the report. It doesn't invoke the Report Designer for you to edit the report. Use the MODIFY REPORT command previously described to edit the report.

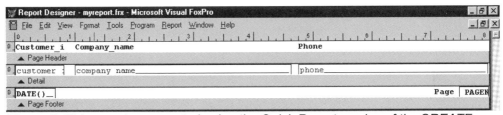

Figure 3. *This report was created using the Quick Report version of the CREATE REPORT command.*

The Quick Report version of the CREATE REPORT command has a few other clauses not shown in the previous example. These are all optional clauses to use at your discretion.

- **FORM or COLUMN:** The FORM clause creates a report that is row-based (each field is on a separate row as shown in Figure 17 in Chapter 2, "The Report Wizard"). The COLUMN clause creates a report that is column-based as shown in Figure 3.

COLUMN is the default; therefore, it's not required in the command. These clauses can't be combined—you may only use one at a time.

- **ALIAS:** Use this clause to tell the VFP Report Designer to precede each field name with the table name. This means the Designer puts "customer.company_name" as the expression of the field instead of "company_name."

- **NOOVERWRITE:** This clause prevents the new report from overwriting any existing report with the same name.

Note: Although the NOOVERWRITE clause prevents the new report from overwriting any existing report, it doesn't notify you that it failed to create the new report.

- **WIDTHS:** This clause doesn't appear to do anything. My guess is it's left over from the old DOS days when reports were character-based. According to the VFP Help, this clause specifies the width of the report page in columns.

When a Quick Report is created, the current default printer settings are used. This means the number of fields that fit on the report depends on the paper size and orientation of the default printer.

Once you've created a report with Quick Report, the report is a regular report that can be modified, manipulated, tweaked, and anything else you can think of to do with the Report Designer. So when you need to get started quickly, use this feature to build a foundation and use the Report Designer to finish the report.

Setting up the page

Now that you know several different ways to invoke the Report Designer, it's time to explore the Report Designer itself. Several report-related menu options appear on the main VFP Menu bar when the Report Designer is active. The first one I'm going to explore is the Page Setup option on the File menu. Select File | Page Setup… from the main VFP Menu bar to display the Page Setup dialog shown in **Figure 4**.

Keep in mind that many of the menu selections are not the same in FoxPro 2.x for Windows. For example, the Page Setup dialog is invoked by selecting Report | Page Layout… instead of File | Page Setup…. Keep this in mind when reading the rest of this chapter. If you can't find the option explained, look around and see whether it or something similar resides on a different menu option.

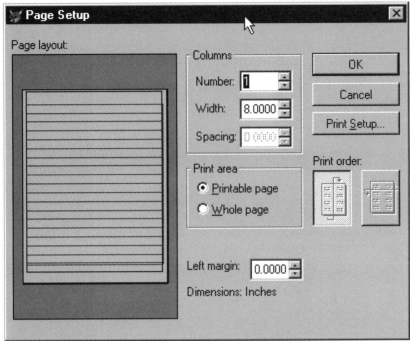

Figure 4. *Use the Page Setup dialog to describe the overall appearance of the pages, such as page size, left margin, and number of columns.*

Columns

The first section on this dialog relates to *columns*. By default, reports are created with one *set* of columns spanning the entire width of the page. This doesn't mean only one column of data exists on the report. It means one set of columns spans across the page. You can choose to have multiple sets of columns on the report by entering a number other than 1 in the Number field. This means multiple sets of columns are created across the page. A prime example of when you would use columns is when you're printing labels.

As soon as you enter a number other than 1, the Report Designer changes the column width to the total page width divided by the number of columns you entered. The Report Designer also takes into account any value for Left margin. Notice the spacing is still zero, which means column two starts immediately to the right of column one with no space between them. If you'd like to add a blank space between the columns, adjust the value of the Spacing field as needed. As you do this, the width of each column is recalculated to allow for the spacing between columns.

Selecting more than one column on a report adds two new bands to the report: Column Header and Column Footer. These bands are only as wide as one column on the report, and the information in these bands is repeated at the top and bottom of each column. Also note that if multiple columns are selected, any Group Header and Footer bands are also shortened to the width of one column.

Print area

The next section of the Print Setup dialog is the Print area section. You have two options: Printable page and Whole page. The Printable page option means that the positioning of the report may vary on the page, depending on which printer you're using. Different printers have different non-printable margins. Selecting this option tells the Report Writer to start the report immediately following the non-printable margin at the top of the page and immediately to the right of the non-printable left margin.

Selecting the Whole page option tells the Report Writer to position the report on the page relative to the upper-left corner of the paper—regardless of the printer being used. When using this option, you have to be very careful to design the report in a way that information doesn't appear outside of the printable areas for all printers accessed by the application. For example, don't put information too close to the left margin or it may be cut off when printed on certain printers.

Notice that as you switch between the two different print area options, the width and left margin values are recalculated accordingly. You can always change them yourself, but the Report Designer attempts to adjust the figures according to the paper size.

Print order

The Print Order section of the Page Setup dialog is only enabled if you've chosen more than one column for the report. This determines whether the records are printed in top-to-bottom order or left-to-right order. See **Figure 5** for an example of the two different options.

Select the Top-to-Bottom button (the leftmost button) to indicate you want the detail lines filled in from top to bottom of the first column before moving on to the top of the next column. Select the Left-to-Right button (the rightmost button) to indicate you want the detail lines filled in across the page before wrapping to the next line.

 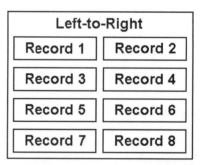

Figure 5. This example shows the difference between the Top-to-Bottom print order and the Left-to-Right print order.

Left margin

The value of the Left margin field determines the leftmost position where printing may begin. However, keep in mind the actual starting position is dependent on the Print area. If Printable page is selected, this value is relative to the first printable position on the paper for the selected printer. If Whole page is selected, this value is relative to the left-hand side of the paper.

Print Setup

Selecting the Print Setup button displays the dialog shown in **Figure 6**. From this dialog, you can select a printer, set the printer properties, select the paper size, select the paper tray, and set the orientation.

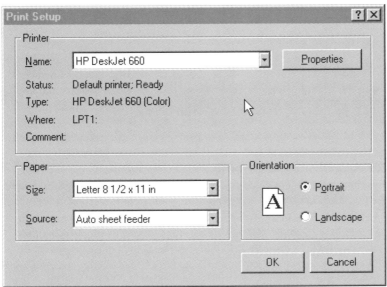

Figure 6. *Use the Print Setup dialog to select a printer, set the printer properties, select the paper size, select the paper source, and set the orientation.*

The Properties button brings up another dialog that varies depending on the selected printer. Each printer has different properties available. For example, some printers may allow duplex printing while others don't. Some printers may allow color printing while others are only black and white. Review your printer manual for a full list of the available properties, keeping in mind that some properties may not be available for configuration from within VFP.

The Report Designer environment

Now that you know how to set up the page, you need to know how to set up the Report Designer environment. The Report Designer is where you'll spend the majority of your time when developing reports. Every developer has different preferences. Fortunately, the VFP Report Designer recognizes this and allows you to set it up in a way that's most productive for you.

Grid Lines

Grid Lines are dotted lines that appear horizontally and vertically on the screen when designing reports (see **Figure 7**). These lines don't appear on the printed or previewed report. The lines only appear in the Designer as a guide to help you position objects in specific positions and relative to other objects. To toggle Grid Lines on or off, select View | Grid Lines from the main VFP Menu bar.

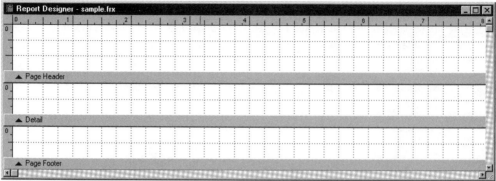

***Figure 7**. Grid Lines help you visually position and align objects on the report.*

Snap to Grid

Snap to Grid is an option that may be toggled on or off by selecting Format | Snap to Grid from the main VFP Menu bar. It helps you place objects on the report by *snapping* your cursor to points on the grid. As you drop an object on the report, the VFP Report Designer moves the object to the closest snap point. A snap point is one of the following: an intersection of the Grid Lines, the midway point on a line between two other lines of the opposite direction, or the center of the square created by the Grid Lines. In other words, if the Grid Lines occur every 12 pixels, a snap point occurs every 6 pixels.

Snapping can occur whether or not you have Grid Lines displayed. When Grid Lines are turned off, snapping occurs as if the lines were there. So keep this in mind—I've been known to tear my hair out when I keep moving an object a few pixels away and it keeps jumping back to the original position. Usually after the third try, I remember to turn off the Snap to Grid option. However, don't let that discourage you. Most of the time, snapping is very helpful in making sure all your objects are lined up exactly on the same horizontal or vertical axis.

Set Grid Scale

Previously, I talked about the Grid Lines representing 12 pixels. Luckily, this number isn't carved in stone as the only scale for grids. Select Format | Set Grid Scale… from the main VFP Menu bar to display the dialog shown in **Figure 8**. With this dialog, you can change the spacing between each Grid Line, which, in turn, sets the snap points. You can also set the unit of measure that appears on the ruler at the top of the Report Designer.

To change the spacing between Grid Lines, change the number in the Horizontal and Vertical fields. Notice that you don't have to use the same number for both fields. This means you could have rectangle shapes created by the Grid Lines instead of the squares shown in Figure 7.

Set Grid Scale
Grid in pixels:
Horizontal:
12
Vertical:
12
OK
Cancel
Ruler scale
System default
Pixels

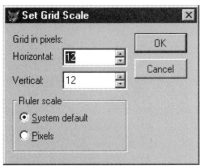

***Figure 8**. Use the Set Grid Scale dialog to change the spacing between each Grid Line and adjust the snap points.*

The Ruler scale portion of this dialog determines what unit of measure is shown on the ruler at the top of the Report Designer. The first option, System default, sets the ruler to inches or centimeters, depending on how your system is set up. The second option, Pixels, sets the rulers to pixels. In Figure 7, you can see the numbers 0-8 at the top of the screen, which represents inches as determined by my system default. Solid lines occur every inch, shorter lines occur every half-inch, even shorter lines occur every quarter-inch, and the smallest of the lines occurs every eighth-inch. Different variations of the hash marks occur depending on which ruler scale you've chosen.

Show Position

The Show Position option may be toggled on or off by selecting View | Show Position from the main VFP Menu bar. Turning this option on tells the VFP Report Designer to show the position of the mouse on the status bar at the bottom of the screen as shown in **Figure 9**. However, if an object is selected, instead of the mouse position being shown on the status bar, the position of the object along with its height and width is shown (see **Figure 10**). This option can be very helpful when you're trying to align several objects perfectly along the x-axis or y-axis.

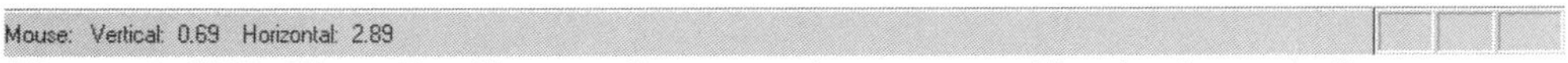

Mouse: Vertical: 0.69 Horizontal: 2.89

***Figure 9**. With Show Position on, the current mouse position is shown in the status bar.*

Object: Top: 0.13 Left: 1.00 Bottom: 0.36 Right: 1.75 Height: 0.24 Width: 0.76

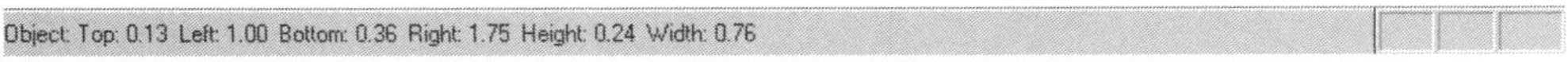

***Figure 10**. With Show Position on, the position of the selected item is shown in the status bar along with the height and width of the object.*

Report bands

Visual FoxPro reports use *bands* to separate the different parts of the report (see the section titled "Parts of a report" in Chapter 1, "Introduction," for more information about each band). Each report, at a minimum, includes a Page Header band, a Detail band, and a Page Footer band. These three bands exist for all reports and can't be removed. Optionally, you can add any of the following bands:

- Title

- Summary

- Group Header

- Group Footer

- Column Header

- Column Footer

Adding and removing bands

The method for adding and removing bands varies depending on which band you're dealing with.

Title and Summary bands

To add or remove the Title or Summary band, select Report | Title/Summary… from the main VFP Menu bar. This invokes the Title/Summary dialog shown in **Figure 11**. To add a Title band to the report, check the Title band check box. To remove an existing Title band from the report, uncheck this check box. Adding and removing the Summary band works the same way, by checking or unchecking the Summary band check box.

> *Note: Removing a Title band or Summary band will remove the band and any objects within the band as soon as you click the OK button. No further warning is given telling you the objects within the band are going to be removed.*

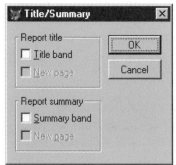

Figure 11. Use the Title/Summary dialog to add or remove a Title band and/or a Summary band from the report and determine whether those bands start on a new page.

If either the Title band or Summary band check box is checked, the corresponding New page check box is enabled. Checking either of these check boxes tells the Report Writer to print the respective band on a separate page all by itself. Be aware that this means the only thing on that page is that band. In other words, Page Header and Page Footer bands do *not* appear on the page with the Title or Summary band. This is one of those *gotchas* that you may have to work around.

For example, let's say the Page Header has a report title and the Page Footer has the page number. The last page of details shows Page 9 in the footer, followed by another page for the summary. However, this last page doesn't have a report title at the top and it doesn't have any page number at the bottom. It looks as if this page is an orphan and doesn't belong to this report. To overcome this issue, you have to repeat the header and footer information within the Title or Summary band. This can be a pain, but it's the only way around this *gotcha* when you need the Title or Summary band on its own page.

Another *gotcha* can occur when you use a Summary band and don't mark the New page check box. If it just so happens that the last detail line prints near the end of the page and causes the Summary band to print on the next page all by itself, the Report Writer ignores any Page Header or Page Footer information and only prints the Summary band on the page.

 Bug Alert! *There's a bug that occurs in the Report Writer when a Summary band is* not *marked as being on its own page. If there's not enough room to fit the Summary band at the bottom of the page, the Report Writer prints it on the next page. However, it behaves as if you've marked it as being on its own page, so it doesn't bother to print the Page Header or Page Detail bands on the page.*

The workaround to this problem is a little more complex and involves using Print When logic and Report Variables, which I haven't discussed yet. However, I think this *gotcha* is important enough to warrant being mentioned here, so without getting into too much detail, here's the gist of what you have to do.

1. Create a Report Variable that counts the number of lines per page (nLines).

2. Copy all the objects from the Page Header band to the top of the Summary band.

3. Copy all the objects from the Page Detail band to the bottom of the Summary band.

4. Change the Print When of the new header and footer objects in the Summary band to only print when nLines = 0 and to remove the object when it's blank.

Once you've read Chapter 5, "Report Objects," and Chapter 8, "Report Variables," this will make more sense—I promise! There's also a second way to work around this problem, which is discussed in the section titled "Fudging another Summary band" in Chapter 7, "Data Grouping."

Group Header and Footer bands

The Group Header and Footer bands are added to or removed from the report when you add or remove Data Groups, respectively. This topic is covered in detail in Chapter 7, "Data Grouping."

Column Header and Footer bands

The Column Header and Footer bands are automatically added to or removed from the report when you change the columns setting in the Page Setup dialog (see the section titled "Columns" earlier in this chapter).

Changing the height of a band

Each band on the report has a corresponding gray bar as shown in **Figure 12**. This bar appears beneath the band and has an arrow pointing upwards to give you a visual indication that it belongs with the band above. The name of the band is to the right of the arrow and is another indication of which band the bar is associated with.

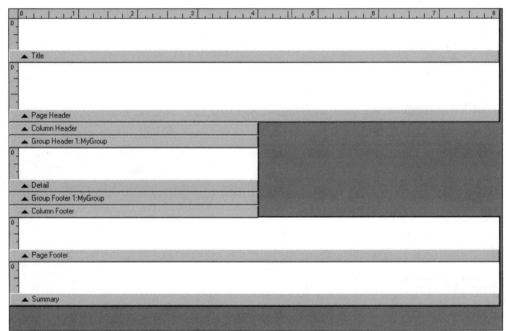

Figure 12. Each band on the report has a corresponding gray bar positioned directly beneath the band it represents.

You may change the height of a band in one of three ways. The first method is to click and drag the corresponding gray bar up or down depending on whether you want to decrease or increase the size of the band. The second method for changing the band height is to select Reports | Bands... from the main VFP Menu bar, which invokes the dialog shown in **Figure 13**.

The Edit Bands dialog lists each band currently defined on the report. Highlight the band you want to change and click the OK button. This invokes the dialog shown in **Figure 14**. From this dialog, change the value of the Height field to represent the height you want. The third method for changing a band height is to double-click the gray bar representing the band, which also displays the dialog shown in Figure 14.

***Figure 13**. Selecting Report | Bands… from the main VFP Menu bar displays the Edit Bands dialog.*

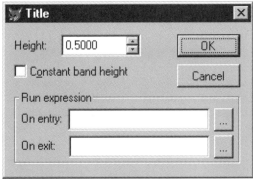

***Figure 14**. This dialog allows you to change the height and other information for a specific band.*

The Constant band height check box on this dialog determines whether the height of this band stays the same or not. It's possible to have objects within a band stretch taller when more room is needed. It's also possible to have items disappear from the report when not needed. In either of these situations, the height of the band changes relative to the objects in it unless the Constant band height check box is checked. When this is checked, the band remains at the defined height regardless of the information in the band.

 In FoxPro 2.x for Windows, you can't click and drag or double-click on the entire gray bar. Instead, a small gray square exists to the left of the bar, and this is the only place where you can click and drag or double-click.

> Note: In some previous versions of FoxPro and Visual FoxPro, you have
> to be careful when defining the height of the bands. If the combined total
> height of the Page Header, Page Footer, Group Header (optional), Group
> Footer (optional), and Detail bands exceeds the total page length, you can either
> get an error message about a band not fitting on the page or the Detail band may
> be truncated when it's printed.

On Entry and On Exit

In addition to changing the band height, the dialog shown in Figure 13 also allows you to enter On Entry and On Exit expressions. The On Entry expression of a band is executed just prior to printing the objects in that band. The On Exit expression of a band is executed just after the objects in the corresponding band have been printed. The expression must be a valid VFP command, a User Defined Function (UDF), or a method call.

These two expressions are extremely valuable when creating complex reports. For example, you can place "MyFunction()" (without the quotes) in the expression for On Entry. MyFunction is a function that is defined somewhere else within your application, but accessible to the report. Or, you can place a method call in the expression such as "_SCREEN.oApp.MyMethod()" (without the quotes). These two options are discussed in greater detail in Chapter 10, "Solutions to Real-World Problems."

The On Entry and On Exit options were introduced with Visual FoxPro. Therefore, these don't exist in FoxPro 2.x for Windows. However, in Chapter 10, "Solutions to Real World-Problems," I'll show you some tricks for imitating this feature in FoxPro 2.x for Windows.

Running the report

When working in the VFP Report Designer, you have the ability to preview the report on the screen by selecting File | Print Preview from the main VFP Menu bar. Another method for previewing the report is to select View | Preview from the main VFP Menu bar. Yet another method is to right-click on any unused area of the report in the Report Designer and select Preview. All three methods do the same thing—they display the report on the screen along with the Print Preview toolbar. This is very helpful because it allows you to see how the report looks as you're designing it.

Besides previewing the report on the screen, you can also print the report from within the VFP Report Designer. As with lots of things in VFP, you have several different ways to print the report. The first method is to use one of the preview methods just described. Then choose the Print button from the Print Preview toolbar. This sends the report to the default printer without prompting you for a printer or any setup options.

A more flexible method for printing is to select File | Print… from the main VFP Menu bar. This invokes the Windows Print dialog, where you can select a printer and set various print options. And once again, you have a few more methods for doing the same thing. You may select Report | Run Report from the main VFP Menu bar, or you may right-click on any unused area of the report in the Report Designer and select Print….

As you can see, you have numerous methods for previewing and printing the report from within the VFP Report Designer. I'm sure at least one or two of those methods will be to your liking!

Wrapping up

By now you should have the foundation of knowledge necessary to start using the VFP Report Designer. This chapter covered how to invoke the Designer, how to set up the page, and how to set up the environment. It also covered how to set up the various bands and how to run the report from within the VFP Report Designer. In the next chapter, you'll learn about where to get the data for creating the report and some different schools of thought about the various methods.

Chapter 4
The Data Source

The bottom line is that a report represents data. So where does the data come from? Well, the answer is, "It depends." There are several different methods and schools of thought on the best way to get the data for reports. Each one has its pros and cons. This chapter describes the different methods and schools of thought so you can decide which is best for your situation. Most likely, no one solution is the best solution for _all_ your reporting needs. Different situations call for different solutions.

In this chapter, I describe the difference between normalized data and denormalized data and how the two methodologies relate to reports. I also discuss issues such as Private Data Sessions and the VFP Report Designer's Data Environment. The Data Environment is what you use to describe the tables, views, and relations you want the VFP Report Writer to open and set each time the report is run. It's the main tool for dealing with report data. Finally, the end of this chapter is dedicated to explaining several different real-world data situations and how to solve them.

Normalized vs. Denormalized

There are two different schools of thought for preparing data for complex reports: Normalized and Denormalized.

Normalized data

Normalized data means that any one piece of information is stored in exactly one place. For example, the Customer Name only resides in the Customer table—not again in the Orders table and not again in the Invoice table. When the customer's name changes, it only needs to be updated in one table—the Customer table. Relational database designs operate on this principle, and because VFP is a relational database, most VFP applications are designed according to this methodology.

The advantage to this methodology is that it greatly improves the performance of updates throughout your application because information only has to be updated in one place. However, that advantage is gained at the expense of retrieval performance—such as in the case of reporting. For example, when creating an order report, you'll quickly discover the Order table only has the Customer ID and not the Customer Name. In order to show the Customer Name for each record, you have to pull that information from the Customer table.

This slight reporting disadvantage is easily overcome with VFP. You can either set a relation between the two tables or use a UDF within the report to access the appropriate Customer Name. Other situations you might have to overcome, such as subtotals and totals for the orders, can also be handled by using the native variables and calculations within the VFP Report Designer. So by all means, don't change the methodology used in the design of your application just for the sake of reporting. Continue to design your VFP applications using normalized data.

Denormalized data

Denormalized data means any one piece of information may be stored in numerous locations in order to speed retrieval performance. If you're familiar with the concept of a Data Warehouse, you're already familiar with denormalization. Most applications do not follow this philosophy, so you're probably asking how this relates to your VFP report.

What it means is that you may build a denormalized cursor, on-the-fly, prior to running a report. In other words, prepare one temporary cursor with all the necessary data pulled from as many tables as necessary. Also, preprocess the data and calculate it, total it, and manipulate it as many times as necessary prior to running the report. Once you've done this, you don't need to use any of the special features such as relations, variables, and calculations within the VFP Report Designer. You just place the desired fields from your cursor on the report and you're done.

Which is better?

So which methodology is better? The answer is both! Each one has its place when creating reports.

The people who subscribe to the Denormalized methodology feel this method is superior mostly because of its flexibility. Once you've created the denormalized cursor, you can do other things with it besides run a report through the VFP Report Writer. For example, you can export the data to a spreadsheet or create XML data. There's definitely merit to this reasoning.

On the other side of the fence are those who subscribe to the Normalized methodology. Performance is usually the biggest reason for this philosophy. Why spend the time to create a new cursor when the data is already there? Set a relation between two tables and *voilà!* You have access to all the information you need and you didn't have to spend any time writing to the disk.

When deciding which methodology to use, you need to evaluate the goals of the individual report you're designing. Most likely, you'll use both philosophies in your application. For a quick list of orders, set a relation to the Customer table and build the report using the Normalized methodology. For a sophisticated forecasting report that pulls information from several tables and has complex formulas, use the Denormalized methodology and create a single cursor for the report.

The main questions you need to ask yourself when making a decision are:

- Will I need to export this information?

- How complex are the calculations and formulas?

- How many tables is the data stored in?

- How much extra data would be created if I built a cursor?

Ask yourself these questions for each and every report you design. Like I said before, you'll probably find situations to use both methodologies within your application. So be open-minded and don't get stuck in one methodology. Remember, one of the great features of Visual FoxPro is the fact that you can skin a cat 12 different ways!

Private Data Session

The Private Data Session may be toggled on or off by selecting Report | Private Data Session from the main VFP Menu bar. In layman's terms, this setting determines whether your report runs inside of its own little world or whether it opens its eyes and recognizes the rest of the world.

The Private Data Session option is not available in FoxPro 2.x reports.

Selecting the Private Data Session option tells the VFP Report Writer to ignore any currently opened tables or views. This means you have to use the VFP Report Designer's Data Environment (described in the next section) to indicate which tables, indexes, and relations are required to run the report. This information is stored with the report, and each time the report is run, the VFP Report Writer opens the appropriate tables and sets the appropriate indexes and relations. In other words, the report is self-contained and is not dependent on anything being set up prior to running the report.

On the other hand, not using a Private Data Session means the report can access any opened tables or views at the time the report is run. This doesn't mean you can't still open one or more tables or views in the Data Environment. It means that in addition to the tables and views opened by the Data Environment, the report can also access any tables or views that were opened prior to running the report.

The Data Environment

The Data Environment is the portion of the VFP Report Designer that is used to describe the tables, indexes, and relations required to run the report. It may be invoked by selecting View | Data Environment… from the main VFP Menu bar. You may also select Data Environment… after right-clicking on any unused area on the report.

The Data Environment in FoxPro 2.x is significantly different from Visual FoxPro. In fact, it's called the Environment and not the Data Environment. Because of the major differences, the FoxPro 2.x Environment is discussed in a separate section titled "The FoxPro 2.x Environment" later in this chapter.

The Data Environment consists of two main areas. The first is the Data Environment window and the second is the Properties window.

The Data Environment window

The Data Environment window shows which tables, views, and relations are opened by the VFP Report Writer.

Adding tables and views

Opening the Data Environment on a new report does nothing more than display an empty Data Environment window. Now you need to add one or more tables. Select DataEnvironment | Add… from the main VFP Menu bar or select Add… after right-clicking on an unused portion of the Report Environment. Note that the DataEnvironment menu option is only available when the Data Environment window is active.

What appears next depends on whether or not you have a database opened in VFP. If you do have a database opened, the Add Table or View dialog is displayed with the appropriate information listed (as shown in **Figure 1**, where I had the TasTrade database opened prior to invoking the dialog). If more than one database is opened, you can use the Database drop-down combo box to select a database. Once a database is selected, its tables are listed in the Tables in database list box.

> *Note: If no database is opened when you first invoke the Add Table or View dialog, the standard Open dialog is displayed and functions just as if you had selected the Other… button (described later).*

Figure 1. *The Add Table or View dialog is used to open the tables and views required by the report.*

Select a table by highlighting the table name and selecting the Add button. This adds the table to the Data Environment as shown in **Figure 2**. You may continue to select as many tables as needed.

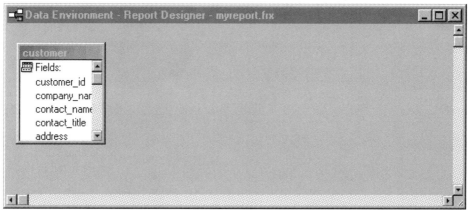

Figure 2. *The Data Environment window shows each table and view required to run the report.*

To add a view to the Data Environment, select Views from the Select option group. This displays all the views that belong to the currently selected database. Select any desired view in the same manner as just described for selecting tables.

To select a free table or a table that belongs to a database currently not opened, select the Other... button on the Add Table or View dialog. This displays a standard Open dialog from which you can navigate to the table you want to open and then select it. Selecting a table in this manner adds the table to the Data Environment. In addition, if the table belongs to a database, the database is opened and its tables are listed in the Tables in database list box.

When you're done adding tables and views to the Data Environment, select the Close button on the Add Table or View dialog.

Adding relations
In situations where multiple tables are required, you may need to set relations between the tables. To do this, click and drag the desired field of the first table over to the second table, dropping it on top of the appropriate index of the second table. **Figure 3** shows an example of a parent-child relation created between the Customer table (the parent) and the Orders table (the child).

> *Note: If relations are already established in the database, the VFP Report Designer will honor these and add the appropriate relation to the Data Environment.*

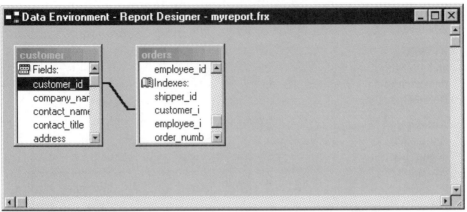

Figure 3. In this example, a relation has been established between the customer_id field in the Customer table and customer_i index of the Orders table.

Removing tables, views, and relations
To remove a table or view from the Data Environment window, right-click the table or view and select Remove. You may also select the table or view, and then select DataEnvironment | Remove from the main VFP Menu bar.

To remove a relation from the Data Environment, click on the line that represents the relation and press the Delete key. You may also use this method to delete a table or view.

Browsing a table or view
You may browse the data in any table or view opened in the Data Environment rather easily. Select the table or view you want to browse and select DataEnvironment | Browse from the main VFP Menu bar. You may also right-click on the table or view and then select Browse.

The Properties window
The standard VFP Properties window can be used to access the Properties, Events, and Methods of the Data Environment itself as well as the tables, views, and relations within the Data Environment. If the Properties window is not already active, you can display it by selecting Window | Properties Window from the main VFP Menu bar. You can also right-click on an open area in the Data Environment window and select Properties.

> *The Properties window may also be displayed from the VFP Command Window. Press Ctrl-F2 to activate the Command Window. Then, enter "ACTIVATE WINDOW properties" (without the quotes).*

Many of the Properties, Events, and Methods (PEMs) used in the Data Environment are the same PEMs used throughout Visual FoxPro and should already be familiar to you. In this section, I'm only going to discuss the PEMs that are unique or special to reports.

The Data Environment PEMs

These PEMs relate to the overall Data Environment.

- **AfterCloseTables event:** This event is fired after the report is finished running and after the tables and views are closed. You can use the method associated with this event to do any special cleanup. It's especially handy if you've used the BeforeOpenTables method to open some tables that need to be closed.

- **AutoCloseTables:** This property determines whether the VFP Report Writer automatically closes the tables and views defined in the Data Environment. The default is true (.t.). If this property is false, the AfterCloseTables event is not fired. An example of when you wouldn't want the tables or views closed is when the program or form that calls the Report Writer needs to access the tables or views when the report is finished.

- **AutoOpenTables:** This property determines whether the VFP Report Writer automatically opens the tables and views defined in the Data Environment. The default is true (.t.). If this property is false, the BeforeOpenTables event and the OpenTables method are not fired. An example of when you wouldn't want the tables and views automatically opened is when the program or form that calls the Report Writer has already set up the tables and views.

- **BeforeOpenTables event:** This event is fired before any tables or views are opened by the Data Environment. This event is extremely useful when you need to open some tables or views yourself, when you need to change the path of the tables or views, or when you need to build data on-the-fly.

- **CloseTables:** This method closes the tables and views defined in the Data Environment. It's run automatically if the AutoCloseTables property is true. However, you may also call this method yourself if needed.

- **InitialSelectedAlias:** This property determines which table or view is made current when the Data Environment is loaded. This is very important, as it determines which table or view is the main table or view driving the report.

- **OpenTables:** This method opens the tables and views defined in the Data Environment. It's run automatically if the AutoOpenTables property is true. As part of this method's default behavior, it fires the BeforeOpenTables method just before it opens the tables.

- **OpenViews:** This property determines which views are opened by the OpenTables method. The valid choices are 0-Local and Remote (the default), 1-Local Only, 2-Remote Only, and 3-None.

The order in which the OpenTables method and the BeforeOpenTables event fire is a little confusing. First, the BeforeOpenTables event fires and processes the custom code within the OpenTables method. Then, just before the OpenTables method exits, it processes the custom code in the BeforeOpenTables method. Lastly, control is returned to the OpenTables method, which, in turn, opens any defined tables and views. Use NODEFAULT and DODEFAULT() within the OpenTables method if you need to circumvent this native behavior.

The cursor PEMs

These PEMs relate to tables and cursors defined in the Data Environment.

- **Alias:** This property determines the alias used to reference this table or view. The default is the same name as the table or view.

- **BufferModeOverride:** This property determines the buffering of the table or view. The valid options are 1-Use Form Setting (the default), 3-Optimistic row buffering, and 5-Optimistic table buffering. You may be asking, "What in the world does this have to do with reports? I'm reading the data, not writing the data!" Usually, this is a true statement and this property would be irrelevant. However, it's possible to write to the data through the use of User Defined Functions within your report.

- **CursorSource:** This property identifies the name of the table or view of this cursor. This is a read-only property.

- **Database:** This property identifies the database that this table or view belongs to. This is a read-only property.

- **Exclusive:** This property determines whether this table is opened exclusively. For tables, the default is false (.f.). For views, this is a read-only property that is set to true (.t.).

- **Filter:** This property is used to enter an expression to apply a filter to the table or view. For example, enter COUNTRY = 'USA' to limit the Customer table to only those records that have a value of "USA" in the Country field.

- **Name:** As tables and views are added to the Data Environment, they're named cursor1, cursor2, cursor3, and so on.

- **NoDataOnLoad:** This property determines whether views are loaded with or without data. A true (.t.) tells the Report Writer to open the view without retrieving any information. The default is false (.f.) for views, and this property is not applicable to tables. An example of when you would set this property to true is when you need to prime some variables for a parameterized view.

- **Order:** This property identifies the index to set for this table or view.

- **ReadOnly:** This property determines whether updates are allowed to the table or view. The default is false (.f.).

If the report is defined with a Private Data Session, do not put code in the Init method of a cursor. Reports do not have a DataSessionID assigned to them, so there's no way to be assured the code will run in the correct Data Session. Therefore, it's suggested (by Microsoft) that you place any Init code in the Init method of the Data Environment instead of the Init method of the cursor.

The relation PEMs

These PEMs relate to the relations defined between tables and/or views.

- **ChildAlias:** This property identifies the alias name of the child table in the relation. It's a read-only property.

- **ChildOrder:** This property identifies the index tag used on the child table.

- **Name:** As relations are added to the Data Environment, they're named Relation1, Relation2, Relation3, and so on.

- **OneToMany:** This property determines whether the record pointer remains on the same parent record until the child table has moved through all the corresponding records. For example, when a Customer table is related to an Order table, it's a one-to-many relation because there may be many records in the Order table that relate to a single record in the Customer table.

- **ParentAlias:** This property identifies the alias name of the parent table in the relation. It's a read-only property.

- **RelationalExpr:** This property identifies the expression used to relate the parent table to the child table.

> *Note: If the report is defined with a Private Data Session, do not put code in the Init method of a relation. Reports do not have a DataSessionID assigned to them, so there's no way to be assured the code will run in the correct Data Session. Therefore, it's suggested (by Microsoft) that you place any Init code in the Init method of the Data Environment instead of the Init method of the relation.*

Mind boggling

By now your mind is probably overloaded with all these PEMs and you're wondering how you're supposed to know when and what to change. Don't worry. For the most part, there's really not much you need to do beyond adding the tables and views and setting the order. In the next section, I'll describe some of the special situations that require you to deal with the PEMs.

Real-world Data Environment issues

In this section, I describe some of the various ways you can manipulate the Data Environment through the use of PEMs. If you're a true beginner to the VFP Report Writer, you may want to skip over this section and come back to it later once you've gotten a better understanding of the VFP Report Writer.

Where's the data?

In many applications, the data resides in a fixed location and never changes—not even between the development environment and the run-time environment. This makes adding tables and views to the Data Environment relatively simple because the path used at design time is the same path used at run time.

> Note: The path is stored in the report as a relative path. So if your development environment is on a different drive than the run-time environment, you don't have to do anything special as long as the same directory structure is used by both.

However, what do you do if your application is a multi-company accounting package where the data for each company is stored in a different directory? It's certainly not practical to define multiple copies of the reports for each company created in the accounting data. Instead, you need to tell the report where to find the data. This can be done by adding code to the BeforeOpenTables method. The following code can be found in the ChangeSource.FRX report included in the source code available with this book:

```
*-- Set the path of the data according to some variable
LOCAL lcPath, loCursors

* For this stand-alone example, I'm hard-coding the path.
* In your real application, you would set this according
* to some global variable or application property.
lcPath = 'c:\rwbook\source\data_x\'

FOR EACH loCursors IN This.Objects
   IF loCursors.BaseClass = 'Cursor' && Skip the relations
      loCursors.Database = lcPath + JUSTFNAME(loCursors.Database)
   ENDIF
ENDFOR
```

This code loops through the cursors in the Data Environment and replaces the path in the database property with a new path. This same type of logic can be used when the data resides in a different location in your development environment than it does in the run-time environment.

May I take your order, please?
Here's another situation that you might encounter. You have a report defined that can be run a number of ways. The user is prompted with a special criteria form to fill out before running the report. The report then has to honor the criteria entered by the user.

For example, the user can choose the sort order and set a filter. Now what do you do? Again, you can use the BeforeOpenTables method to set the appropriate properties at run time. Loop through the cursors in the same manner shown in the previous code sample and set the Order and Filter properties of each table or view according to the criteria entered by the user.

Don't you dare open that table
When would you *not* want the Report Writer to open the tables and views? Well, consider the situation where the data is stored in multiple tables with the exact same structure. For example, customers from the Sprockets division of the company are stored in a table called SPR_CUST. The customers from the Widgets division of the company are stored in a table

called WID_CUST. Depending on which division the report is being run for, the data has to be pulled from the appropriate table.

This presents a very unique situation. You want to put tables in the Data Environment so you can take advantage of the benefits of quickly adding fields to the report. However, when the report is run, you don't want the Report Writer to open the tables and views defined in the Data Environment because it doesn't know which table to open.

To solve this sticky situation, add one of the tables to the Data Environment and design your report as needed. However, be sure when you add objects to the report, you do *not* use any table aliases on your field names. For example, use customer_id instead of wid_cust.customer_id. You must also be sure the Private Data Session option (discussed earlier in this chapter) is *not* checked.

To eliminate the tables from the Data Environment at run time, you may either set the AutoOpenTables and the AutoCloseTables properties to false (.f.) or delete the tables and views from the Data Environment after you've finished designing the report. I prefer to leave the tables in the Data Environment and set the two properties to false. This makes it easier for me to maintain the report later because the table or view is still in the Data Environment.

To run this report, make sure the calling program or form opens the appropriate table or view, sets the index order, and positions the record pointer to the top of the file. Now call the report. The VFP Report Writer won't bother to open any of the tables or views defined in the Data Environment and will run based on whatever tables or views are opened at the time the report is called.

A fly on the wall

Another example of when you might want to do some special coding in the Data Environment is when you need to build a cursor on-the-fly. Maybe your report needs to scan through one or more tables and build a summarized set of data to print. Or maybe your report needs to list some random numbers generated based on the current date and time. The reasons are endless, but the solution is very simple. Put the code to generate the cursor in either the BeforeOpenTables method or the OpenTables method.

However, if the Data Environment has any other tables or views defined—and you want the newly created cursor as the main table—you have to use the following code in the OpenTables method:

```
*-- Suppress the default behavior that occurs at the end of this method
NODEFAULT

*-- Invoke the default behavior which opens the tables and views
*-- in the Data Environment
DODEFAULT()

*-- Create your cursor
* (Do whatever is necessary to create the cursor)

*-- Set the InitialSelectedAlias
This.InitialSelectedAlias = 'MyNewCursor'
```

You might be asking, "Why in the world did she use NODEFAULT and DODEFAULT() in this code? Has she lost her mind?" Well, some may argue that, yes, I have lost my mind.

But that doesn't have anything to do with why I combined both of these commands in this method code.

The native behavior of this method is to process any custom code first. Then, as the method exits, it opens the tables defined in the Data Environment and sets the InitialSelectedAlias. In this situation, I want *my* cursor set as the InitialSelectedAlias. This means I need to have the Data Environment tables opened first. That's why I used DODEFAULT() prior to my custom code to force the native behavior to happen when I wanted it to happen.

So why did I use NODEFAULT at the beginning of the method code? Without this command, the native behavior will happen *again* at the end of the custom code—even though I've already forced the native behavior to execute earlier in the code. As you can imagine, this can cause problems when the tables are already opened. As a side note, the NODEFAULT command doesn't have to appear prior to the DODEFAULT() command. As long as the NODEFAULT command resides anywhere within the method code, the native behavior will not execute again at the end of the method.

The FoxPro 2.x Environment

In the FoxPro 2.x Report Designer, the whole concept of a Private Data Session and a Data Environment is completely different. First of all, there's no such thing as a Private Data Session. Secondly, there's no Data Environment window to interactively add tables and relations to the report.

In FoxPro 2.x, the current environment is *captured* and *saved* with the report. This means you first use the FoxPro Command Window (or any another means) to open the tables, set the orders, and establish the relations between tables. Then, with the tables still opened, you create the report. Once in the FoxPro 2.x Report Designer, you *save* the environment by selecting Report | Page Layout... from the FoxPro system menu bar. This invokes the Page Layout dialog, from which you select the Environment... button to display the Environment dialog shown in **Figure 4**.

Figure 4. The Environment dialog in FoxPro 2.x is used to save, restore, and clear the report Environment.

The Save button takes a snapshot of the current FoxPro 2.x environment and saves it with the report. Each time the report is run, the Report Writer will open the same tables, set the same index tags, and set the same relations to match what they are at this exact moment.

The Restore button restores the environment to what is currently stored with this report. In other words, any changes you've just saved in this editing session are thrown out and the original settings are restored.

The Clear button clears everything from the report environment. No tables, indexes, or relations are created when the report is run.

The Cancel button returns to the Page Layout dialog without making any changes to the environment stored with the report.

Selecting any of the buttons performs the appropriate action, closes the Environment dialog, and returns control to the Page Layout dialog.

Use your imagination

I've only shown you a few examples of how to manipulate the Data Environment through its PEMs. I'm sure you can come up with a whole lot more on your own. That's what's great about FoxPro—its extensibility. You're not locked into just one way of doing things. You can get as creative as you want or need to be to solve the situation at hand.

Chapter 5
Report Objects

Now that you know what all the parts of a report are, you're probably asking, "Yeah, but how do I get the data on the report?" After all, isn't that the whole point of a report—to represent data in a visually pleasing way for humans to understand? In this chapter, you'll learn what the different types of objects are and how to place them on the report.

In the previous two chapters, I discussed how to set up the Report Designer's environment and where the data comes from, but I didn't discuss how to actually put the data on the report. This chapter describes how to put the data on the report along with other objects such as text, lines, boxes, and graphics so your reports look pleasing to the human eye.

Types of controls

The term *control* is used to describe an individual object placed on a report. A control may be a piece of data, it may be a fixed piece of text, it may be a line or box, or it may even be a picture. All these different types of objects are called controls and may be placed on any band of the report.

Labels

A *Label* object is a piece of static text placed on the report. It's commonly used to enter report titles, column headings, and special text such as "Page Number:" to precede the actual page number. The content of the label is fixed and appears the same every time the report is printed.

Fields

A *Field* object is used to print data on the report, and it's the most powerful of all the Report objects. It contains an expression that is evaluated each time the object is printed. For example, when a Field object is placed in the Detail band, the expression is evaluated for each record processed by the Report Writer. When a Field object is placed in the Page Footer band, the expression is evaluated once at the end of each page.

Shapes

Shape objects come in the form of lines, rectangles, and rounded rectangles. Lines can be horizontal or vertical. Rectangles can be tall and skinny, short and fat, and any other combination you can think of. Rounded rectangles, like rectangles, can be of various sizes, but unlike rectangles, the corners are rounded instead of being crisp 90° angles.

Pictures and ActiveX Bound controls

Often times, you need to print pictures on reports. Using the *Picture/ActiveX Bound* control is the way to do this. The valid picture formats are BMP, JPG, and ICO files. Pictures may also be printed from general fields in a table when APPEND GENERAL has been used to store the graphic image to the table.

In FoxPro 2.x, the only valid formats are BMP and ICO files. Sorry—no JPG files allowed!

At this point, you might be asking what the *ActiveX* portion of this control means. How can a report have an ActiveX control? The answer is, it doesn't. The title of this object in older versions of FoxPro was *Picture and OLE Bound control*. It appears to be the victim of a massive search-and-replace of the entire VFP source code, replacing the word *OLE* with *ActiveX*. In any event, what it means is that you can place an OLE Bound object, such as a Microsoft Word or Excel document, on the report.

Using the Report Controls toolbar

Now that you know *what* the controls are, wouldn't it be nice to know *how* to put them on the report? The most common method for placing controls on a report is to use the Report Controls toolbar shown in **Figure 1**. You can display the Report Controls toolbar with one of three methods. The first method is to select View | Report Controls Toolbar from the main VFP Menu bar. The second method is to select the Report Controls Toolbar button from the Report Designer toolbar. The third method is to right-click on an unused portion of any *docked* toolbar and then select Report Controls.

Figure 1. The Report Controls toolbar is used to place objects on the report.

The buttons on this toolbar, from left to right, are:

- Select Objects
- Label
- Field
- Line
- Rectangle
- Rounded Rectangle
- Picture/ActiveX Bound Control
- Button Lock

 In FoxPro 2.x, the Report object buttons are displayed on the left-hand side of the screen and are not moveable. They aren't contained within a toolbar whose positioning you can control. In addition, there is no Button Lock button.

Select Objects

This button is not used to place an object on the report. Instead, this button is used to select existing objects on the report so you can edit them. It's discussed in more detail later in this chapter.

Label

To add a Label object from the Report Controls toolbar, select the Labels button. Then position the cursor on the report, click with the mouse, and start typing the text you want printed on the report. When you're done typing, click anywhere else on the screen to tell the Report Designer that you're done with that label.

That's all there is to adding a label. Click, point, and type.

> *Note: When typing the text for a label, you can press the Enter key to wrap the text to the next line.*

Field

To add a Field object from the Report Controls toolbar, select the Fields button. Position the cursor on the report and click with the mouse to display the Report Expression dialog shown in **Figure 2**. Many of the options on this dialog are common to other types of objects placed on reports. Therefore, I'm only going to discuss the unique options here and I'll discuss all the common options later (see the "Common options" section later in this chapter).

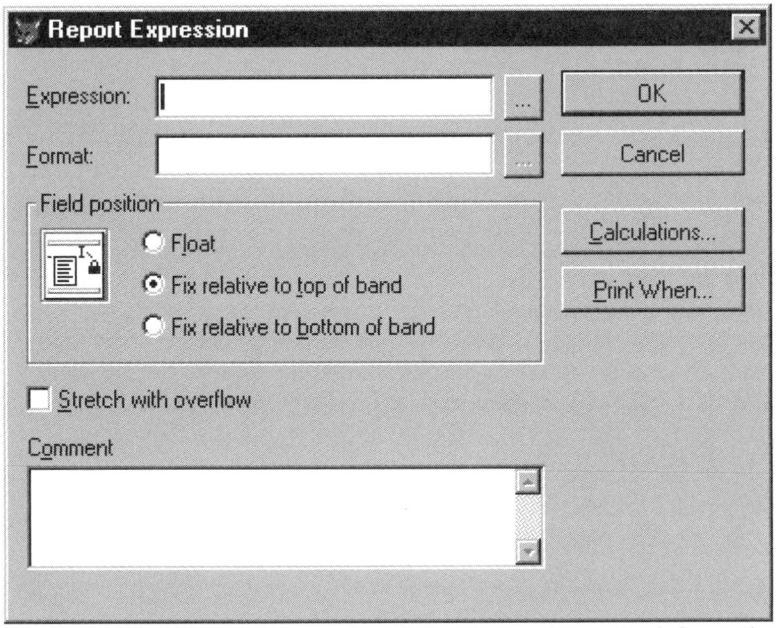

Figure 2. The Report Expression dialog is used to enter information for Field objects.

Expression

The most important part of this dialog is the Expression text box, which tells the Report Writer what to print for this Field object. The expression can be any valid VFP expression. It can be a field from a table, for example, *MyTable.MyField*. It can be a function such as *Date()*. It can be a combination of a field and a function, such as *PADR(MyField, 35, '*')*. These are all valid expressions.

A Field object may also be used to print text as long as it's entered as a valid expression. For example, you may enter *"The Big Important Report"*, with the quotes, as an expression. Or you may enter *IIF(MyField, "Yes", "No")* to show Yes and No for logical fields.

I've said that any valid expression can be used. One of the most important and powerful implications of this fact is that you can use UDFs, method calls, and references to properties as an expression. For example, use *MyUDF()* to print whatever value MyUDF returns. When using a UDF, you need to make sure it's either defined in a program that resides in the current calling stack or it's defined in a program that is set as a current procedure file (SET PROCEDURE TO MyProc).

To use a method or a property, enter the expression just as you would within any other program or class. For example, *oApp.cCompanyName* prints the value stored in the cCompanyName property of the oApp object. Use *oApp.MySpecialMethod()* to print the value returned by the method named MySpecialMethod of the oApp object. You can also reference the _SCREEN object, such as *_SCREEN.caption*. And even more powerful, if you're running a report from within a VFP form, you can reference any property or method defined in the form such as *ThisForm.cTitle* or *ThisForm.GetClient()*. This is extremely useful when you need to use some information based on some criteria the user entered.

The use of UDFs and method calls is very powerful, and you need to realize the possibilities that they present. As I've said, the Report Writer prints the value returned by the UDF, but what goes on *inside* of the UDF is left to your wild imagination. You can select another table, seek a specific record, and return the value of one of its fields. You can access another table and scan through a series of records adding the value of some field and return the grand total. You can even scan through the same table being used to drive the report and return the value of another record or the total of several records.

> Note: If you select another table within a UDF or method call, be sure to restore the original table before returning. Otherwise, if you leave a different table as the current table, the rest of the report continues to process using that table instead of the one it should be using. Also, if you move the record pointer of the current table, be sure to put it back before exiting the UDF or method—that is, unless you want to change the current record pointer. This valuable, but sometimes dangerous trick gives you additional flexibility to manipulate the report data.

Special characters

When building an expression, you can embed special characters using the CHR() function. For example, use CHR(64) to print the @ symbol. Or use CHR(13) to concatenate several fields, forcing a line feed between each one. A classic example of this is shown in the following example that builds a mailing address.

```
Name+CHR(13)+Address1+CHR(13)+Address2+CHR(13)+City+' '+State+' '+Zip
```

However, this expression has two flaws. The first is that you have blank lines whenever a field is empty, such as the second address line. The second flaw is that when any of the City, State, or Zip fields are empty, you end up with extra spaces. You could add a bunch of IIF() functions to weed out the unwanted line returns and spaces, but that gets real ugly real quick.

A better solution is to use the two special characters available to Field expressions. The comma may be used to add two fields together with a space between them, yet it eliminates the space if either of the fields is blank. The semicolon may be used to add two fields together with a line feed between them, yet it eliminates blank lines caused by empty fields. Use these two special characters as shown in the following example.

```
Name;Address1;Address2;City,State,Zip
```

This expression is not only shorter and easier to enter, it also eliminates blank lines and extra spaces.

Expression Builder
When entering long expressions, it can be difficult to see the entire expression in the area allowed on the Report Expression dialog. If you need more room, or want more help with building an expression, select the ellipse button (…) to the right of the Expression text box. This displays the Expression Builder dialog shown in **Figure 3**.

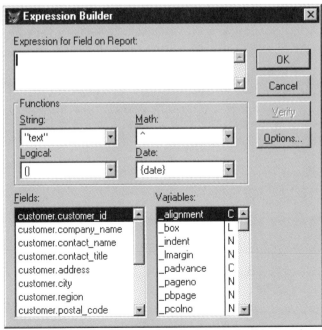

Figure 3*. Use the Expression Builder to build complex expressions for Field objects.*

If you already know the expression you want to enter for this Field object, type it in to the Expression for Field on Report edit box. When done, you may press the OK button to save the expression and return to the Report Expression dialog.

If you don't know the exact expression and want help from the Report Designer, you're in luck. You can select items from the four Functions drop-down combo boxes, items from the Fields list box, and items from the Variables list box. As you select these items, the function, field, or variable appears in the Expression for Field on Report edit box just as if you had typed it yourself. It's a great way to reduce your typing or to look up a function, field, or variable when you can't remember exactly what you're looking for.

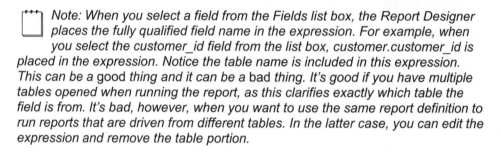

Note: When you select a field from the Fields list box, the Report Designer places the fully qualified field name in the expression. For example, when you select the customer_id field from the list box, customer.customer_id is placed in the expression. Notice the table name is included in this expression. This can be a good thing and it can be a bad thing. It's good if you have multiple tables opened when running the report, as this clarifies exactly which table the field is from. It's bad, however, when you want to use the same report definition to run reports that are driven from different tables. In the latter case, you can edit the expression and remove the table portion.

The Functions drop-down combo boxes list all the valid functions in Visual FoxPro, separated into four categories to make it easier to find the right function. What's listed in the Fields list box is every field of every table in the Data Environment. What's listed in the Variables list box is every system variable, every user-defined variable within the current scope, and every Report Variable defined within this report. In addition to the names of each variable, the variable type is also included in the Variables list box.

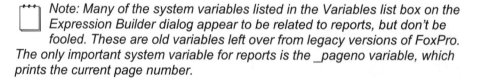

Note: Many of the system variables listed in the Variables list box on the Expression Builder dialog appear to be related to reports, but don't be fooled. These are old variables left over from legacy versions of FoxPro. The only important system variable for reports is the _pageno variable, which prints the current page number.

As previously mentioned, only the fields of tables in the Data Environment are listed in the Fields list box. However, if you'd like to see fields from other tables, enter the following commands in the Command Window prior to opening the Report Designer.

```
USE <MyTable>
SCATTER MEMVAR MEMO
```

This causes all the fields from the table to appear in the Variables list box in the Expression Builder dialog. Notice that I said the *Variables* list box and not the *Fields* list box.

Verify

The Verify button is used to *test* the expression to make sure it's valid. Select the Verify button and the VFP Report Designer evaluates the expression. If the expression is valid,

"Expression is valid" is displayed on the VFP Status Bar at the bottom of the screen. If the status bar is not turned on, the message is displayed in a WAIT WINDOW. If the expression fails validation, a message box is displayed with the appropriate error message.

Be aware, however, that the validation may fail even though the expression is valid. This happens when a variable, object property, object method call, or UDF is used in the expression, but it's not available to the Report Designer. For example, you may use oApp.cCompanyName in the expression to print the cCompanyName property of your Application object. However, when you're in the Report Designer, your Application object isn't instantiated, therefore, it's properties aren't available. So, to reiterate, the validation may return an error, when in fact, the expression is valid.

Expression Builder options
Previously, I said that *every* valid VFP function is listed in one of the four Functions drop-down combo boxes and *all* the system variables are listed in the Variables list box. Now I'm going to retract that statement—sort of. As long as you haven't changed any of the default options, the statement is true. However, if you've changed some options, it *may* not be true.

To change the options, select the Options... button from the Report Expression dialog, which displays the Expression Builder Options dialog shown in **Figure 4**.

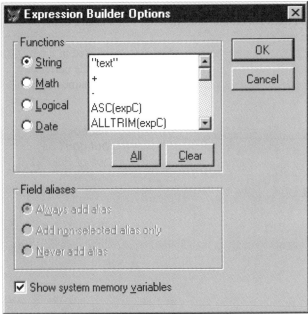

Figure 4. *The Expression Builder Options dialog allows you to control which functions and system memory variables appear in the Expression Builder dialog.*

To control which functions appear on the Expression Builder dialog, select one of the options in the Functions option group (String, Math, Logical, or Date). This displays the appropriate functions in the list box to the right. You may now select as many items as you wish using standard selection methods (for example: click, Shift-click, or Ctrl-click). To select all the items at once, select the All button. To unselect all the items, select the Clear button. Continue selecting which functions you want for each of the four categories.

Bug Alert!   *The Field aliases option group on the Expression Builder dialog is disabled and for the life of me, I can't figure out any way to enable it. I'm writing this one off as being a bug in the Visual FoxPro Report Designer.*

The "Show system memory variables" check box determines whether or not the system memory variables are displayed in the Variables list box on the Expression Builder dialog. If this box is unchecked, only the user-defined variables and Report Variables are displayed.

Once you've made all the changes you want to the options, select the OK button to return to the Expression Builder dialog. Be aware that the changes you make to the options are permanent in the Report Designer from this point forward (at least until you decide to change them again). This means that any time you bring up the Expression Builder dialog for any Field object on this report or any other report, the changes you just made remain in effect and control what is displayed. However, don't get worried about any existing expressions in reports. Just because a function or system variable is not listed in the Expression Builder dialog, it doesn't mean that you can't use that function or variable in an expression. It only means it won't be displayed in the Expression Builder dialog.

The Expression Builder Options are not available in the FoxPro 2.x Report Designer.

Wow!

Wow—all that discussion of the Expression text box, the Expression Builder dialog, and the Expression Builder Options dialog got pretty intense. Don't let the enormity of it all scare you. The bottom line is that you enter an expression for Field objects. That expression can be as simple as a table field or as complex as several VFP functions combined with table fields and method calls. You can enter the expression directly or let VFP help you build an expression. Either way, once again, the bottom line is that you enter an expression.

Format

The Format text box on the Report Expression dialog (see Figure 2 earlier in this chapter) is used to describe how the Report Writer should format the value that is obtained from evaluating the expression. For example, for numeric data, you may use *$999,999,999.99* to format the value as a dollar amount, or you may use *(999) 999-9999* to format the data as a phone number. With character data, you may use *@!* to force the data to all uppercase, or you may use *@R* to right-justify the data, or you may use *@!J* to do both. You may combine any number of formatting characters.

For a full list of valid formatting characters, see the InputMask Property entry and the Format Property entry in the Visual FoxPro Help system.

For a full list of valid formatting characters in FoxPro 2.x, see the @ ... GET entry and the @ ... SAY entry in the FoxPro Help system.

Keep in mind that when you enter an expression for formatting, such as $999,999.99, the Field object must be wide enough to accommodate the entire format expression. If the Field object isn't wide enough, the report displays asterisks (*) across the entire width of the Field object. To resolve this problem, either widen the Field object (discussed in the section titled "Resizing controls," later in this chapter) or shorten the format expression.

Format dialog

Similar to the Expression text box, you can press the ellipse button (...) to the right of the Format text box to display the Format dialog. The Editing options displayed on the bottom of the dialog vary depending on what type of field has been indicated in the option group under the Format text box. **Figure 5** shows the Format dialog with a *character* field. **Figure 6** shows the Format dialog with a *numeric* field. And **Figure 7** shows the Format dialog with a *date* field. Select Character, Numeric, or Date from the option group to select one of the three different Editing options.

The Editing options are pretty self-explanatory so I'm not going to go through each one. However, I do want to mention that not all options are available at all times. For example, with character data, if the Left justify, Right justify, or Center justify check box is checked, the other two are disabled (for obvious reasons).

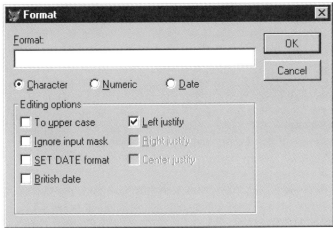

Figure 5. This Format dialog shows all the Editing options for character data.

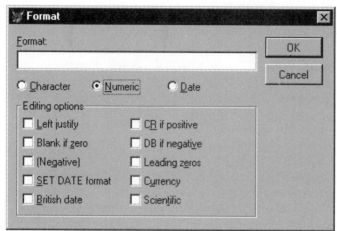

Figure 6. *This Format dialog shows all the Editing options for numeric data.*

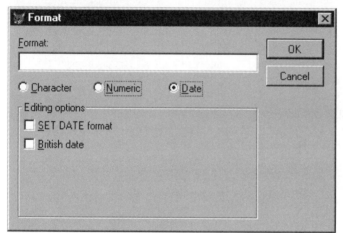

Figure 7. *This Format dialog shows all the Editing options for date data.*

Stretch with overflow

The setting of the "Stretch with overflow" check box (again, in Figure 2) is very important when printing a large number of characters or memo fields. For example, you may have a notes field in your table that could be empty, could contain one small phrase, or could be several paragraphs of information. You don't want to waste a large block of real estate on the report and designate a fixed-sized Field object that's large enough to accommodate the biggest possible size of the memo field. Instead, you want the report to expand the size of this Field object to accommodate the information in the expression.

Checking the "Stretch with overflow" check box does just that. If the expression is too big to fit within the size of the Field object on the report, the Report Writer expands the object as tall as necessary to accommodate the data in the expression. The width, however, always remains the same.

> The "Stretch with overflow" option is not available for Field objects placed in the Page Footer band. VFP needs to figure out how much room should be reserved at the bottom of the page so it knows when to do page breaks. If the height of the footer were to vary, the VFP Report Writer couldn't figure out how much room to reserve in advance for each different page. Therefore, the "Stretch with overflow" option is disabled for objects in the Page Footer.

One thing you don't have easy control over when stretching fields is the *leading*, which is the height of one single line plus the blank space between it and the next line. The Report Writer uses a complex formula for determining the leading, which is based on the defined height of the object and the particular font selected for the object. Making the object taller doesn't necessarily mean that the leading is increased. In fact, sometimes the opposite is true and a taller object has less leading. In Chapter 11, "Hacking the FRX," I reveal the formulas used by VFP so you can reverse engineer them to obtain a specific leading when necessary.

Calculations

The Visual FoxPro Report Designer has seven built-in mathematical calculation options: Count, Sum, Average, Lowest, Highest, Standard deviation, and Variance. The calculations allow you to process data from all the detail records and print information such as subtotals for each customer or grand totals at the end of the report.

The calculation is initiated when the first detail record is processed and the value of the expression is used by the calculation. Then, each subsequent detail record is processed in the same manner. The calculation continues until the Report Writer reaches the *reset* point for that calculation. Once the reset point is reached, the calculation is set to zero and resumes building the calculation again with the next detail record.

To add a calculation to a Field object, start by selecting the Calculations... button from the Report Expression dialog. This displays the Calculate Field dialog shown in **Figure 8**.

Figure 8. The VFP Report Writer has seven built-in calculations at your disposal.

The first item on the dialog is the Reset drop-down combo box. Use this to tell the VFP Report Writer what the reset point is for this calculation. The three standard values are End of

Report, End of Page, and End of Column. The End of Column option is only available if multiple column sets exist on the report. In addition to these three options, one additional option appears for each Data Grouping defined with the report (Data Grouping is discussed in detail in Chapter 7, "Data Grouping").

To help make all this clearer, I'm going to give you some examples of different ways to use the internal calculations of the VFP Report Writer. I'll start with a simple grand total of a quantity field at the end of the report. Place a Field object in the Summary band of the report. Enter *quantity* as the expression. Now select the Calculations... button, set the Reset value to End of Report, and select the Sum option. That's it. When the Summary band prints, the VFP Report Writer doesn't print the value of the last record processed, as one might think when looking at the expression of the Field object. Instead, it prints the total sum of all the detail records as indicated by the calculation options set up on that Field object.

Now I'll show you an example of how the Reset at End of Page option might be used. I want to create a report that prints the line number of each detail record on the page. Whenever a new page starts, I want the line number to start over. To accomplish this task, I create a Field object in the Detail band. For the expression, I can enter any valid expression. It doesn't matter what I enter because it's just a placeholder for the calculation. I usually make it something simple like the number 0. Now select the Calculations... button, set the Reset value to End of Page, and select the Count option. When the report prints, the 0 I entered in the expression is not printed. Instead, the running count created by the calculation is printed, thus giving me line numbers for each detail record. When the end of a page is reached, the calculation is reset to 0 so it starts over with 1 for the first detail line on the next page.

> The Count option is the only option that may be performed on character data. In the event that you indicate a calculation on a character field, the VFP Report Writer prints all asterisks (*) on the report for this object. Some of the calculations may be performed on date data, but not all of them. For example, it makes no sense to Sum a date field, but the Highest option prints the latest date. In the event you use an invalid calculation for a date, the VFP Report Writer prints an empty date (/ /).

The last example I'm going to explain has to do with Data Grouping. I haven't talked much about Data Grouping yet, but I'll do so in greater detail in Chapter 7, "Data Grouping." It's an important example to understand because it's one of the most commonly used types of calculation. I want to create a report that lists the order number, order date, and order amount of each order. I sorted the data by the customer and prepared a Data Grouping that *breaks* whenever the value of the *customer* field changes. The Data Grouping added a Group Footer band to the report that I'm going to take advantage of. In this band, I add five Field objects that all have an expression of *orderamt*. This may seem strange, but bear with me and it will make sense in a minute.

For each of these new Field objects, use the Calculations... button to invoke the Calculate Field dialog. Set the Reset option to *Customer* for all five objects. Select Count for the first object, Sum for the second object, Average for the third object, Lowest for the fourth object, and Highest for the fifth object. Is it starting to make sense now? Even though each of the five Field objects has the exact same expression, the value that prints is completely different for each of them. The first object prints the total number of orders for the customer. The second object prints the total amount of all the orders for the customer. The third object prints the average order amount of all the orders for this customer. The fourth object prints the lowest order amount for this customer… and you guessed it… the fifth object prints the highest order amount for this customer.

You've probably guessed by now that native variables and calculations are very powerful features of the Visual FoxPro Report Writer. This is why I can't fully subscribe to the denormalized methodology discussed in Chapter 4, "The Data Source." It would be a shame to ignore all this power!

Line

To add a horizontal line to the report, select the Line button from the Report Controls toolbar. Click on the report at the position you want to start the line, but don't release the mouse button yet. Drag the mouse left or right and let go of the mouse button when the line is the length you want. To add a vertical line, repeat the process, dragging the mouse up or down instead of left or right.

A vertical line placed within the Detail band repeats for each detail record. As long as the line starts at the very top of the band and ends at the very bottom of the band, it appears as a solid line on the report. However, it starts on the first detail record and ends with the last detail record. It doesn't fill up the entire page from top to bottom. But don't worry. I'm going to show you a trick that stretches a line from the top of the page to the bottom of the page.

Start the line anywhere in the Page Header band and end the line anywhere in the Page Footer band. This trick causes the line to stretch from the starting position, past all the detail records, and it continues all the way to the ending position in the Page Footer. Keep in mind that even if the line is only one pixel in the Header band and one pixel in the Detail band, the trick works. So you can fudge the appearance of a vertical line through the entire detail section of a report, even if the page isn't entirely filled with detail records.

This same trick that is used to stretch a line from one band to another can also be used to stretch a Rectangle or a Rounded Rectangle object.

Rectangle

Adding a Rectangle object is very similar to adding a line. Select the Rectangle button from the Report Controls toolbar and click on the report where you want one corner of the rectangle anchored. While still holding down the mouse button, drag the mouse to the opposite diagonal corner of where you want the rectangle to stop. Let go of the mouse button when the rectangle is the size you want.

Rounded Rectangle

Add a Rounded Rectangle object in exactly the same manner just described for a Rectangle object. If you want to change the radius used on the object, invoke the Round Rectangle dialog, shown in **Figure 9**, by double-clicking on the newly created Rounded Rectangle.

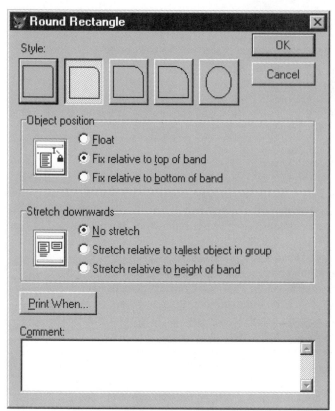

Figure 9. The Round Rectangle dialog is used to change the radius on the corners of the rectangle.

At the top of the Round Rectangle dialog there are five buttons that represent various degrees of rounding. Select the leftmost button for the least amount of rounding. Select any of the middle three buttons for softer rounding. Select the rightmost button for an ellipse.

The rest of the options in the Round Rectangle dialog are discussed later in this chapter in the section titled "Common options."

Picture/ActiveX Bound controls

To add a picture to the report, select the Picture/ActiveX Bound Control button from the Report Controls toolbar and click somewhere on the report. This inserts a small Picture object at the position of the mouse. You can also use the same click, stretch, and release method used with shapes to size the picture as you add it to the report. As soon as the Picture object is added to the report, the Report Picture dialog shown in **Figure 10** is displayed.

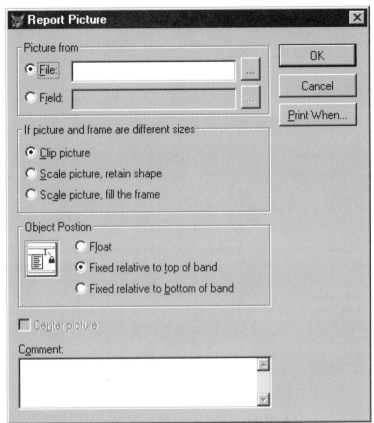

Figure 10. *The Report Picture dialog is used to set up the properties of a picture so it prints in the manner you desire.*

The first thing you need to describe to the Report Designer is where to get the picture. This is done with the Picture from option group and either the File text box or the Field text box.

Picture from File

The File option tells the VFP Report Writer that the picture is a physical file, such as MyPicture.JPG. Depending on how your application is designed, you may need to qualify the file name with a partial or full path. If the file resides in a directory that is within the current VFP search path, you won't need the path. However, if the file doesn't reside within VFP's search path, you need to qualify the file name with enough path information for the Report Writer to find the file.

You may also select the ellipse (…) button to the right of the File text box to invoke the standard Open dialog. From this dialog, you can navigate to the directory that contains the picture and select it. Upon returning from the Open dialog, the File text box contains the name of the file you selected—with the full path name.

> *It's important to realize that only the minimum relative path needed to find the file is saved with the report. The full path is only displayed in the text box for your benefit.*

Besides entering a file name in the File text box, you may also enter an expression that returns the file name of the picture to print. This is a very powerful feature! Consider the following situation.

You have an inventory table with hundreds of items. You have pictures to associate with each of the items in the table. Sometimes, the same picture is used for several items. For example, you have a widget that comes in red, white, and blue. The item exists in the inventory table three times because the part number varies depending on the color. But you only have one picture that shows all three widgets. You could design the Inventory table with a *General* field and use APPEND GENERAL to insert the picture into each and every Inventory item, but this would result in a lot of wasted space when the same picture is used for multiple items.

A better approach is to leave the pictures as stand-alone files. In your inventory table, add a field called *PictureFile* as a character or memo field. What is stored in this field is the *name* (and path if necessary) of the picture that relates to this item. The picture itself is not stored in the Inventory table. When you add the Picture object to the report, enter *Inventory.PictureFile* in the File text box. Once the file name is obtained from the expression, the Report Writer continues in its normal fashion looking for the file and printing it on the report.

> *Note: A common mistake when implementing this scenario is to enter Inventory.PictureFile in the* Field *text box instead of the* File *text box. But you have to realize that the picture itself is not contained in a field. It's contained in a stand-alone file and you're just using an expression, which happens to use a field, to point to the file.*

Another example of when to use an expression is when you have to conditionally print a picture. For example, assume your application is a multi-company application that prints invoices. The company logo that prints at the top of the invoice differs based on which company the particular invoice is for. For this situation, you can use an IIF() function to determine which file to print, as shown here:

```
IIF(Invoice.Company = 'A', 'LogoA.JPG', 'LogoB.JPG')
```

If there are too many possibilities that make an IIF() function too complex, use a UDF or method call to return the appropriate file name as shown here:

```
oApp.CompanyLogo(Invoice.Company)
```

Either of these examples tells the VFP Report Writer to evaluate the expression and print the picture whose file name is returned by the expression. So, like I said previously, being able to enter an *expression* for the file name is a very powerful feature!

Sorry! The ability to enter an expression for the file name is a feature that was added to Visual FoxPro. Older FoxPro 2.x applications can't use this trick.

Picture from Field

The Field option tells the VFP Report Writer that the picture is stored within a *General* field in a VFP table. The Report Writer extracts the picture file from the indicated field and prints it on the report. If you've never used general fields to store pictures, don't worry. It's really easy. Use the following code to create a table and add a few records with pictures.

```
CREATE TABLE Test (pk I, MyPicture G)
INSERT INTO Test (pk) VALUE (1)
APPEND GENERAL MyPicture FROM c:\pictures\LogoA.JPG
INSERT INTO Test (pk) VALUE (2)
APPEND GENERAL MyPicture FROM c:\pictures\LogoB.JPG
```

The picture files you append into the general fields still have to be one of the supported formats of BMP, JPG, or ICO. Or *do* they? Hmmm…

This is where the ActiveX... er... I mean the OLE Bound stuff comes into play. What happens if you append a Microsoft Word document or Excel spreadsheet into the general field? As long as you have the associated application installed, the document prints on the VFP Report. Now that is really cool! Think of the possibilities. However, keep in mind it only prints within the area defined for the Picture object. So a multi-page Word document won't print in its entirety without you pulling some major tricks to break the document down into separate documents appended into separate records.

The Picture Frame

There are three options in the "If picture and frame are different sizes" option group (see Figure 10). These options allow you to tell the VFP Report Writer what to do when the size of the picture does not match the size of the Picture object (frame) you placed on the report.

- **Clip picture:** This option tells the VFP Report Writer to position the upper left corner of the picture in the frame and to chop off any portion of the picture that extends beyond the right and bottom edges of the frame.

- **Scale picture, retain shape:** This option tells the VFP Report Writer to expand or shrink the picture so that it fills the frame. However, it will retain the proportional height and width of the picture, and thus, the original dimensions of the frame may be changed.

- **Scale picture, fill the frame:** This option tells the VFP Report Writer to expand or shrink the picture so that it fills the frame both horizontally and vertically. Because the *ratio* between the height and width of the picture is probably different from the *ratio* between the height and width of the frame, the picture may become distorted.

Center Picture

OLE objects that come from general fields of a table can vary in shape and size. By default, the object is anchored in the upper left corner of the frame. Check the Center Picture check box to center the object within the frame you've designed. This option is only available for Picture from Fields, not Files.

Button Lock

The Button Lock button is used to help you quickly add objects of the same type to the report. Select the Button Lock button from the Report Controls toolbar to toggle the Lock mode on. Select the Label button from the Report Controls toolbar. Click on the report and start typing the text for the first label. When finished, click on another portion of the report and start typing the text for the second label. Continue in this manner until you've added all the labels you need. Turn the Lock mode off by selecting the Button Lock button again or selecting the Select Objects button from the Report Controls toolbar. The lock feature is available for all the Report objects (Label, Field, Line, Rectangle, Rounded Rectangle, and Picture/ActiveX Bound controls).

In addition to using the Button Lock button, you can also toggle Lock mode on by double-clicking any of the Report object buttons in the Report Controls toolbar. This does the same as selecting the Button Lock button, followed by selecting an individual Report object button. You should also note that once the Lock mode is on, you can bounce back and forth between different Report objects. For example, turn Lock mode on, select the Label object, and add five labels, and then select the Field object and add three Field objects, and then select the Rectangle object and add two Rectangle objects. It's a real time-saver when adding lots of objects to a report.

Common options

Many of the different types of Report objects have common options and settings, so I'm being efficient and describing those here in one common place. You may have jumped ahead in your reading and still have a particular Report object's dialog on the screen, but most likely, you've closed the dialogs by now and are wondering how to bring them back up. One simple way is to double-click the object with the mouse. Other ways are discussed in the section titled "Changing properties," later in this chapter.

Field/Object position

The Field position option group (used by Field objects) and Object position option group (used by all other types of objects) determine where this object prints within the band (see **Figure 11**). It is extremely important when dealing with data that contains long character or memo fields that may wrap to two or three lines.

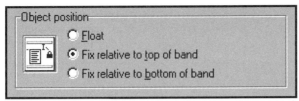

Figure 11. *The Object position (and Field position) option group determines where this object prints within a band.*

The three choices are:

- **Float:** This option tells the VFP Report Writer to move the object relative to the other objects that appear directly above it. For example, if one Field object is stretched an additional three lines, any objects positioned underneath it that are marked as *float* are moved down three lines.

- **Fix relative to top of band:** This option tells the VFP Report Writer to maintain the top starting position of this object, relative to the top of the band, regardless of whether or not other objects within the band stretch. For example, if you placed the object exactly 0.25" below the top of the band, it *always* prints 0.25" below the top of the band.

- **Fix relative to bottom of band:** This option tells the VFP Report Writer to maintain the top starting position of this object, relative to the bottom of the band, regardless of whether or not other objects within the band stretched and regardless of whether the band itself stretched. For example, if you placed the object exactly 0.5" from the bottom of the band, it *always* prints 0.5" away from the bottom of the band.

 In the FoxPro 2.x Report Designer, the "Stretch with overflow" option and the Object position options are combined into one option group, which means you have fewer possible combinations. The "Top— Constant Field Height" option is the same as VFP's "Fix relative to top of band" without the "Stretch with overflow" option. The "Top—Field Can Stretch" option is the same as VFP's "Fix relative to top of band" combined with the "Stretch with overflow" option. FoxPro 2.x's third option, Bottom, is the same as VFP's "Fix relative to bottom of band" without the "Stretch with overflow" option.

Float and Stretch with overflow

The *Float* option and the *Stretch with overflow* option are used hand-in-hand. However, unless you fully understand how objects float, you might not get the results you're looking for. When deciding whether an item needs to float, the Report Writer only looks at objects that are directly above the object in question. Objects that are to the right or left of the current object are not considered in the decision. The report definition, Products.FRX, produces the example shown in **Figure 12** and **Figure 13** and is included in the source code available with this book.

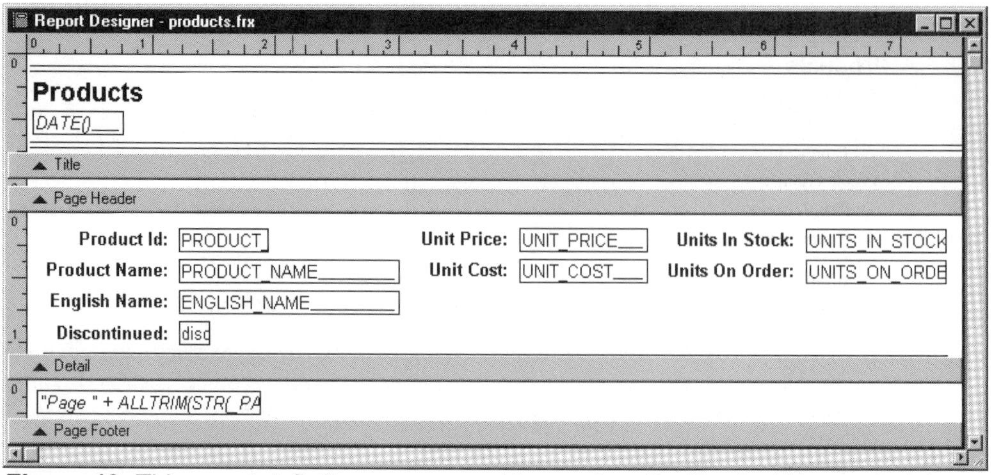

Figure 12. *This report definition causes problems when the Product Name stretches to multiple lines.*

The Product_Name, English_Name, and Discontinued Field objects are all marked as *Float*. In addition, the English Name and Discontinued Label objects are also marked as *Float*. However, when the report is printed, you don't exactly get what you wanted (see Figure 13).

At first sight, you may think everything looks okay. But look again, particularly at Product ID 4, Chef Anton's Cajun Seasoning. The Product Name was too long for one line and it stretched to the second line. The English Name and Discontinued fields underneath it floated down just as you expected. But look at the label for the "English Name." It didn't float down and it's no longer lined up with the Field object it's supposed to. The same thing happens for Product ID 6 and Product ID 7.

So why did this happen? The reason is that the Report Writer only checks objects that are directly above to determine whether an object needs to float. In this situation, when the Report Writer processed the English Name Label object, it only looked at the Product Name Label object and the Product ID Label object—neither of which had stretched. Therefore, the English Name Label object had no reason to float down. The Report Writer didn't realize that you wanted the English Name Label object to float *along with* the English_Name Field object.

So now what? Well, you have two options for solving this dilemma. The first is to change the Label objects to Field objects and make them wide enough that they extend into their corresponding data objects. Make sure that the new objects are wide enough to extend at least one pixel beyond the beginning of the Field objects. Also, be sure to use the *Send to Back* option on the new Field objects being substituted for the Label objects to ensure the actual data objects show in their entirety. The sample report definition shown in **Figure 14** is included in the source code available with this book and is named Products1.FRX. Now, when the Report Writer checks to see whether anything above the label (which is now a Field object) stretched, the Product_Name Field object *does* appear in the space directly above the label.

Products
03/16/2002

Product Id:	1	Unit Price:	18.00	Units In Stock:	39.000
Product Name:	Chai	Unit Cost:	12.60	Units On Order:	0.000
English Name:	Dharamsala Tea				
Discontinued:	N				

Product Id:	2	Unit Price:	19.00	Units In Stock:	17.000
Product Name:	Chang	Unit Cost:	13.30	Units On Order:	40.000
English Name:	Tibetan Barley Beer				
Discontinued:	N				

Product Id:	3	Unit Price:	10.00	Units In Stock:	13.000
Product Name:	Aniseed Syrup	Unit Cost:	7.00	Units On Order:	70.000
English Name:	Licorice Syrup				
Discontinued:	N				

Product Id:	4	Unit Price:	22.00	Units In Stock:	53.000
Product Name:	Chef Anton's Cajun Seasoning	Unit Cost:	15.40	Units On Order:	0.000
English Name:	Chef Anton's Cajun Seasoning				
Discontinued:	N				

Product Id:	5	Unit Price:	21.35	Units In Stock:	0.000
Product Name:	Chef Anton's Gumbo Mix	Unit Cost:	14.94	Units On Order:	0.000
English Name:	Chef Anton's Gumbo Mix				
Discontinued:	Y				

Product Id:	6	Unit Price:	25.00	Units In Stock:	120.000
Product Name:	Grandma's Boysenberry Spread	Unit Cost:	17.50	Units On Order:	0.000
English Name:	Grandma's Boysenberry Spread				
Discontinued:	N				

Product Id:	7	Unit Price:	30.00	Units In Stock:	15.000
Product Name:	Uncle Bob's Organic Dried Pears	Unit Cost:	21.00	Units On Order:	0.000
English Name:	Uncle Bob's Organic Dried Pears				
Discontinued:	N				

Figure 13. This sample report demonstrates the problem that can occur with stretchable fields.

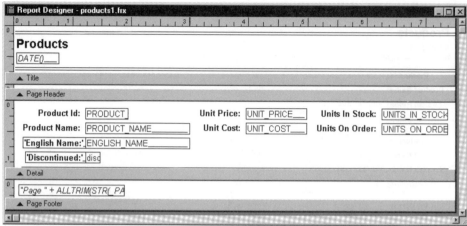

Figure 14. Change Label objects to Field objects and make them wide enough to extend into the Field objects they correspond with.

The second method is to add an invisible horizontal line between the two sets of Label and Field objects. To create an invisible line, add a horizontal line and either change its foreground color to white or change its pen style to None (Chapter 6, "Adding Pizzazz to the Objects," discusses how to change the color and pen style). **Figure 15** shows an example of this technique; however, it wouldn't do you any good if you couldn't see the *invisible* line, so I made it a dotted line instead. When you apply this technique, be sure to change the foreground color to white or the pen style to None. The report definition is included in the source code available with this book and is named Products2.FRX.

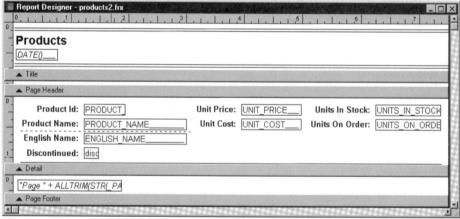

Figure 15. Use an invisible horizontal line to make Label objects and Field objects float together.

Using either of the two methods just described will overcome the problems of stretching and floating objects, as shown in the sample report in **Figure 16**.

Products
03/16/2002

Product Id:	1	Unit Price:	18.00	Units In Stock:	39.000
Product Name:	Chai	Unit Cost:	12.60	Units On Order:	0.000
English Name:	Dharamsala Tea				
Discontinued:	N				

Product Id:	2	Unit Price:	19.00	Units In Stock:	17.000
Product Name:	Chang	Unit Cost:	13.30	Units On Order:	40.000
English Name:	Tibetan Barley Beer				
Discontinued:	N				

Product Id:	3	Unit Price:	10.00	Units In Stock:	13.000
Product Name:	Aniseed Syrup	Unit Cost:	7.00	Units On Order:	70.000
English Name:	Licorice Syrup				
Discontinued:	N				

Product Id:	4	Unit Price:	22.00	Units In Stock:	53.000
Product Name:	Chef Anton's Cajun Seasoning	Unit Cost:	15.40	Units On Order:	0.000
English Name:	Chef Anton's Cajun Seasoning				
Discontinued:	N				

Product Id:	5	Unit Price:	21.35	Units In Stock:	0.000
Product Name:	Chef Anton's Gumbo Mix	Unit Cost:	14.94	Units On Order:	0.000
English Name:	Chef Anton's Gumbo Mix				
Discontinued:	Y				

Product Id:	6	Unit Price:	25.00	Units In Stock:	120.000
Product Name:	Grandma's Boysenberry Spread	Unit Cost:	17.50	Units On Order:	0.000
English Name:	Grandma's Boysenberry Spread				
Discontinued:	N				

Product Id:	7	Unit Price:	30.00	Units In Stock:	15.000
Product Name:	Uncle Bob's Organic Dried Pears	Unit Cost:	21.00	Units On Order:	0.000
English Name:	Uncle Bob's Organic Dried Pears				
Discontinued:	N				

Figure 16. This sample report shows it's possible to overcome float issues.

Print When

Print When controls... well... when the object prints. Each of the different types of Report objects has a Print When... button on its associated dialog, which invokes the Print When dialog shown in **Figure 17**.

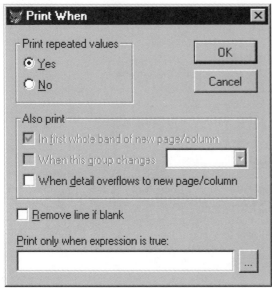

Figure 17. The Print When dialog allows you to tell the VFP Report Writer when an object should or shouldn't be printed.

The "Print repeated values" option group and the Also print check boxes work together to determine when an item prints. Their combined behavior depends on whether the object is a Field object or one of the other objects, and it gets pretty complicated to sort out. **Figures 18-20** show a three-page report that demonstrates the difference in behavior between a Rectangle object and a Field object with the various combinations selected. Use these examples as you read through the following explanations to help sort it all out.

Print repeated values

This option tells the Report Writer what to do when the value of this object is exactly the same as the previous record that was processed. A *Yes* indicates that you want this object printed each and every time, even if it's the same as the previous record. However, the meaning of *No* changes, depending on whether this is a Field object or one of the other Report objects. For a Field object only, *No* indicates you want this object suppressed if its value is exactly the same as the previous record. You can see the difference between these two objects in the sample report shown in Figure 18. The first Customer ID column has the "Print repeated values" option set to *Yes* and the second Customer ID column has it set to *No*.

 A *No* option for all non-Field objects, such as a line or rectangle, means this object never prints—that is, unless one of the Also print check boxes triggers the object to print. So if you use the *No* option and forget to check any of the Also print check boxes, the object *never* prints, as shown in the sample report in Figure 18. The report definition for this sample is included in the source code for this book and is named PrintWhen1.FRX.

Orders
03/16/2002

Order Number	Print Repeated Values = Yes Customer Id	Print Repeated Values = No Customer Id	Ship To Name
63	ALFKI	ALFKI	Alfred's Futterkiste
644	ALFKI		Alfred's Futterkiste
693	ALFKI		Alfred's Futterkiste
703	ALFKI		Alfred's Futterkiste
836	ALFKI		Alfred's Futterkiste
953	ALFKI		Alfred's Futterkiste
309	ANATR	ANATR	Ana Trujillo Emparedados y helados
626	ANATR		Ana Trujillo Emparedados y helados
760	ANATR		Ana Trujillo Emparedados y helados
927	ANATR		Ana Trujillo Emparedados y helados
29	ANTON	ANTON	Antonio Moreno Taquería
45	ANTON		Antonio Moreno Taquería
102	ANTON		Antonio Moreno Taquería
138	ANTON		Antonio Moreno Taquería
143	ANTON		Antonio Moreno Taquería
219	ANTON		Antonio Moreno Taquería
366	ANTON		Antonio Moreno Taquería
508	ANTON		Antonio Moreno Taquería
536	ANTON		Antonio Moreno Taquería
574	ANTON		Antonio Moreno Taquería
678	ANTON		Antonio Moreno Taquería
683	ANTON		Antonio Moreno Taquería
857	ANTON		Antonio Moreno Taquería
1126	ANTON		Antonio Moreno Taquería

Page 1

Figure 18. *The "Suppress repeated values" option controls whether or not a Field object prints if its value is the same as the previous record. However, for non-Field objects, it controls whether the object prints at all.*

Also print

There are three Also print check boxes, and each one offers another opportunity for the object to print, even if the "Print repeated values" option has suppressed it. Consider it an *override* feature to Print repeated values. This can be very confusing to understand, so bear with me here. You can refer to Figures 19-20 and **Figure 21** as you read through the following explanation and hopefully, they'll help you grasp the whole concept a little better.

In first whole band of new page/column

Checking this check box tells the Report Writer to go ahead and print this object in the first band that prints in its entirety on a new page (or column, if applicable). That's the official definition. But what really happens is slightly different. Besides printing the object in the first *full* band on a page, it also prints when a band has been continued from the previous page.

To understand how this works, follow the fourth column of boxes through all three pages shown in the sample report (Figures 19-21). The report definition for this report is included in the source code for this book and is named PrintWhen.FRX. On page 1, the word *Hello* prints for the first record because it's the first occurrence of the value *Hello*. The box also prints on page 1, but for a different reason. It's printing because the "In first whole band of new page/column" option is selected, which means that because this is the first record of the page, the box prints.

Now look at the second page of the report (Figure 20). The box and text print for the first record—even though this band is not printing in its entirety (it overflowed from the previous page). This is where the official definition doesn't quite match the behavior. The box and text print for the second record of page 2 (Figure 20) and for the first record on page 3 (Figure 21) because they're the first full band on their respective pages.

When this group changes

This option is only enabled when Data Grouping (discussed later in Chapter 7, "Data Grouping") has been used on the report. It tells the Report Writer to print this object whenever the selected Data Group changes. You can use this option, combined with the "Suppress repeated values" option, to only print an item for the first record in each Data Group.

When detail overflows to new page/column

Checking this check box tells the Report Writer to go ahead and print this object on the next page when a Detail band overflows. The fifth column of boxes on page 2 (Figure 20) demonstrates this overriding feature. The first row of data was started on the previous page (Figure 19) and overflowed to this page. Because the "When detail overflows to new page/column" check box is checked, the box and the word *Hello* are printed for this row again.

Example of Print When situations   Page: 1

	Box 1	Box 2	Box 3	Box 4	Box 5
Customer: ALFKI — Print Repeated Values...........	Yes	Yes	No	No	No
Also print in first whole band of new page/column......	X	X		X	
Also print when detail overflows to new page/column		X			X
Company Name: Alfreds Futterkiste	Hello	Hello	Hello	Hello	Hello
Customer: ANATR — Print Repeated Values...........	Yes	Yes	No	No	No
Also print in first whole band of new page/column......	X	X		X	
Also print when detail overflows to new page/column		X			X
Company Name: Ana Trujillo Emparedados y helados	Hello	Hello			
Customer: ANTON — Print Repeated Values...........	Yes	Yes	No	No	No
Also print in first whole band of new page/column......	X	X		X	
Also print when detail overflows to new page/column		X			X
Company Name: Antonio Moreno Taquería	Hello	Hello			

Figure 19. On page 1 of this sample report, the last customer is about to overflow to the next page.

Example of Print When situations   Page: 2

	Box 1	Box 2	Box 3	Box 4	Box 5
Print Repeated Values...........					
Also print in first whole band of new page/column......					
Also print when detail overflows to new page/column		Hello		Hello	Hello
Customer: AROUT — Print Repeated Values...........	Yes	Yes	No	No	No
Also print in first whole band of new page/column......	X	X		X	
Also print when detail overflows to new page/column		X			X
Company Name: Around the Horn	Hello	Hello		Hello	
Customer: BERGS — Print Repeated Values...........	Yes	Yes	No	No	No
Also print in first whole band of new page/column......	X	X		X	
Also print when detail overflows to new page/column		X			X
Company Name: Berglunds snabbköp	Hello	Hello			

Figure 20. On page 2 of this sample report, the last customer from page 1 has overflowed to this page.

Example of Print When situations	Page: 3	Box 1	Box 2	Box 3	Box 4	Box 5
Customer: BLAUS	Print Repeated Values...........	Yes	Yes	No	No	No
	Also print in first whole band of new page/column......	X	X		X	
Company Name:	Also print when detail overflows to new page/column		X			X
Blauer See Delikatessen		Hello	Hello		Hello	
Customer: BLONP	Print Repeated Values...........	Yes	Yes	No	No	No
	Also print in first whole band of new page/column......	X	X		X	
Company Name:	Also print when detail overflows to new page/column		X			X
Blondel père et fils		Hello	Hello			
Customer: BOLID	Print Repeated Values...........	Yes	Yes	No	No	No
	Also print in first whole band of new page/column......	X	X		X	
Company Name:	Also print when detail overflows to new page/column		X			X
Bólido Comidas preparadas		Hello	Hello			

Figure 21. On the third page of this sample report, all three customers are fully contained on this page. No previous customer has overflowed to this page and the last customer completely fit on this page.

Remove line if blank

Checking this check box tells the Report Writer to completely remove this item from the band if it has no value or is not being printed because of any of the Print When settings. It then checks to see whether any other objects occupy the same horizontal space that this object would have occupied. If no other objects are being printed within the same horizontal space, the Report Writer collapses the band to reclaim the unused space.

A classic example of when you would use this feature is when you're printing names and addresses. Assume your table has the following fields: Name, Address1, Address2, City, State, and Zip. When stacking the fields, you place the Name first, followed by the first address line, followed by the second address line, and finish up with the City, State, and Zip combined on the last line. However, many addresses in the table don't have a second address line filled in and appear as follows:

```
Mary Smith
100 Main Street

Anytown, MI 49341
```

Not only does this *look* funny, but it also wastes a lot of space on the report. By marking the second address line as *Remove line if blank*, the empty second address line is removed and the space is reclaimed as follows:

```
Mary Smith
100 Main Street
Anytown, MI 49341
```

This looks much more professional and it doesn't use as much room on the report.

Print only when expression is true

This feature allows you to tell the Report Writer to only print this object when the expression entered in the "Print only when expression is true" text box evaluates to true. The expression can be any valid VFP expression from a simple *.t.* to something as complex as a method call, within another method call, using a form property as a parameter.

If you need help with building the expression, you may press the ellipse (…) button to the right of the text box. This displays the Expression Builder dialog discussed earlier in this chapter.

> *Note: Using the "Print only when expression is true" feature negates the settings of the "Print repeated values" option group and the Print also check boxes. This expression becomes the sole determination of whether or not this object is printed.*

> *Note: It's important to realize that "Print only when expression is true" is evaluated after Report Variables but prior to the On Entry expression of the band. So don't plan to use On Entry to set any variables used in the "Print only when expression is true" expression.*

Stretch Downwards

This option group is only available for Lines (vertical only), Rectangles, and Rounded Rectangles. It tells the Report Writer what to do if any of the objects within the same band stretch.

No Stretch

The No Stretch option means this object remains as defined. Its size is unaffected by any other stretched objects.

Stretch relative to tallest object in group

The "Stretch relative to tallest object in group" option means the Report Writer stretches this object to accommodate all other objects that have been *grouped* with this object. Grouping is discussed in greater detail in Chapter 6, "Adding Pizzazz to the Objects." This should not be confused with Data Groups, which are discussed in Chapter 7, "Data Grouping."

Stretch relative to height of band

The "Stretch relative to height of band" option tells the Report Writer that if the band itself has been stretched to accommodate some objects, this object should be stretched the same amount as the band.

The Stretch Downwards option group is not available as a separate option in the FoxPro 2.x Report Designer. It's combined with the Stretch option (see the note in the section titled "Field/Object position" earlier in this chapter).

Comment

The Comment edit box is just for informational purposes and does not affect the report in any way. You can use this to describe this particular object and document any special quirks or information that would be helpful to the next developer who has to maintain this report. (Or to help you remember what in the world you were thinking when you put this report together six months ago.)

Manipulating the controls

Now that you know how to add the different types of controls to the report, wouldn't it be nice to know how to change them? After all, we don't always get it right the first time!

Selecting controls

The first step in changing an existing control is to select the desired control. You can do this a number of different ways. First, you can select the Select Objects button on the Report Controls toolbar and then click the object you want to select. This changes the border of the object to give you a visual clue that the object is selected. To select multiple objects, start by selecting the first object. Then, use the Shift key at the same time you click on a second object. The first object remains selected as the second object is selected. You can continue in this manner selecting as many objects as desired. If you select an object that is already selected, it's unselected, while the other selected objects remain selected.

You can also use a *selection marquee*, which selects all objects within a rectangular area. First, select the Select Objects button on the Report Controls toolbar. Next, click somewhere on the report, but don't release the mouse button yet. Drag the mouse to create a rectangular area that encompasses the objects you want to select. When finished, release the mouse button. All objects that are within the selection marquee are selected. Note that objects don't have to be fully contained within the selection marquee to be selected. As long as any portion of the object is within the selection marquee, the object is selected.

To select an object with the keyboard, use Ctrl-Tab to put the Report Designer in *Tab mode*. Once Tab mode is initiated, you may press the Tab key to navigate through the objects one at a time, selecting each one. As you tab to the next object, the first object is unselected and the next object is selected. In other words, only one object is selected at a time. There doesn't appear to be any way to select multiple objects with the keyboard. In addition to the Tab key, you may press Shift-Tab to navigate backwards through the objects.

As with any standard Windows application, you can also use Ctrl-A to select all objects on the report.

Moving controls

To move a control, click and drag the control to the new position. However, be sure the cursor is *not* positioned on one of the resizing squares around the border of the object. For more refined movement, select the object (using any method just described) and use the up, down, left, and right arrow keys to move the object one pixel at a time. You can also use the Ctrl key along with the arrow keys to move the object several pixels at a time. However, the number of pixels isn't consistent. It seems to be approximately 10, give or take a few. Also, when moving right or left, I've noticed that sometimes it also moves up or down one or two pixels as well.

Resizing controls

To resize a control, start by selecting the control. Once selected, use the mouse to click on one of the resizing squares around the border of the object and drag to the desired size. The four corner resizing squares allow you to change both the height and width of the object at the same time. Select either the top or bottom square to just change the height of the object, or select either the left or right square to just change the width.

For more controlled resizing, select the object and then use the Shift key in combination with one of the arrow keys. Each stroke of the arrow key changes the size by one pixel. The up arrow decreases the height of the object, the down arrow increases the height of the object, the left arrow decreases the width of the object, and the right arrow increases the width of the object. However, be aware that if the *Snap to Grid* option is on, you cannot change the height of the object with this method.

For those of you who are more comfortable using the mouse, you can click on any of the non-corner resizing squares. The height and width of the object will be increased or decreased a pixel at a time, depending on which square was clicked. Left and top squares *decrease* the dimension of the object; right and bottom squares *increase* the dimension of the object. If you want to get real fancy, you can click on the corner resizing squares and complete two actions with one motion. Just be aware that both the height and width of the object will be affected— maybe *not* in the direction you anticipated.

Duplicating controls

To copy a control, you must first select it and then use Ctrl-C to copy it to the report clipboard. Use Ctrl-V to paste a copy of the object on the report. You may also copy objects between two different reports using this method.

Deleting controls

To delete a control, start by selecting it. Once selected, you may either press the Del key or the Ctrl-X key combination.

Changing properties

As you've seen throughout this chapter, each of the different types of controls has some type of dialog window associated with it. These dialogs are used to set properties for the objects. There are several different methods for bringing up the dialogs associated with an existing control. The first method is to use the mouse to double-click the object. Another method is to right-click the object with the mouse and select Properties from the right-click menu.

To use the keyboard to invoke a particular object's dialog, start by selecting the object as described earlier in this chapter in the section titled "Selecting controls." Once a control is selected, you may press Alt-Enter to invoke the dialog associated with the object.

Editing a Label object

The one last thing you need to know about editing objects is how to edit the text of a Label object. You may have already noticed that the text of a label is *not* one of the items in the Text dialog associated with a label. At first thought, you may think that once you've typed the text, that's it and you can't ever change it again. If this is the case, you're not alone. The way to edit a label is not so obvious and has eluded many developers over the years.

Select the Label button from the Report Controls toolbar. Only this time, instead of placing the mouse cursor on an unused portion of the report, place it on top of the label you want to change. This switches to an Edit mode where you can begin inserting, deleting, and overwriting characters at the point of the cursor. You can even use the left and right arrow keys to move within the text.

To accomplish the same task with the keyboard, start by selecting the object as described earlier in the section titled "Selecting controls." Once the label is selected, press Ctrl-E to turn Edit mode on. This places your cursor at the end of the text and allows you to start editing it. When you've finished editing the text, press Esc to exit Edit mode.

More ways to add controls

Now that you know how to add all the different types of controls, it's time you learn a few more ways to skin a cat. After all, you can't just learn *one* method for adding controls. That wouldn't be the FoxPro way!

Insert Control

Earlier in this chapter, I described how to add each of the controls through the Report Controls toolbar using the mouse. For those who are rodently-challenged, you can also add items through the menu. Select Report | Insert Control from the main VFP Menu bar. This displays a submenu with the six different types of Report objects. Select any one of them and the selected object's associated dialog appears. Once you've entered the properties and selected OK from the dialog, the object is added to the upper left corner of the report. You can use any of the methods described in the section titled "Moving controls," earlier in this chapter, to move the object to the desired position.

The Data Environment

In the section titled "The Data Environment" in Chapter 4, "The Data Source," I described how to add tables to the Data Environment of a report. One of the advantages of doing this is that you can quickly add objects to the report using drag-and-drop.

If the Data Environment is not open, go ahead and open it with the method of your choice. To add an individual field from a table to the report, select the field with the mouse, drag it to the desired position on the report, and release the mouse button. Notice how the Report Designer made a very good attempt at sizing the field based on the defined length of the field in the table. It also sets the formatting of the object to character, numeric, or date based on the type of the field in the table. Unfortunately, it doesn't add any captions or formatting that are set up in the database.

To add multiple fields from the same table, select all the desired fields and drag and drop them together as one on the report. The fields are added to the report, each one below the previous field. To add all the fields from the table to the report, select the Fields: icon at the top of the table and drag and drop it to the report. When adding multiple fields to a report using this drag-and-drop technique, the height of the band is automatically expanded to accommodate all fields, if necessary.

 Reminder: The FoxPro 2.x Report Designer does not have a Data Environment; therefore, you can't add Field objects to a report using this method.

Quick Report

In the section titled "Create a Quick Report" in Chapter 3, "Learning the Basics," you learned how to create a *Quick Report* from the VFP Command Window. Would it surprise you at all to learn there's another way to create a Quick Report?

While in the Report Designer, select Report | Quick Report... from the main VFP Menu bar to invoke the Quick Report dialog shown in **Figure 22**.

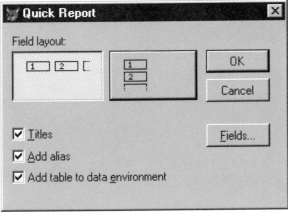

Figure 22. The Quick Report dialog allows you to tell the VFP Report Designer what fields you want included on the report and how it should add them.

The first two buttons on the Quick Report dialog let you determine whether the fields should be added as columns (across the page) or rows (down the page). Only one of these buttons may be selected at a time.

Check the Titles check box if you want a Label object added along with the field as a column or row title. The text for the Label object is the field name of each of the corresponding fields. If you've chosen a Column layout, the Label objects are added in the Page Header band directly above each of the corresponding Field objects. If you've chosen a Row layout, the Label objects are added down the leftmost edge of the report. Each of the corresponding Field objects are added to the right of the labels, with all Field objects aligned and starting in the same horizontal position.

Check the Add Alias check box to tell the VFP Report Designer to add the fully qualified field name as the expression. In other words, *MyTable.MyField* is used instead of just *MyField*. When designing reports with multiple tables opened, it's good to qualify the field names to avoid any confusion. On the other hand, if you design a report without the table aliases in the expressions, the report becomes more flexible. You can then run the same report from different tables as long as the structures of the tables are the same.

Check the "Add table to data environment" check box to tell the VFP Report Designer to add the currently selected table to the Data Environment, if it doesn't already exist.

So by now you might be asking, "What table *does* the VFP Report Designer use to create a Quick Report?" Well, it depends. If you have any tables defined in the Data Environment, the first table listed is the one it uses. If no tables are opened in the Data Environment, it uses whatever table is the currently selected table in VFP. If no tables are opened in the Data Environment *and* no tables are opened in VFP, you're prompted to select a table with the standard Open dialog as soon as you choose the Quick Report option.

But what if you want fields from a table other than the first table listed in the Data Environment? Or what if you only want a few fields from a table? Or what if you want some fields from one table and a few other fields from a second table? Don't worry—you can do all of these. Select the Fields… button from the Quick Report dialog to display the Field Picker dialog shown in **Figure 23**.

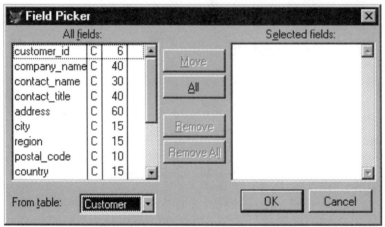

Figure 23. The Field Picker dialog allows you to pick and choose which fields to include on the report when generating a Quick Report.

The From table drop-down combo box at the bottom of the Field Picker dialog lets you choose which table is used to list the fields in the All Fields list box. All tables in the Data Environment are included in this combo box along with any tables currently opened in Visual FoxPro.

Move fields from the All fields list box to the Selected fields list box by either double-clicking the field or selecting the field and then selecting the Move button. You may also move the fields from the Selected fields list box back into the All fields list box if you change your mind. When you have all the fields you desire listed in the Selected fields list box, select the OK button to return to the Quick Report dialog.

Once you've entered all the criteria you want in the Quick Report dialog, select the OK button and the VFP Report Designer creates the Quick Report right before your very eyes. All the selected fields (or all fields if you haven't specifically selected any) are added to the report. The detail band is resized according to the amount of information added by the Quick Report. In addition, a Field object for the date and a Label and Field object for the page number are added to the Page Footer of the report.

 Note: The FoxPro 2.x Report Designer disables the Quick Report option from the menu if any objects already exist on the report. You must be working from a clean slate to use this option.

Conclusion

By now your head is probably spinning because this chapter was chock-full of information and covered a lot of ground. You learned all about the different types of Report objects and saw the great potential of the VFP Report Writer. In the next chapter, you'll learn how to add pizzazz to all these Report objects. After all, you don't want to create dull and boring reports, do you? Wouldn't you rather present your clients and end users with really great-looking reports? If so, read on.

Chapter 6
Adding Pizzazz to the Objects

Dull and boring reports are *not* **what our users deserve. They deserve reports that have pizzazz and are easy to read and understand. This means you have to get creative with formatting, alignment, and the placement of all the objects. The report should be visually pleasing to the human eye—like a fine piece of art. This chapter teaches you how to transform your artistic ideas into reality.**

Compare the report shown in **Figure 1** to the report shown in **Figure 2**. They both show the exact same data, but the second report looks much better. Why is that? It's because the layout and appearance of the first report is plain, while the layout and appearance of the second report is much more polished. The report definitions for the samples shown in Figure 1 and Figure 2 are included in the source code available with this book, and are named Pizzazz1.FRX and Pizzazz2.FRX, respectively.

```
03/16/2002              Inventory Value Report                  Page      1

                                                         Discontinued
                                    Unit Cost  Quantity on Hand  Unit Cost
 Product Id  Product Name
       1     Chai                      12.6000         39.000      491.4000 N

       2     Chang                     13.3000         17.000      226.1000 N

       3     Aniseed Syrup              7.0000         13.000       91.0000 N

       4     Chef Anton's Cajun Seasoning  15.4000    53.000      816.2000 N

       5     Chef Anton's Gumbo Mix    14.9450          0.000        0.0000 Y

       6     Grandma's Boysenberry Spread  17.5000   120.000     2100.0000 N

       7     Uncle Bob's Organic Dried Pears  21.0000  15.000     315.0000 N

       8     Northwoods Cranberry Sauce   28.0000      6.000      168.0000 N

       9     Mishi Kobe Niku           67.9000          1.000       67.9000 Y

      10     Ikura                     31.7000         31.000      672.7000 N
```

Figure 1. This report contains all the necessary data, but it's very plain and boring.

Product ID	Product Name	Unit Cost	Quantity on Hand	Inventory Value	
				Inventory Value Report	Page: 1
1	Chai	12.6000	39.000	$491.40	
2	Chang	13.3000	17.000	$226.10	
3	Aniseed Syrup	7.0000	13.000	$91.00	
4	Chef Anton's Cajun Seasoning	15.4000	53.000	$816.20	
5	Chef Anton's Gumbo Mix	14.9450	0.000	$0.00	Discontinued
6	Grandma's Boysenberry Spread	17.5000	120.000	$2,100.00	
7	Uncle Bob's Organic Dried Pears	21.0000	15.000	$315.00	
8	Northwoods Cranberry Sauce	28.0000	6.000	$168.00	
9	Mishi Kobe Niku	67.9000	1.000	$67.90	Discontinued
10	Ikura	21.7000	31.000	$672.70	
11	Queso Cabrales	14.7000	22.000	$323.40	
12	Queso Manchego La Pastora	26.6000	86.000	$2,287.60	

03/16/2002

Figure 2. This report is much more pleasing to look at than the report shown in Figure 1.

Layout

In the previous chapter (Chapter 5, "Report Objects"), you learned how to place objects on the report. You also learned how to move them around and resize them. Now, wouldn't it be nice if you could tell the VFP Report Designer to align a bunch of objects on the same vertical axis instead of having to move each one individually? Or wouldn't it be nice to tell the VFP Report Designer to make a bunch of objects the exact same size? Well, you're in luck. The VFP Report Designer has several different layout options to help you do this and more.

The layout options may be accessed individually through the Format option on the main VFP Menu bar or through the layout options on the Layout toolbar (shown in **Figure 3**). You can display the Layout toolbar using one of three methods. The first method is to select View | Layout Toolbar from the main VFP Menu bar. The second method is to select the Layout Toolbar button from the Report Designer toolbar. The third method is to right-click on an unused portion of any *docked* toolbar and then select Layout.

Figure 3. Use the Layout toolbar to access most of the layout options.

The layout options on the Layout Toolbar are as follows (from left to right):

- Align Left Sides

- Align Right Sides

- Align Top Edges

- Align Bottom Edges

- Align Vertical Centers

- Align Horizontal Centers

- Same Width

- Same Height

- Same Size

- Center Horizontally

- Center Vertically

- Bring to Front

- Send to Back

> *Note: Not every layout option is available on the Layout toolbar, so you have to use the Format option on the main VFP Menu bar to access some of the lesser-used options. Also note that format options are only enabled when applicable. For example, the Align Left Sides option is only enabled when two or more objects are selected.*

> *FoxPro 2.x is not quite as rich as Visual FoxPro when it comes to the layout options. Not all of the options discussed here are available in FoxPro 2.x.*

Align

There are six different options that allow you to align objects relative to each other, and there are two additional options that allow you to center objects within a report band. The first step in aligning multiple objects at the same time is to *select* the objects. Next, select one of the align options from the Layout toolbar or select Format | Align | <your choice> from the main VFP Menu bar.

> *Note: The Snap to Grid setting is ignored when using any of the align options.*

Align Left Sides

This option tells the VFP Report Designer to position all the *selected* objects so their left sides are all flush. By default, the leftmost object is used as the reference point for aligning the objects. If you'd rather align the objects using the left edge of the object whose left edge is the farthest right on the report, hold down the Ctrl key while you select the Align Left Sides button from the Layout toolbar.

Align Right Sides

This option tells the VFP Report Designer to position all the *selected* objects so their right sides are all flush. By default, the object with the rightmost edge is used as the reference point for aligning the objects. If you'd rather align the objects using the right edge of the object whose right edge is the farthest left on the report, hold down the Ctrl key while you select the Align Right Sides button from the Layout toolbar.

Align Top Edges

This option tells the VFP Report Designer to position all the *selected* objects so their top edges are all flush. By default, the object with the topmost edge is used as the reference point for aligning the objects. If you'd rather align the objects using the top edge of the object whose top edge is the lowermost edge on the report, hold down the Ctrl key while you select the Align Top Edges button from the Layout toolbar. Although you can align any of the objects on the report in this manner, you should be careful when selecting objects from more than one band. There's a good chance that one or more of the objects will *jump* bands and this may not be what you wanted.

Align Bottom Edges

This option tells the VFP Report Designer to position all the *selected* objects so their bottom edges are all flush. By default, the object with the bottommost edge is used as the reference point for aligning the objects. If you'd rather align the objects using the bottom edge of the object whose bottom edge is the uppermost edge on the report, hold down the Ctrl key while you select the Align Bottom Edges button from the Layout toolbar. As with the Align Top Edges option, you should exercise caution when selecting objects in more than one band.

Align Vertical Centers

This option tells the VFP Report Designer to position all the *selected* objects with their centers, width-wise, positioned in the same column. To determine where the centers of the objects are placed on the report, the Report Designer looks at the leftmost edge of all the selected objects and then looks at the rightmost edge of all the selected objects. It uses the center of those two points as the column position for centering all the selected objects.

Align Horizontal Centers

This option tells the VFP Report Designer to position all the *selected* objects with their centers, height-wise, positioned in the same row. To determine where the centers of the objects are placed on the report, the Report Designer looks at the topmost edge of all the selected objects and then looks at the bottommost edge of all the selected objects. It uses the center of those two points as the row position for centering all the selected objects.

Center Vertically

This option tells the VFP Report Designer to position the *selected* object so it's equally spaced between the top and bottom edges of the band. If multiple objects are selected at the time you choose Format | Align | Center Vertically from the main VFP Menu bar, the entire group of selected objects is treated as one object for the purpose of centering. In other words, each object retains its relative position to the other objects. However, sometimes when multiple objects are selected, the VFP Report Designer freaks out and moves the objects to a position that's completely unexpected. I can't seem to pinpoint exactly what triggers this unexpected behavior. Sometimes it works as expected and other times it doesn't.

Center Horizontally

This option tells the VFP Report Designer to position the *selected* object so it's equally spaced between the left and right edges of the band. If multiple objects are selected at the time you choose Format | Align | Center Horizontally from the main VFP Menu bar, the entire group of selected objects is treated as one object for the purpose of centering. In other words, each object retains its relative position to the other objects.

> Note: Whenever the VFP Report Designer attempts to align multiple objects at the same time, it takes care to never move an object outside the left, right, top, or bottom edge of the report.

Size

There are four different options that allow you to size objects relative to each other, and there's one option that allows you to size objects relative to the grid.

 Sorry, but no sizing options are available in FoxPro 2.x.

Size to Grid

Select Format | Size | Size to Grid to change the width of each *selected* control so that its rightmost edge touches one of the Snap Points on the grid. If the closest Snap Point is to the left of the object's right edge, the object is shortened. If the closest Snap Point is to the right of the object's right edge, the object is lengthened. If multiple objects are selected, each object is resized individually.

Size to Tallest

Select Format | Size | Size to Tallest from the main VFP Menu bar to change the height of all the *selected* objects to match the height of the tallest object that is selected. You may also select the objects and then select the Same Height button from the Layout toolbar to accomplish the same task.

Size to Shortest

Select Format | Size | Size to Shortest from the main VFP Menu bar to change the height of all the *selected* objects to match the height of the shortest object that is selected. You may also select the objects and then hold down the Ctrl key while you select the Same Height button from the Layout toolbar to accomplish the same task.

Size to Widest

Select Format | Size | Size to Widest from the main VFP Menu bar to change the width of all the *selected* objects to match the width of the widest object that is selected. You may also select the objects and then select the Same Width button from the Layout toolbar to accomplish the same task.

Size to Narrowest

Select Format | Size | Size to Narrowest from the main VFP Menu bar to change the width of all the *selected* objects to match the width of the narrowest object that is selected. You may also select the objects and then hold down the Ctrl key while you select the Same Width button from the Layout toolbar to accomplish the same task.

Same Size

Select the Same Size button from the Layout toolbar to perform the Size to Tallest and Size to Widest options on all the *selected* objects at once. Press the Ctrl key at the same time you select the Same Size button from the Layout toolbar to perform the Size to Shortest and Size to Narrowest options on all the selected objects at once.

> Note: Whenever the VFP Report Designer attempts to size multiple objects, it takes care to never resize an object too large, causing it to extend outside the edges of the report.

Horizontal spacing

There are three horizontal spacing options in the Report Designer that may be accessed by selecting Format | Horizontal | <your choice> from the main VFP Menu bar.

Sorry, but no horizontal spacing options are available in FoxPro 2.x.

Make Equal

This option repositions each of the *selected* objects so the distance between each object is equal. It first figures out what the smallest horizontal gap is right now (ignoring any objects that overlap) and uses that as the new spacing. The leftmost object stays in its current position, and each of the remaining selected objects is positioned using the new spacing. The order in which the objects are repositioned is determined by the current order of their leftmost edges.

Increase

This option increases the horizontal gap between each *selected* object by two pixels. The leftmost object stays anchored in its current position, and each of the remaining objects is bumped two pixels to the right, then two more pixels (four pixels total), then two more pixels (six pixels total), and so on.

Decrease

This option decreases the horizontal gap between each *selected* object by two pixels. The leftmost object stays anchored in its current position, and each of the remaining objects is moved two pixels to the left, then two more pixels (four pixels total), then two more pixels (six pixels total), and so on.

Vertical spacing

There are three vertical spacing options in the Report Designer that may be accessed by selecting Format | Vertical | <your choice> from the main VFP Menu bar.

 Sorry, but no vertical spacing options are available in FoxPro 2.x.

Make Equal

This option repositions each of the *selected* objects so the distance between each object is equal. It first figures out what the smallest vertical gap is right now (ignoring any objects that overlap) and uses that as the new spacing. The topmost object stays in its current position, and each of the remaining selected objects is positioned using the new spacing. The order in which the objects are repositioned is determined by the current order of their topmost edges.

Increase

This option increases the vertical gap between each *selected* object by two pixels. The topmost object stays anchored in its current position, and each of the remaining objects is bumped two pixels down, then two more pixels down (four pixels total), then two more pixels down (six pixels total), and so on.

Decrease

This option decreases the vertical gap between each *selected* object by two pixels. The topmost object stays anchored in its current position, and each of the remaining objects is moved up two pixels, then two more pixels up (four pixels total), then two more pixels up (six pixels total), and so on.

Z-order

The term *Z-order* refers to the position of objects on the Z-axis. You can think of it as layers where each object is on its own layer. Object one is placed on the report, then object two is placed on a layer on top of object one's layer, then object three is placed on a layer on top of object two's layer, and so on.

The natural Z-order of Report objects is the order in which they were placed on the report. In other words, the first object you added is on the bottommost layer, then the second object is on the next-to-last layer, and so on, with the last object you added assigned to the topmost layer. To rearrange the Z-order of objects, don't look for an option on the menu or a toolbar called *Z-order* because you won't find it. Instead, use the *Bring to Front* and *Send to Back* options.

Bring to Front

To bring a *selected* object to the topmost layer, select Format | Bring to Front from the main VFP Menu bar. You may also select the Bring to Front button from the Layout toolbar or press Ctrl-G to move the selected objects to the top layer.

Send to Back

To send a *selected* object to the bottommost layer, select Format | Send to Back from the main VFP Menu bar. You may also select the Send to Back button from the Layout toolbar or press Ctrl-J to move the selected objects to the bottom layer.

> *Note: Keep in mind that only one object at a time resides on any individual layer. For example, assume you have Name, Address, and Phone Number objects on the report, residing on layers one, two, and three, respectively. When you select the Phone Number and choose Send to Back, the Phone Number is moved to layer one, the Name is bumped forward to layer two, and the Address is bumped forward to layer three.*

Disappearing objects

As long as no object overlaps another object, the Z-order is usually irrelevant to the outcome of the report. However, when objects overlap each other, the Z-order determines which objects are placed *on top of* each other. For example, consider the situation where you place a Field object that contains a total amount on the report and then place a Rectangle object on top of the Field object. When you run the report, you see the amount, surrounded by a rectangle just as you expected.

Now change the color of the rectangle to gray (see the section titled "Colors," later in this chapter) and run the report, and you may be quite surprised by what you see. You only see the gray box and not the total amount. Where did the total amount go? Well, it didn't go anywhere. However, the gray box is on top of the total amount, thus, covering it up so it isn't visible anymore. You need to either move the gray box to the bottom layer or bring the total amount Field object forward to the top layer. Either of these would solve the problem and allow the total amount to print on top of the gray box as you intended.

Express yourself

Another example of when the Z-order is significant to the outcome of the report is when you have UDFs and method calls in the expression of Field objects. Assume you're pulling some special tricks in the UDF, such as moving the record pointer in another table to the record that corresponds with the current detail record and returning a value from the second table. You also have three other Field objects in the Detail band that each print data from the second table.

It's imperative that the object with the UDF call is processed first so the other three objects print the data from the proper record. Otherwise, if the UDF is processed last, the three other Field objects would print the data from the record that corresponds to the previous Detail band. To ensure the correct processing order, make sure the object with the UDF is *Sent to Back* so that it gets processed before all the other objects.

Gotcha

It's important to realize that the Z-order of the objects is relative to one specific band. In other words, the objects within the Page Header band have their own Z-order, which has nothing to do with the Z-order of the objects in the Page Footer band. Selecting *Send to Back* for an object in the Page Footer only sends it to the first layer of the Page Footer band. It doesn't mean that the object is now processed before any of the Page Header objects. The bands are still processed in order (see the section titled "Parts of a report" in Chapter 1, "Introduction," for a detailed description of when the bands are processed).

So why is this section titled "Gotcha"? Well, consider the following situation where you have a gray Rectangle object in the Page Footer band of the report. You also have a vertical line that stretches from the Page Header band, continues through the Detail band, and ends in the Page Footer band. The vertical line goes right through the middle of the Rectangle object. Are you starting to see the gotcha yet?

The objects in the Page Header band are processed first. Then the Detail objects are processed, and finally, the objects in the Page Footer band are processed. This means the vertical line is printed first, and then the gray box is printed on top of it, covering a portion of the vertical line. So even though you may have selected *Send to Back* on the gray box, it doesn't help because it was only sent to the back of the Page Footer objects. The Page Header objects are still printed first.

A tricky workaround to this problem is to place a shorter line on top of the current line where it covers the rectangle, making sure to use *Bring to Front* on the shorter line. Because the shorter line is fully contained within the Page Footer band, just as the gray rectangle is, the problem is solved. The VFP Report Writer still prints the larger vertical line first. It then places the rectangle on the report, covering the line. Now it prints the shorter line right on top of the first line and on top of the rectangle, giving the appearance of one solid line that spans from the top of the report to the bottom of the report.

Group/Ungroup

Often times, several objects on the report are tightly associated with each other. For example, a Field object and its corresponding Label object could be considered one object in the overall scheme of things. When you move one of the objects, you need the other object to move right along with it, maintaining the relative position between the two objects. This can be done with the Group option.

Select the objects you want grouped together, and then select Format | Group from the main VFP Menu bar. The Report Designer now treats the objects as one single object. Whenever you move or align it, all the objects maintain their respective positions to each other.

However, now that the objects are grouped, you may not access any of the individual objects within the group to change their properties or settings, nor to resize them. If you need to do this, select the grouped objects and ungroup them by selecting Format | Ungroup from the main VFP Menu bar. This removes the grouping so the VFP Report Designer once again treats each object individually. You can now make your change and, if desired, select all the objects and group them together again.

Note: The Group/Ungroup option discussed here is not the same as the Data Grouping feature discussed in Chapter 7, "Data Grouping." The terminology is very confusing, and I wish the developers of the Report Designer had chosen something less similar for the two, such as Control Breaks instead of Data Grouping. Unfortunately, they didn't ask me, so I guess we have to live with the confusion.

Bug Alert! *There's a bug with grouped objects that can be very annoying at times. If you have objects grouped together and you add or delete a Data Group, the reference to grouped objects gets confused. The next time you select the grouped objects, the marquee appears in the wrong spot. Instead of surrounding all the grouped objects, it's offset by the height of the gray bar of the band that was added to or deleted from the report. To work around this bug, ungroup any grouped objects prior to adding or deleting Data Groups.*

Appearance

As you saw earlier in the sample reports shown in Figure 1 and Figure 2, the appearance of each object makes a world of difference in how a report is perceived. This section explains how to spiff up the objects on the report. The appearance of objects may be changed individually for each object on the report. You can also select several objects at once and change their appearance at the same time. This feature is a real time-saver.

Font

Label objects and Field objects each have a font associated with them. You may change the font of any object (or several selected objects) by selecting the object and selecting Format | Font... from the main VFP Menu bar. This invokes the Font dialog shown in **Figure 4**.

From the Font dialog, you may select the Font (such as Arial), the Font style (such as Bold), and the Size (such as 10) by selecting the desired value from the appropriate list box or typing the value into the appropriate text box. You may also select some special effects, such as Strikeout and Underline, by checking their associated check boxes. Finally, you may set the color of the text by choosing a color from the Color drop-down combo box at the bottom of the Font dialog.

To improve the speed when printing reports, design your reports with only those fonts that are native to the specific printers you'll be printing to.

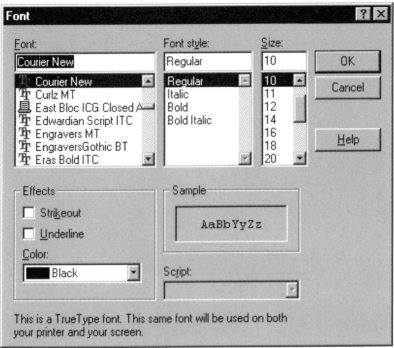

Figure 4. *Use the Font dialog to change the font properties of a Label object or a Field object.*

Default Font

You may have wondered why the Report Designer chooses to use the Courier New, Regular, 10 font when objects are first added to the report. The answer is because that's the default font. However, you can change the default font of any given report by selecting Report | Default Font… from the main VFP Menu bar. This invokes the same Font dialog shown in Figure 4.

Once you change the default font of a report, any newly added objects—to this report only—use the new default font. All previously added objects, and all previously defined reports, remain unaffected by the change. If you wish to change the font of existing objects, use the method just described in the section titled "Font."

The default font is saved with the report, so each time you edit a particular report with the VFP Report Designer, the same default font remains in effect for the given report. Unfortunately, there's no way to change what the default setting is for Default Font. Each new report you create always starts out with a default font of Courier New, Regular, 10.

 In FoxPro 2.x the default font is accessed by selecting Report | Page Layout… from the FoxPro system menu bar. Then select the Font… button from the Page Layout dialog.

Color

With today's wide variety of color printers, our users often want a lot of color on their reports. But even if you're limited to just a black and white printer, don't think the color options don't apply to you. The color options are still important because often the user wants a gray box here or reverse text there to make things stand out.

The coloring of objects is broken out into two different colors, the foreground color and the background color. The foreground color determines what color is used for the text of Label and Field objects and the lines used to draw Line, Rectangle, and Rounded Rectangle objects. The background color determines what color is used to fill the inside of a Rectangle or Rounded Rectangle object as well as the background of a Label or Field object.

 In FoxPro 2.x, you only have access to 16 basic colors and are not allowed to describe any custom colors as you can with Visual FoxPro.

Basic colors

To change the foreground color of an object, select the object. Then select Format | Foreground Color... from the main VFP Menu bar. This displays the Color dialog shown in **Figure 5** (although it's just not the same when printed on a black and white page in a book). You may select any of the basic 48 colors from this dialog and then select the OK button to return to the Report Designer with the foreground color of the selected object changed.

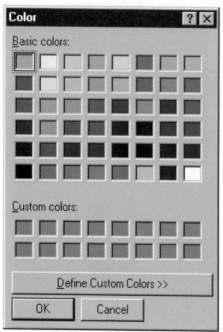

Figure 5. *Use the Color dialog to choose a wide variety of standard colors.*

You may change the background color of an object in much the same manner. Select the object, and then choose Format | Background Color... from the main VFP Menu bar. This displays the same Color dialog shown in Figure 5, from which you can select a color for the background of the selected object.

Custom colors

Besides the 48 basic colors, you may also define custom colors. To expanded the Color dialog with the custom options, select the Define Custom Colors >> button from the Color dialog. As shown in **Figure 6**, the left side of the dialog is still the same. However, the right side of the dialog is filled with everything necessary to create custom colors.

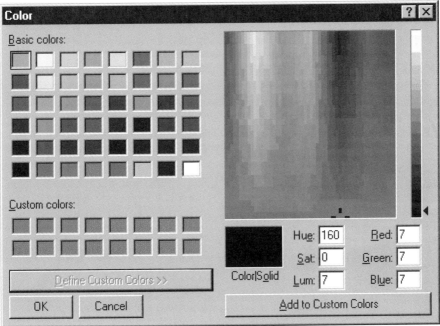

Figure 6. Use the expanded Color dialog to define very specific colors for objects.

The large rainbow-filled square on the right-hand side of the dialog is a matrix of all the possible colors. Moving across the X-axis of the matrix changes the Hue of the current custom color. Moving up or down the Y-axis of the matrix changes the Saturation level of the current custom color. To the right of the matrix is a narrow vertical bar. Moving within this bar changes the luminous value of the current custom color. As you move within either the matrix or luminous bar, the current color is displayed in the Color|Solid box underneath the matrix.

All these terms (hue, saturation, and luminous) are probably foreign to you. In FoxPro, we refer to colors by the Red/Green/Blue value, or RGB value. This is just another way to represent a color. The Color dialog shows both the HSL value and the RGB value of the current color in text boxes next to the Color|Solid box. You may tweak any of these values and the newly identified color appears in the Color|Solid box.

Once the exact color you're looking for is defined, select the Add to Custom Colors button on the expanded Color dialog. This adds the current color to one of the 16 Custom colors boxes. If all the custom color boxes are currently filled, the Report Designer overwrites the first custom color, then the second custom color, and so on. When you have all the necessary custom colors defined, select the OK button to apply the currently selected color to the selected object or select the Cancel button to return to the Report Designer without applying a new color to the selected object.

Now that you have custom colors defined, each time you invoke the Color dialog, those custom colors remain at the bottom of the dialog so you can apply them to objects. These custom colors are stored with the report. The next time you edit the report, the same custom colors appear.

Even though there are only 16 positions on the Color dialog for custom colors, it doesn't mean you can only use 16 custom colors on the report. Once the color of an object is changed, that information is permanently saved with that object. It doesn't rely on a *custom* color set up in the Color dialog. You can define a bunch of objects using the current custom colors. Then you can change the colors in the Custom colors section of the Color dialog and apply the new colors to a bunch of different objects. Changing the colors in the Custom colors section of the Color dialog does not affect any of the objects that are already defined.

The Color Palette toolbar

You can also change the foreground and background color of objects using the Color Palette toolbar shown in **Figure 7**. You can display the Color Palette toolbar with one of three methods. The first method is to select View | Color Palette Toolbar from the main VFP Menu bar. The second method is to select the Color Palette Toolbar button from the Report Designer toolbar. The third method is to right-click on an unused portion of any *docked* toolbar and then select Color Palette.

Figure 7. Use the Color Palette toolbar to change the foreground and background color of objects.

Learning to use this toolbar is somewhat tricky and confuses a lot of developers. The first two buttons, Foreground Color and Background Color, are used to toggle the foreground and background modes, respectively. When a foreground or background mode is on, its associated button is sunken. The next 16 buttons are used to choose a specific color. The last button, Other Colors, is used to invoke the Color dialog shown in Figure 5.

To change the foreground color of an object using the Color Palette toolbar, follow these steps:

1. If the Foreground Color button isn't sunken, select it so it is.

2. If the Background Color button is sunken, select it so it isn't.

3. Select the object you want to change.

4. Select one of the 16 colors from the Color Palette toolbar.

To change the background color of an object using the Color Palette toolbar, follow these steps:

1.   If the Foreground Color button is sunken, select it so it isn't.

2.   If the Background Color button isn't sunken, select it so it is.

3.   Select the object you want to change.

4.   Select one of the 16 colors from the Color Palette toolbar.

It's really quite simple once you get the hang of it. What usually throws developers is that they try to select the object and color first, then select the Foreground Color or Background Color button, which is completely opposite of what you need to do.

> Note: When you change the background color of a Field object, you also have to change the Mode (discussed later in this chapter) to opaque or the color doesn't show up on the report even though you see it in the Report Designer.

You can also toggle both the Foreground Color and Background Color buttons on and select an object and a color to change both the foreground and background color at the same time. I know what you're thinking: "That's stupid. If the foreground and background color is the same, how would I see the text?" While that statement is true for text, you haven't thought about rectangles. The foreground color of a rectangle is used to draw the line around the outside of the rectangle. The background color of a rectangle is used to fill in the rectangle. So when you don't want a border around the rectangle, you can make the foreground color the same as the background color.

Color tricks
There are two tricks I'd like to mention that have to do with color. The first trick involves gray boxes and the second trick involves dynamically changing the color of an object.

Gray boxes
When designing a report that requires light gray boxes, you can use yellow boxes as long as the report is only printed on a black and white printer. When yellow is converted to black and white, it comes out as a lighter shade of gray than the standard light gray color you can select with the Color dialog. When your users need to fax reports, the lighter shade of gray faxes much better than the regular gray.

Dynamic color
It's not possible to truly change the color of a Report object dynamically. However, you can create the appearance by using *Print When* logic. For example, say you want to print a dollar amount that is black when it's positive or red when it's negative. Start by adding two Field objects to the report with the same expressions (MyTable.DollarAmt). Next, change the color of one of the objects to red and leave the other object black. Now change the Print When expression of the black object to *MyTable.DollarAmt >= 0* and change the Print When expression of the red object to *MyTable.DollarAmt < 0*. For the final step, place one object

directly on top of the other object, making sure they are aligned perfectly with each other. When the report prints, either the red dollar amount prints or the black dollar amount prints, but not both of them.

Text Alignment

Text Alignment controls how the text within a Label object or Field object is aligned within the defined width of the object. Select the object you wish to alter. Then select Format | Text Alignment | <your choice> from the main VFP Menu bar. The three options are:

- **Left:** This option positions the text flush with the left edge of the object.

- **Center:** This option centers the text within the object.

- **Right:** This option positions the text flush with the right edge of the object.

At first thought, you may be wondering why in the world you would need to use Text Alignment on a Label object. After all, the object is only as wide as the text. Well, I've learned over the years that what you see is not always what you get. The visual representation of the label on the screen doesn't always match what is printed on the report. For example, let's say I want a label lined up flush with the right edge of a numeric field. I could use the Align Left Sides option from the Layout toolbar to make sure the Label object is flush with the left edge of my Field object. However, this might not work as expected.

The reason it doesn't always work is that the fonts displayed on the screen are not always TrueType fonts and can't always be accurately displayed. In these situations, a close match is used to display the font. It's possible that the close match isn't quite the same width as the real font that is used when the report is printed. This means that my right-aligned label looks great on the screen, but prints a slightly different width on the report and isn't flush like I expected.

The point to this explanation is to use Text Alignment on your Label objects as well as your Field objects to ensure that what you see on the screen is also what you see on the printed report.

> *You may have noticed that there are three additional options on the Text Alignment submenu that I haven't discussed: Single Space, 1 1/2 Space, and Double Space. The reason I didn't discuss them is because you can't select them. I'm guessing that these options are intended to let you select the spacing of Field objects that span multiple lines. Unfortunately, they're not implemented and they just sit there and tease us!*

Reading Order

Unless you're running a Middle Eastern version of Microsoft Windows, this option is not enabled. It's used to control whether the text is displayed in left-to-right order or right-to-left order.

In FoxPro 2.x, you cannot change the Reading Order.

Fill

The Fill option is used to control what pattern is used to fill the inside of shapes, such as Rectangles and Rounded Rectangles. Select the object you want to fill and then select Format | Fill from the main VFP Menu bar. This displays the submenu shown in **Figure 8**. The first item on this submenu fills the object with nothing. So no matter what color you've chosen as a background color, nothing ever appears. The second item on the submenu fills the object solid with the background color.

Figure 8*. Use the fill options to control what pattern is used to fill the inside of a Rectangle or Rounded Rectangle object.*

The last six options on the Fill submenu fill the object with the chosen pattern, using the background color to draw the lines of the pattern. Keep in mind, however, that the foreground color of the object is still used to draw the border around the object.

Although you cannot control the color of the *white space* between the pattern lines, here's a trick to get around that. Draw two rectangles of the same size on the report. For the first rectangle use a solid fill, choosing the color you want as the white space. Then, on the second rectangle, set the fill pattern of your choice using the background color of your choice to draw the lines. Be sure to set the second rectangle (the one with the patterned fill) as Transparent (see the section titled "Mode" later in this chapter) so the solid-filled rectangle can bleed through the pattern-filled rectangle.

Pen

The Pen option is used to control what style of line is used when drawing lines and the border of rectangles and rounded rectangles. Select the object you want to affect, and then select Format | Pen from the main VFP Menu bar. This displays the Pen submenu shown in **Figure 9**.

Select any one of the 10 different Pen options from the Pen submenu. A sample of the different options is shown in **Figure 10**. The *None* option tells the VFP Report Writer to suppress the border around Rectangle and Rounded Rectangle objects. For Line objects, the *None* option creates an invisible line (which is sometimes necessary to force the VFP Report Writer to do what you want).

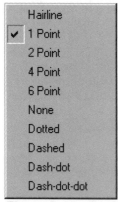

Figure 9. *Use the Pen submenu to select the type of line used to draw lines, rectangles, and rounded rectangles.*

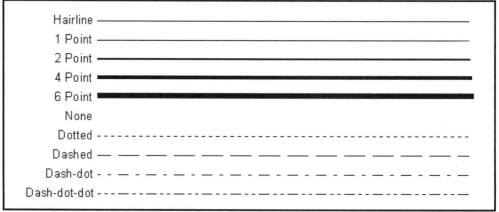

Figure 10. *These 10 different Pen options control how lines are drawn as well as the border around rectangles and rounded rectangles.*

Mode

The Mode controls whether the object is transparent or opaque. Transparent means that it's see-thru and objects underneath it can bleed through. Opaque means that the object is solid and nothing underneath it bleeds through. In other words, this object completely covers and overpowers any objects underneath it.

To change the Mode of an object, select the object. Then select Format | Mode | <your choice> from the main VFP Menu bar.

Programming is an art

We've all heard this phrase before, and when it comes to reports it's very true. You have to use your artistic talents to design reports that are visually pleasing to look at. I urge you to take the extra time required to do just that. In the end, it pays off because your users are much happier. And if having happy users isn't enough to motivate you, better reports can make executive management happier too. I don't know about you, but it's the manager who signs my check, so I want to make sure that person is *very* happy!

Chapter 7
Data Grouping

Data Grouping is essential to many different reports. Customer Lists can be grouped by State, Sales Reports can be grouped by Sales Rep, Packing Lists can be grouped by Warehouse Number and then again by Shelf Number. A large number of reports require data to be grouped in some fashion, and Visual FoxPro's Data Grouping feature allows you to accomplish this. In addition, you can use Data Grouping to solve several *problems* you might encounter with the VFP Report Writer, such as spanning a Detail band across several pages. You can even pull off some cool tricks to create dynamic Data Grouping or to add white space to your reports.

 Data Grouping means that certain records in the report are grouped together because of some similarity. For example, a Customer List is grouped by Country when you want to see all the customers for a particular country grouped together. In addition to seeing the records grouped together, each time the country changes, you may want to do something special, such as print the country name in bold at the beginning of each new country or print a total at the bottom of each country as shown in **Figure 1**. That's the true definition of Data Grouping. It's not the fact that the records are sorted by Country, it's the fact that you're going to do something special when the Country changes. The report definition for creating the sample shown in Figure 1 is included in the source code available with this book, and is named DataGroup.FRX.

Personally, I think the term *Data Grouping* is misleading. It's confusing because it's very similar to the term *Group*, which is used to combine several Report objects into one Report object for the purposes of moving and aligning them. I'd prefer to use the term *Control Break* to indicate that a *break* occurs each time the value of a *control* changes. Unfortunately, I didn't get to make the decision, so we have to live with the terminology as it is. In any event, Data Grouping is a very powerful feature of the Visual FoxPro Report Writer and one that is used often.

Sorting it all out

The first, and most important, thing you need to understand about Data Grouping is that the data *must* be sorted in the proper order. Using the VFP Report Designer to set up Data Groups does *not*, I repeat, does *not* set the index order on the table used to drive the report. This is a common misconception by many developers.

Defining a Data Group in the VFP Report Designer only tells the Report Writer to *break* each time the specified Data Group changes. It's up to you to make sure that all the records for specific groups appear together in the table. This may be done by setting an index on the table. In situations where no index is available, you may either create a temporary index just for the purpose of running the report, or you can build a temporary cursor with the data already sorted.

Customers by Country

03/16/2002

Customer Id	Company Name

Argentina

	CACTU	Cactus Comidas para llevar
	OCEAN	Océano Atlántico Ltda.
	RANCH	Rancho grande

Total Customers in Argentina: 3

Austria

	ERNSH	Ernst Handel
	PICCO	Piccolo und mehr

Total Customers in Austria: 2

Belgium

	MAISD	Maison Dewey
	SUPRD	Suprêmes délices

Total Customers in Belgium: 2

Brazil

	COMMI	Comércio Mineiro
	FAMIA	Familia Arquibaldo
	GOURL	Gourmet Lanchonetes
	HANAR	Hanari Carnes
	QUEDE	Que Delícia
	QUEEN	Queen Cozinha
	RICAR	Ricardo Adocicados
	TRADH	Tradiçao Hipermercados
	WELLI	Wellington Importadora

Page 1

Figure 1. *This sample Customer by Country report uses Data Grouping. The Country is printed in the Group Header, followed by each Customer within the Country, followed by a total count of Customers in the Group Footer.*

Note: The sample report shown in Figure 1 appears to be sorted by Customer within each Country. However, it's just a coincidence because the natural order of the records in the table just happens to coincide with the alphabetical order of the Customers.

Use an existing index

If the table resides in the report's Data Environment, you may set the index through the Properties window. Open the Data Environment window (select View | Data Environment... from the main VFP Menu bar or select Data Environment... after right-clicking on an unused portion of the report).

Right-click on the table that drives the report and select Properties. In the Properties window, scroll down to the property called *Order*. Change this property to the name of the desired index tag already defined for this table.

Create a temporary index

When the table doesn't have an index that matches the Data Grouping you want, you can create a temporary index just for the purpose of running the report and then you can remove the index when the report is done.

No Data Environment

 If you're not using the Data Environment and are setting the table up prior to running the report, you may use code similar to the following example to create the index, run the report, and remove the index when done. The program, DataGroup1.PRG, and report definition, DataGroup1.FRX, are included in the source code available with this book.

```
*-- Create a temporary index on the Customer table
*-- and run the Customer by Country Report

* Get a unique name
LOCAL lcIndex
lcIndex = SYS(2015) + '.idx'

* Create the index
USE data\customer
INDEX ON country TO (lcIndex)
GOTO TOP

* Run the report
REPORT FORM reports\DataGroup1 TO PRINTER PROMPT PREVIEW

* Erase the temporary index
SET INDEX TO
ERASE (lcIndex)

* Close the table
USE
CLOSE DATABASES
```

Using a Data Environment

If you're using the Data Environment to open the table, you can create a temporary index using the following code in the *OpenTables* method of the Data Environment.

```
*-- Data Environment / OpenTables method
*-- Create a temporary index on the Customer table

* Open the tables now, instead of at the end of this method
NODEFAULT
DODEFAULT()

* Get a unique name
LOCAL lcIndex
lcIndex = SYS(2015) + '.idx'

* Create the index
SELECT Customer
INDEX ON country TO (lcIndex)
GOTO TOP
```

In addition to creating the index in the OpenTables method, you also have to remember to remove the index in the *CloseTables* method with the following code.

```
*-- Data Environment / CloseTables method
*-- Erase the temporary index on the Customer table

* Get the name of the temporary index file
LOCAL lcIndex
SELECT customer
lcIndex = NDX(1)

* Erase the file
SET INDEX TO
     ERASE (lcIndex)
```

 The previous two code samples are included in the DataGroup2.FRX report definition, which is included with the source code available with this book.

Use SQL to create a temporary cursor

In situations when you need to build a temporary cursor to run the report, you can use a SQL statement to build the cursor with the data already sorted in the proper order. For example, the following code builds a temporary cursor, runs the report, and closes the cursor when done. The program, DataGroup3.PRG, and report definition, DataGroup1.FRX, are included in the source code available with this book.

```
*-- Create a temporary cursor with SQL SELECT
*-- and run the Customer by Country Report

* Create the cursor
SELECT * ;
  FROM data\customer ;
  ORDER BY country ;
```

```
     INTO CURSOR tmpCust

* Run the report
SELECT tmpCust
REPORT FORM reports\DataGroup1 TO PRINTER PROMPT PREVIEW

* Close the table
SELECT tmpCust
USE
SELECT customer
USE
CLOSE DATABASES
```

Your choice

It's up to you to decide which method of sorting the data works best for the specific report you're designing. Different situations warrant different solutions. The bottom line is, you have to make sure the data is sorted or Data Grouping won't work as expected. With that said, it's time to move on and learn *how* to do Data Grouping.

Creating a Data Group

The first step in creating a Data Group is to decide what the *group* is. For example, if you're printing a report of customers by country, the group is the *Country*. If you're printing sales orders, the group is the *Order Number* because you need to print the order header information each time a new order is encountered and you also need to print totals at the end of each order. In essence, whenever you need to *break* on some condition, the condition is considered the Data Group.

You may create a Data Group using one of three methods. The first method is to select Report | Data Grouping… from the main VFP Menu bar. The second method is to select the Data Grouping button from the Report Designer toolbar. The third method is to right-click on an unused portion of the report in the Report Designer and then select Data Grouping… Regardless of the method you choose, the Data Grouping dialog shown in **Figure 2** is invoked.

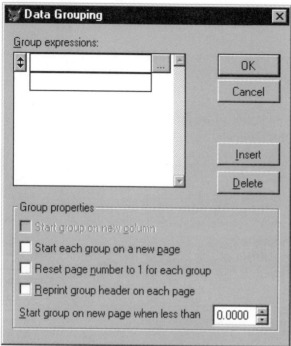

Figure 2*. Use the Data Grouping dialog to describe the condition that controls a break and set other properties that control the appearance of the report when these breaks occur.*

Group expressions

The first and most important part of the Data Grouping dialog is the Group expressions section. This is where you enter the actual expression that defines each specific Data Group. In case you were wondering, the answer is "Yes, you may have more than one Data Group on a report." I'll discuss "Nesting Data Groups" later in this chapter, but for now, I want to show you how to create a report with a single Data Group.

Enter the *expression* that defines this Data Group in the first text box in the Group expressions section of the Data Grouping dialog. You may also use the ellipse button (…) to the right of the text box to invoke the Expression Builder dialog. The expression may be any valid VFP expression. For example, in the Customer by Country and the Sales Order examples mentioned previously, the expressions are *Customer.Customer.ID* and *Orders.Order_Number*, respectively. You may enter the expression with or without the table name (I just included it here for clarity).

You can also use VFP commands in the expression. For example, enter *LEFT(Company_Name,1)* to create a Data Group that breaks each time the first letter of the Company Name changes (like a telephone book does). If the case of the data isn't consistent, you can enter *UPPER(MyField)* as the expression to ensure that the Data Group is not case-sensitive. You can even use UDFs and method calls to return values to the expression. I'll discuss some good examples of these later in this chapter. Of course, it's important to remember that the data has to be sorted in a fashion that's consistent with the Data Group you're defining.

So *when* is this expression evaluated? Well, the Report Writer evaluates it each time a record is processed. It's evaluated *after* the Detail band of a record to determine whether the *next* record belongs to the same Data Group as *this* record. This means the Report Writer jumps ahead to the next record, evaluates the expression, and then jumps back to the record it was on. If the Report Writer determined that the next record triggers a new Data Group, then the Group Footer band is processed for this record. It then moves the record pointer ahead to the next record, and the Group Header band is processed for the new record before the normal Detail band processing occurs. Of course, the Group Header also prints prior to the first record in the table. In addition, other processing, such as page breaks and column breaks, may occur in the middle of all this.

Group properties

The bottom half of the Data Grouping dialog is used to set up several different options associated with Data Groups.

Start group on new column

The "Start group on new column" check box is only enabled if you have multiple column sets defined for this report. Checking this check box tells the VFP Report Writer to jump to a new column each time a new value is encountered for this Data Group. First, the Group Footer is printed in the current column. Then, the Report Writer jumps to a new column before printing the Group Header of the new record. Note that checking this check box disables the "Start each group on a new page" check box.

Start each group on a new page

Checking the "Start each group on a new page" check box tells the VFP Report Writer to jump to a new page each time a new value is encountered for this Data Group. First, the Group Footer is printed on the current page. Then, the Report Writer jumps to a new page before printing the Group Header of the new record. Note that checking this check box disables the "Start group on new column" check box.

Reset page number to 1 for each group

This option tells the VFP Report Writer that each time a new value for a Data Group is encountered, the Page Number should be reset to 1. Checking this check box automatically unchecks the "Start group on new column" check box and then disables it. Checking the "Reset page number to 1 for each group" check box also implies that you want the "Start each group on a new page" check box selected as well. Therefore, that check box is checked and then disabled. After all, it wouldn't do any good to reset the page counter if you aren't jumping to a new page.

Reprint group header on each page

When the "Reprint group header on each page" check box is *not* checked, the Group Header band is only printed once at the beginning of each new Data Group. However, when this check box is *checked*, the VFP Report Writer prints the Group Header band on each page of any given Data Group. In other words, if the Data Group flows over to the next page, the Group Header is reprinted, following the Page Header.

Start group on new page when less than

This option is available to help you prevent orphaned Group Headers. An orphaned Group Header is the term used to describe the situation where the Group Header prints at the bottom of a page, and then because there's no more room left, the first detail band of that group is printed at the top of the next page. The Group Header is just sitting at the bottom of a page without any details to go with it.

To prevent an orphaned Group Header, enter a value into the Start group on new page when less than spinner. The value you enter depends on the height of the Group Header band, the height of the Detail band, and the minimum number of Detail bands you want printed. For example, if the Group Header band is 1" tall and the Detail band is 0.25" tall, a value of 1.5 would make sure that the Group Header and two Detail bands fit on the bottom of the page (1" + 0.25" + 0.25"). The Report Writer checks to see whether 1.5" is remaining on the page, and if not, it jumps to the next page before printing the Group Header and any Detail bands of the new Data Group. When determining how much room is remaining on the page, the Report Writer takes into account the amount of room needed to print the Column Footer band and the Page Footer band.

> Note: If you have objects in the Group Header band or the Detail band that have been marked as Stretch, there's no guarantee that you can always prevent orphaned Group Headers. The reason is that you can only designate a given amount a space. You meticulously calculate that space as the total height of the Group Header band plus x number of Detail bands. However, when the Group Header band or one of the Detail bands stretches to accommodate long fields, your calculation doesn't match the true height of the bands anymore.

After you've finished entering all the properties, you can select the OK button. This saves the Data Grouping information and adds a Group Header band and a Group Footer band to the report.

Group Header and Footer bands

When a Data Group is added to a report, an empty Group Header band and an empty Group Footer band are automatically added to the report. You cannot remove these bands. However, you don't have to put anything in the bands. You can leave them empty and assign a height of zero to them. Then again, what would be the point of creating a Data Group! Well, actually there are situations where you would want to do this. Data Groups have other properties, such as On Entry and On Exit expressions, that you can take advantage of without having to put anything in the Group Header or Group Footer bands.

The Group Header band appears just above the Detail band, and the Group Footer band appears just below the Detail band (as shown in **Figure 3**). In the gray bar that represents the Group Header, the words *Group Header* appear, followed by a number, and then followed by the expression used to define the Data Group. The number is a sequential number that represents which Data Group this is (see "Nesting Data Groups" later in this chapter). The gray bar representing the Group Footer band also displays similar information, except that it says *Group Footer*.

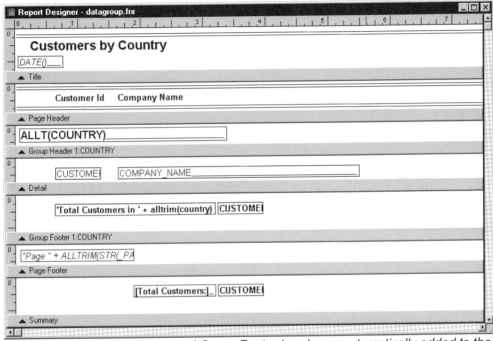

Figure 3. The Group Header and Group Footer bands are automatically added to the report when you create a Data Grouping.

Group Header band

Commonly, the Group Header band is used to print information about the group. For example, in the sample Customers by Country report (shown in Figure 1 earlier in this chapter), I used the Group Header to print the name of the country. Notice the country name prints on its own separate line—not on the same line as the customer information. I also used the Group Header to provide a little extra white space whenever a new country is encountered.

Group Footer band

The Group Footer band is most commonly used to print total and summary information about the group. For example, when printing Sales Orders, the Group Footer band may be used to print the total amount of the order. Or as in the Customer by Country example, I used the Group Footer to print a total count of the number of customers within each particular country.

Run expression

Consider the Run expression as a special type of *hook* into the Group Header and Group Footer bands. You can set up an *On entry* and an *On exit* expression for each Group Header and each Group Footer. Enter the expressions into the Group Header and Group Footer dialogs (the Group Header dialog is shown in **Figure 4**). To invoke either of these dialogs, double-click on the gray bar representing the band.

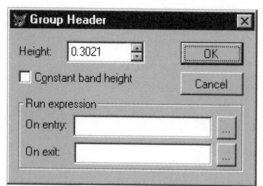

Figure 4. Use the Group Header (or Group Footer) dialog to set up the On entry and On exit expressions for a Data Group.

 Sorry! On entry and On exit expressions are not available in FoxPro 2.x.

You can also access the Group Header and Group Footer dialogs by selecting Report | Bands… from the main VFP Menu bar. This displays the Edit Bands dialog shown in **Figure 5**. The list box includes an entry for each Group Header and each Group Footer on the report. However, there's a bug in this dialog. Can you spot it?

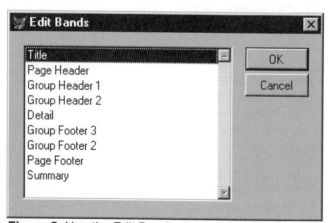

Figure 5. Use the Edit Bands dialog to invoke the Group Header or Group Footer dialog. However, be careful not to overlook the Group Footer numbering bug and select the wrong Data Group.

Bug Alert! *There's a harmless bug in the Edit Bands dialog. Each Group Header has a corresponding Group Footer entry in the list box. However, the Group Footer entries are numbered incorrectly. Group Footer 2 actually corresponds to Group Header 1 and Group Footer 3 actually corresponds to Group Header 2. The number associated with each Group Footer entry is off by one. But don't worry, just do the math in your head and select the Group Footer that is numbered one more than the one you really want.*

The Edit Bands dialog is new to VFP 7. Previous versions of Visual FoxPro, as well as FoxPro 2.x versions, do not have this feature.

The *On entry* expression is evaluated prior to processing any of the objects in the corresponding band. The *On exit* expression is evaluated after printing all the objects in the corresponding band. The values returned by the expressions are meaningless, as these do not print on the report. It's what happens inside of the expressions that makes this feature powerful.

For example, in the *On entry* of a Group Header band, you can call a UDF that finds a particular record in another table so objects within the Group Header band can access the data in that record. Another really slick use of the *On entry* expression is to print totals up front in the Group Header instead of waiting until the Group Footer. The following code shows an example of how to do this for the Customers by Country report. This code can be found in the program called DataGroupUDF.PRG, which runs the report called DataGroupUDF.FRX, both of which are included with the source code available with this book.

```
*-- Initialize a variable
PRIVATE pnTotalCust
pnTotalCust = 0

*-- Call the report
REPORT FORM reports\datagroupudf TO PRINTER PROMPT PREVIEW

RETURN


*---------------
*-- Define a UDF
*---------------
PROCEDURE TotalCust

*-- Remember this country and record position
LOCAL lcCountry, lnRec
lcCountry = country
lnRec = RECNO()

*-- Count the customers for this country
COUNT REST WHILE country == lcCountry TO pnTotalCust

*-- Restore the record position
GOTO lnRec

RETURN
```

Enter *TotalCust()* as the Group Header On entry expression. Next, place a Field object in the Group Header band of the report. For its expression, enter *pnTotalCust*. When the report is run, the UDF is called when a new value is encountered for the Data Group. The UDF counts the records in the table for that Country and saves the count in the *pnTotalCust* variable. The Field object on the report prints the value of the *pnTotalCust* variable. *Voilà!* You now have a total count in the Group Header.

> Note: Be sure to declare any variables used on the report as either private or public. If you use a local variable, the VFP Report Writer can't see it.

I'm sure you're beginning to see the power of the On entry and On exit expressions. Having these *hooks* gives you the opportunity to run just about any code you can come up with. Just think about it. You can even manipulate the data in the table as you're printing it. Wow!

> Note: One important thing to point out is that the On entry and On exit expressions are evaluated each time a band is processed. This means if the Group Header is reprinted on subsequent pages, the On entry and On exit expressions are evaluated again. Be very careful to remember this fact, especially when you're resetting variables through these expressions.

Nesting Data Groups

As I mentioned earlier, you can have multiple Data Groups on a report. In fact, you can have up to 20 different Data Groups on one report—although I wouldn't want to be the one who has to write that report!

Adding more Data Groups

To add additional Data Groups to the report, start by invoking the Data Grouping dialog as explained earlier. To add a new Data Group immediately underneath the current one, just enter the expression in the text box underneath the current Data Group. To insert a Data Group ahead of an existing one, place your cursor on the text box of the Data Group you want to insert above. Then press the Insert button, which adds a new Data Group above the cursor.

Deleting Data Groups

To delete an existing Data Group, place the cursor on the text box of the Data Group you want to delete. Now press the Delete button, which deletes the Data Group from the report. If the Group Header or the Group Footer bands of the selected Data Group contain any objects, you're prompted with a dialog reminding you that you have objects in those bands and asking you if you're really sure you want to delete it.

Moving Data Groups

You may change the order of any existing Data Groups by dragging the mover button to the left of the text box up or down within the other Data Groups. However, you should be aware of one important thing that happens when you reorder Data Groups. Any native calculations defined in Field objects and Report Variables may be inadvertently affected by the change.

When the VFP Report Designer saves the Reset value of a calculation as one of the Data Groups, it does *not* store the expression of the group with the calculation. Instead, it stores the Data Group Number. This means that if you define a calculation to reset at the first Data Group, and then switch Data Groups 1 and 2, the calculation still resets at Data Group 1. Only now Data Group 1 isn't the same one anymore. This may or may not be what you want. I just want you to be aware of this so that any time you move around Data Groups, you go back and check your calculations and Report Variables to make sure they reflect what you want.

How Nested Data Groups are processed

When multiple Data Groups exist on a report, they're nested within each other. This means that Data Group 2 is nested inside of Data Group 1, Data Group 3 is nested inside of Data Group 2, and so on (see **Figure 6**).

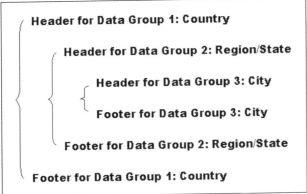

Figure 6. Each new Data Group is nested within the previous Data Group.

When the Report Writer checks the next record to see whether it belongs to the same group as the current one, it first checks Data Group 1 to see whether it has changed. If not, it then checks Data Group 2, and then Data Group 3, and so on. If any one of these triggers the start of a new group, a chain reaction occurs.

> Reminder: You're still responsible for sorting the data in the same order as the Data Groups. For this sample of Data Groups nested three-deep, your index expression should be COUNTRY + REGION + CITY.

For example, using the three Data Groups shown in Figure 6, assume the current record is for Country = USA, Region = Michigan, and City = Detroit. The next record is for Country = USA, Region = Michigan, and City = Grand Rapids. The Report Writer checks the Country and determines that it's the same. Then it checks the Region and again confirms it's the same. But when it checks the City, it realizes it's different. This triggers the Group Footer for Data Group 3 (City), followed by the Group Header for Data Group 3 (City), and then the detail record for the new City.

Now take the following example. The current record is for Country = USA, Region = Michigan, and City = Detroit. The next record is for Country = USA, Region = Washington, and City = Seattle. The Report Writer first checks the Country and determines it's the same. Then it checks the Region, realizes it's different, and triggers the change. Only this time, here's what occurs. First, the Group Footer of Data Group 3 (City) prints, then the Group Footer of Data Group 2 (Region) prints, then the Group Header of Data Group 2 (Region) prints, then the Group Header of Data Group 3 (City) prints, and then, finally, the new detail record for Seattle prints.

In this situation, the Data Group that triggered the change wasn't the innermost level. Therefore, the Report Writer started at the innermost level of all the Data Groups and worked its way out toward the Data Group that triggered the change. Along the way, it executed the Footer for each Data Group it encountered. It then executes the Header of the Data Group that triggered the change and continues inward executing each Header of each Data Group it encounters until the Header of the innermost Data Group is executed. In essence, it executes a loop starting with the innermost Data Group Footer, continuing outward until it reaches the Data Group that triggered the change, and then circles back in to the center, processing each Header along the way (see **Figure 7**).

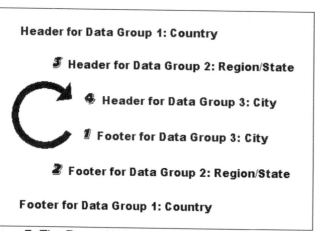

Figure 7. The Report Writer processes the Data Groups in a loop, starting with the Footer of the innermost Data Group, moving outwards to the Data Group that triggered the change, and then circling back in toward the center, processing each Header along the way.

Has all of this confused you yet? I think the best way for you to understand this is to actually see a report with nested Data Groups. The sample Customer List shown in **Figure 8** demonstrates the three levels of Data Groups just discussed. This report, called DataGroupNest.FRX, is included in the source code available with this book.

Customers by Country, Region and City

03/16/2002

Customer Id	Company Name

Country: Argentina

    Region:

        City: Buenos Aires

CACTU	Cactus Comidas para llevar
OCEAN	Océano Atlántico Ltda.
RANCH	Rancho grande

        Total Customers in City Buenos Aires: 3

      Total Customers in Region: 3

    Total Customers in Country Argentina: 3

Country: Austria

    Region:

        City: Graz

ERNSH	Ernst Handel

        Total Customers in City Graz: 1

        City: Salzburg

PICCO	Piccolo und mehr

        Total Customers in City Salzburg: 1

      Total Customers in Region: 2

    Total Customers in Country Austria: 2

Country: Belgium

    Region:

        City: Bruxelles

MAISD	Maison Dewey

        Total Customers in City Bruxelles: 1

        City: Charleroi

SUPRD	Suprêmes délices

        Total Customers in City Charleroi: 1

      Total Customers in Region: 2

    Total Customers in County Belgium: 2

Page 1

Figure 8*. This sample report shows Data Groups nested three-deep (Country, Region, and City).*

Cool tricks with Data Groups

Now that you know all about Data Groups, it's time to get really fancy. There are some really cool tricks you can do if you just let your imagination run wild.

Dynamic Data Groups

Have you ever been asked by a customer to create a report, but they want to be able to control how it's sorted and grouped? You probably created the report for the first sorting option, and then copied the report and changed a few things for the second sorting option. Although this solves the problem at hand, maintenance becomes double the work whenever you have to change something because two reports have to be changed. Wouldn't it be nice to create just one report that's smart enough to sort and group both ways?

Consider a report of Employees (I'm getting really bored with the Customer table). You want to be able to sort and group it by either the Country or Group_ID fields. The only thing different between the two reports is how it's grouped and whether you print the Country or the Group ID in the Detail band. The Employee report shown in **Figure 9** is sorted and grouped by Group ID. The Employee report shown in **Figure 10** is sorted and grouped by Country. Yet both reports were run from the exact same report definition.

Employees
03/16/2002

	Country	Employee Name	Title
Group ID: 1			
	UK	Buchanan, Steven	Sales Manager
	USA	Fuller, Andrew	Entry Clerk
	USA	Smith, Tim	Mail Clerk
Group ID: 2			
	France	Pereira, Laurent	Advertising Specialist
	UK	Dodsworth, Anne	Sales Representative
	USA	Davolio, Nancy	Applications Developer
	USA	Leverling, Janet	Applications Developer
Group ID: 3			
	France	Brid, Justin	Marketing Director
	UK	King, Robert	Sales Representative

Figure 9. This Employee report is sorted and grouped by the Group ID field.

Employees

03/16/2002

	Group ID	Employee Name	Title

Country: France

	2	Pereira, Laurent	Advertising Specialist
	3	Brid, Justin	Marketing Director
	4	Martin, Xavier	Marketing Associate

Country: UK

	1	Buchanan, Steven	Sales Manager
	2	Dodsworth, Anne	Sales Representative
	3	King, Robert	Sales Representative
	4	Callahan, Laura	Inside Sales Coordinator
	4	Suyama, Michael	Sales Representative

Country: USA

	1	Fuller, Andrew	Entry Clerk
	1	Smith, Tim	Mail Clerk
	2	Davolio, Nancy	Applications Developer

***Figure 10**. This Employee report is sorted and grouped by the Country field.*

I bet you'd like to know how I did this. Well, it's actually quite simple (like most things in life), once you know the secret. I started by creating a program that prompts the user for the way he or she wants to see the report. The program then opens the Employee table and creates a temporary index based on the user's choice. It also sets some private variables for the report to use. It then runs the report, closes the table, and removes the temporary index. The following code is included in the source code available with this book, and is called Employee.PRG.

```
PRIVATE pcGroupExpr, pcGrpTitle, pcColTitle, pcColField, pcSortBy
LOCAL lcIndex
lcIndex = ''

*-- Get the user's sort option
pcSortBy = 'G'
CLEAR
@ 10,10 SAY 'Sort by [G]roup ID or [C]ountry: ' ;
  GET pcSortBy ;
  PICTURE '!' ;
  VALID pcSortBy $ 'GC' ;
  MESSAGE 'Invalid - enter G or C'
READ

*-- Open the table
```

```
USE DATA\employee

*-- Sort the table and set the private variables
*-- based on the selected sort option
lcIndex = SYS(2015) + '.idx'

DO CASE

  CASE pcSortBy = 'G' && by Group
    pcGroupExpr = 'group_id'
    pcGrpTitle = 'Group ID: '
    pcColTitle = 'Country'
    pcColField = 'country'
    INDEX ON group_id + country + last_name TO (lcIndex)
    GOTO TOP

  CASE pcSortBy = 'C' && by Country
    pcGroupExpr = 'country'
    pcGrpTitle = 'Country: '
    pcColTitle = 'Group ID'
    pcColField = 'group_id'
    INDEX ON country + group_id + last_name TO (lcIndex)
    GOTO TOP

ENDCASE

*-- Print the report
REPORT FORM reports\Employee TO PRINTER PROMPT PREVIEW

*-- Close the table and erase the index
SELECT employee
USE
ERASE (lcIndex)
```

Next, I turned my attention to defining the report. The key pieces to this trick are the expression for the Data Group, the expression used in the Group Header, the expression used for the first column of data, and the expression used for the heading of the first column of data. Do you see a pattern here? *Expressions* are the key to all of this. The report definition, Employee.FRX, is included in the source code available with this book.

The Data Group

If you were defining a static Data Group, you'd probably set the expression of the Data Group to a field in the table, such as *Group_ID*. However, in this situation, we don't know what field should be controlling the Data Group because it's determined when the user makes a choice in the calling program. So how in the world can we tell this Report definition to change the Data Group based on what the user chooses?

The trick is to use VFP's EVALUATE() command. Look at the sample code again and you'll notice that I set a private variable, *pcGroupExpr,* to the name of the field that should control the Data Group. Combine this variable with the EVALUATE() command as shown here and the Data Group suddenly becomes dynamic:

```
EVALUATE(pcGroupExpr)
```

Cool trick, don't you think? Any valid VFP expression can be used, including the EVALUATE() command. Thus, the end result is that this expression returns either the Group_ID or the Country of the current record.

The Group Header

Now that the Data Group is defined, you need to put an object in the Group Header. Add a Field object using the following as the expression.

```
pcGrpTitle + EVALUATE(pcGroupExpr)
```

This uses two of the private variables defined in the calling program to print the value of the field that controls the Data Group preceded by a descriptive label.

The first column of data

Now that you have the Data Grouping taken care of, you need to turn your attention to what prints in the Detail band. The first column on the report needs to be the opposite field of what the report is grouped by. For example, if the report is sorted and grouped by Group_ID, the first column needs to be Country. Or if the report is sorted and grouped by Country, the first column needs to be Group_ID.

This is done by using one of the private variables defined in the calling program as follows.

```
EVALUATE(pcColField)
```

Now for the label associated with that column, you have a problem. You can't use a Label object because Label objects are static. The information can't be changed. I supposed you could add two Label objects, one for Group ID and one for Country, and change their Print When logic to conditionally print one or the other, but I don't like to add more objects than necessary. Instead of using a Label object, use a Field object in the Page Header band with the following expression.

```
PcColTitle
```

Remember, Field objects can contain any expression and don't necessarily have to be used to print fields from tables.

Easy maintenance

This may all seem like a lot of work right now, but down the road, this may save you time. I don't know about you, but my customers hardly ever leave things alone. There's always just one more change to make to the report. Using this technique, you'll only have to make that change in one place because there's only one report definition, not two.

A group of one

Is a group of one really a group? Those of you who are philosophers can hash that out among yourselves, but when it comes to reports, there are situations where you really do need a group of one. A group of one is easily achieved by using *RECNO()* as the expression. This assures that a Data Group is triggered for *each* record in the table.

Spanning multiple pages

A great example of when to use a Data Group of RECNO() is when you want to print the information for each record spanned across two or more pages. Sometimes a table has so many fields in it that it's impossible to get them to all fit on one page. Not to mention the fact that you want to control when the information flows to the next page because there are certain groups of fields that belong together.

To solve this problem, add a Data Group with RECNO() as the expression. Change the height of the Group Header band to the height of your page, less some room for the Page Header and Page Footer. Mark the Group Header as *Start group on new page*. Now add all the objects in the Group Header that you want to appear on the first page.

Next, change the height of the Detail band to accommodate the objects you want on the second page (remembering to allow for the Page Header and Page Footer). Add all the objects to the Detail band that you want to appear on the second page. And if you need a third page, you still have the Group Footer that you can expand and use.

If you need even more pages, just add another Data Group with the same expression of RECNO(). Each time you create a new Data Group, you get two more bands, which means you get two more pages. Let's see… you can have 20 Data Groups, which gets you 40 pages, plus the one page for the Detail band… by my calculations, you can have up to 41 pages for each detail record in the table. And if you need more than 41 pages, I discuss another way to span multiple pages in Chapter 10, "Solutions to Real-World Problems." However, I'd like to have a serious talk with the person who designed a table with so many fields it takes 41 pages to print!

Variable height Detail band

In Chapter 5, "Report Objects," you learned how to use Print When logic to suppress objects from printing. This gives you the ability to add lots of objects to the report, yet only print certain objects for certain conditions. This is great—but it does have one flaw.

Before printing a band, the VFP Report Writer checks to see how much room is needed based on all the objects in that band. However, it *doesn't* consider the Print When logic when it does this check. For example, assume you've defined a report and made the Detail band tall enough to accommodate 15 objects, each on its own line. Each of the objects has different Print When logic that controls whether it prints. In most cases, only 3-5 of the objects actual print on the report. However, when the Report Writer checks to see how much room is needed to print the next Detail band, it assumes all 15 objects need to be printed; therefore, it may trigger a new page even though the next one or two Detail bands would have fit.

To overcome this, create one or more Data Groups with an expression of RECNO() and move some of the objects to the Group Header or Group Footer bands. For example, you could create four Data Groups, each with RECNO() as the expression. Place the first three objects in the Detail band, the next three objects in the Group Footer #4 band, the next three objects in the Group Footer #3 band, the next three objects in the Group Footer #2 band, and the last three objects in the Group Footer #1 band.

Now, when the Report Writer checks to see whether enough room is left on the page, it only checks for three lines at a time, instead of the full 15 lines. However, this trick comes with its own flaw. Using this method, you can't guarantee that all objects related to one record appear on the same page. It's possible to print the first three objects on Page 1 and the next three objects on Page 2. This is something you'll have to consider when creating the report. Is the wasted space more of an issue than keeping the objects together... or... is it more important to always keep the objects together?

Fudging another Summary band

Have you ever wanted two summary bands, one immediately following the Detail band and the other on its own page? Or have you ever wanted to include stretchable fields in the Summary band, only to find out you can't do that in the Summary band? Or have you ever been bitten by the bug in the VFP Report Writer that causes a Summary band to flow to the next page, but it doesn't print the Page Header or Page Footer information?

   All of these problems can be overcome with a Data Group using *EOF()* as the expression. The Group Footer band of this Data Group can be now be used as an additional Summary band or in place of the native Summary band.

Maintaining a fixed location

Group Footer bands print immediately following the last Detail band belonging to the Data Group. So what do you do if you want the Group Footer to print at a specific location on the report? For example, what if you want to print Sales Orders 2-up on a page as shown in **Figure 11**? Notice that even though the first order has one detail line and the second order has three detail lines, the rectangle around each order is the same size and the Total Amount prints in the same position relative to the bottom of the rectangle.

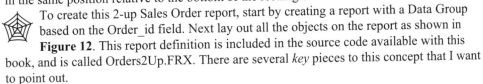 To create this 2-up Sales Order report, start by creating a report with a Data Group based on the Order_id field. Next lay out all the objects on the report as shown in **Figure 12**. This report definition is included in the source code available with this book, and is called Orders2Up.FRX. There are several *key* pieces to this concept that I want to point out.

- The positions of the objects in the Detail band are butted up tight against the top of the band, and the height of the band is only as tall as the objects within the band. No extra white space is included in the Detail band.

- There are *no* stretchable objects on this report. This is imperative to successfully fixing the bottom of the order in the exact same spot. No exceptions! Well, there's one, but I'll explain that in a minute.

- Define a Report Variable, called *nLines*, as a Count variable with a Reset at value of the order_id Data Group.

- The "Total Amount" label, the Field object that prints the total amount, and the gray Rectangle object in the Group Footer are all set as *Fix relative to bottom of band*.

Order Number	Order Date	Customer	Ship-To			
1	05/09/1992	BSBEV	B's Beverages			

Product	Product Name		Unit Price	Quantity	Extended Price
10	Ikura		31.0000	5.000	155.00

				Total Amount	155.00

Order Number	Order Date	Customer	Ship-To			
2	05/12/1992	CACTU	Mère Paillarde			

Product	Product Name	Unit Price	Quantity	Extended Price
40	Boston Crab Meat	18.4000	998.000	18,363.20
59	Raclette Courdavault	38.5500	24.000	925.20
64	Wimmers gute Semmelknödel	33.2500	10.000	332.50

				Total Amount	19,620.90

Figure 11. Use CHR(13)s in a Group Footer to force it to a fixed position on the page.

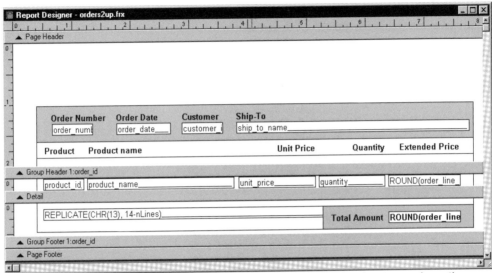

Figure 12. *Use the Report Designer to create this report definition to produce the 2-up Sales Orders shown in Figure 11.*

The final piece to this solution is the Field object in the Group Footer that forces the extra lines. For this example, a maximum of 14 lines can print on a Sales Order. To fudge the extra lines, enter the following expression for the Field object.

```
REPLICATE(CHR(13), 14-nLines)
```

This uses the Report Variable nLines to see how many lines have already printed. It subtracts this number from the maximum lines (14) and uses the REPLICATE() function to force multiple carriage returns to make up the difference. Remember when I said there's one stretchable object on the report. Well, this is the one. Mark this Field object as *Stretch with overflow* and you're done.

Be aware that this example assumes there are no more than 14 lines per order. If this situation might occur in your data, you have to get a little more complex with building the cursor and the Data Groups to overflow to the next order form whenever the maximum number of lines is exceeded. Chapter 10, "Solutions to Real-World Problems," offers more information on how to accomplish this.

Creating white space with Data Groups

Numbers, numbers, numbers! Reports are full of numbers, and often times your vision goes blurry trying to read them all. Wouldn't it be nice to add some extra white space to your reports, say, every fifth line or so? Well, guess what—you can with Data Groups!

Start by creating a Report Variable to track the line number. I know I'm jumping ahead here, because I haven't told you how to create a Report Variable yet. Report Variables are covered in great detail in Chapter 8, "Report Variables," but this trick is so cool I couldn't wait to tell you about it. Select Report | Variables... from the main VFP Menu bar and fill in the information so it looks like the Report Variables dialog shown in **Figure 13**.

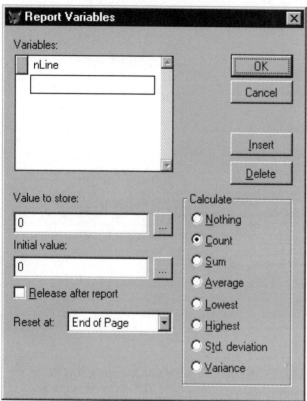

Figure 13. *Use the Report Variables dialog to create a line counter for each detail record.*

Now create a Data Group with the following expression.

```
INT(nLine/5)
```

The "5" represents the number of lines I want grouped together. You can change this to any number you wish.

Expand the height of the Group Header band to the same height as the amount of white space you want between each group of lines. But wait—you're not done yet. You might be thinking that this is all you have to do, but you're wrong. Because of the way the Group Headers and variables are processed, you're not quite finished. If you were to run the report right now, you'd get white space before the first record on page one and double white space before the first record of each subsequent page.

However, with a little ingenuity, you can trick the Report Writer to do what you want. Add a Rectangle object in the Group Header band. Make the rectangle as tall as the Group

Header band (it doesn't matter how wide you make it). Change the Print When logic of the Rectangle object to *nLine <> 0* and check the "Remove line if blank" check box.

By now you're probably thinking, "Great. What in the world is she thinking? I don't want a rectangle between each group of records. I want white space!" The key word in that thought is *white*. Change the Foreground color of the Rectangle object to white and *voilà!* It prints, but you can't see it. And the Print When logic takes care of the unwanted white space at the top of each page. The complete report is included in the source code available with this book, and is called Customer5.FRX.

See! I told you this was a cool trick!

There's power in groups

Data Grouping is a very powerful feature of the Visual FoxPro Report Writer. By now, you're probably tired of hearing me say *powerful*, but I can't help it. Once you fully understand how the Report Writer works, you can take advantage of so many things and create reports that wow your clients. It can be so satisfying to successfully create a very complex report—especially after another developer has told the client, "No way. That can't be done."

Chapter 8
Report Variables

Variables are essential to developing software. It would be impossible to create a practical application without them. Reports are no different! There are many situations when variables are essential to developing reports. You might need a variable to count the number of lines on a page or to track the total sales amount for each customer. Perhaps, you need to count the number of customers for each Sales Rep. Whatever the reason, the Visual FoxPro Report Writer provides a mechanism for creating and maintaining variables within a report.

The Visual FoxPro Report Writer has the ability to use *built-in* Report Variables. Some developers avoid this feature at all costs and adhere to the practice of preparing the data, including calculations, prior to running the report. The reasoning behind this practice is that your code is more flexible to other forms of output. Once the data has been prepared, it's a quick change to send the results to a spreadsheet instead of Visual FoxPro's report engine. If you have variables and calculations in your report, the change becomes much more complex.

That said, I still use Report Variables on many of the reports I design. Sometimes, I prepare the data in advance, but not always. I just can't bring myself to justify building a temporary cursor of 50,000 records when it contains the exact same data as the original table and one additional field that is the result of a simple count or sum function. I know FoxPro is fast, but one of my main concerns when I develop software is maximizing performance for my users, and making them wait while that cursor is built just rubs me the wrong way. So it just depends on the situation and needs of the report I'm designing as to which method I use.

Report Variables are similar to other variables in Visual FoxPro in that they can contain data of different types such as character, numeric, or dates. They also have a *scope*, which is public. This means you can access a VFP Report Variable from outside of the report, such as a UDF or a method call made by the report.

There are two main reasons for using Report Variables. The first is to take advantage of having the Report Writer perform one of its built-in calculation functions. You simply define a Report Variable, set it up as a calculated variable, and that's it. The Report Writer takes care of processing the variable for each record, such as incrementing a Count variable or totaling a Sum variable. The second reason for using Report Variables is to extend the built-in calculation functions on Report objects. See a pattern here? Report Variables are most often used for performing calculations.

Creating variables

Report Variables are created through the Report Variables dialog (shown in **Figure 1**), which can be displayed by selecting Report | Variables… from the main VFP Menu bar. The Variables list box in the upper left corner of this dialog lists all the Report Variables defined for this report. As you select an item from the list, the rest of the information on the dialog refreshes to reflect the properties of the selected Report Variable.

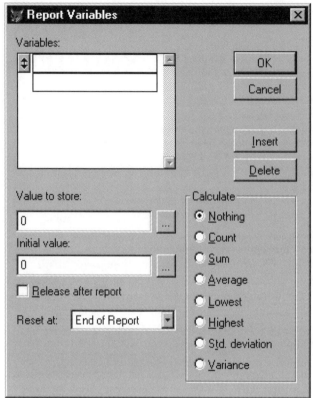

Figure 1. *Use the Report Variables dialog to create variables used within a report.*

Variable name

To create the first Report Variable, enter a name in the first box of the Variables list box. To create the second Report Variable, enter the name in the second box of the Variables list box. Each time you add a new Report Variable, an additional box is added in the list box so there's always an empty box to enter a new Report Variable.

The rules for naming a Report Variable are the same rules for naming any other VFP variable and are as follows.

- Use only letters, underscores, and numbers.

- Use 1-128 characters.

- Begin the name with a character or underscore.

- Avoid Visual FoxPro reserved words.

My Tech Editor, Dave Aring, brought up a very good point in regards to naming Report Variables. We're all accustomed to the *standard naming conventions* of prefixing variables with a character to identify the scope. For example, global variables are prefixed with "g", private variables are prefixed with "p", local variables are prefixed with "l", and parameters are prefixed with "t". So shouldn't we prefix Report Variables with something to identify them as Report Variables? Thanks, Dave! That's a great suggestion and from now on, I'm going to start prefixing my Report Variables with "r". Of course, don't hold me to this as you read through the rest of the book—old habits are hard to break.

Insert and Delete

To insert a new Report Variable in a position other than the end of the list, position the cursor in the list box and then select the Insert button. This moves the current item and any subsequent items down and inserts a new item at the cursor position.

To delete an existing Report Variable, position the cursor on the Report Variable and select the Delete button.

Value to store

The Value to store text box is where you assign a value to the Report Variable by entering any valid VFP expression. As each record is processed by the Report Writer, the expression is evaluated and the results are assigned to the Report Variable.

The expression can be as simple as static information such as *"Fox Rocks!"*, a field such as *MyTable.MyField*, a complex expression such as *INT((MyField + 20) / 100)*, or it can even use UDFs or method calls such as *MyUDF(MyField)*. You may also select the ellipse button (…) to the right of the Value to store text box to invoke the Expression Builder dialog to help you enter a more complex expression.

Release after report

The "Release after report" check box is *supposed* to determine whether or not the Report Variable is released when the report is done. Remember, Report Variables are defined as public, which means they stay in memory until CLEAR ALL, CLEAR MEMORY, RELEASE <variable>, or RELEASE ALL is executed. However, the VFP Report Writer has a bug and never bothers to release the Report Variables.

Bug Alert! *The VFP Report Writer ignores the "Release after report" check box and never releases the Report Variables. If you intend to reference the Report Variables after the report is finished, make sure this option is not checked (just in case this bug is fixed in a future version of Visual FoxPro). For now, the only foolproof way to release Report Variables is to use the RELEASE command after calling the report.*

Using calculations

Report Variables have seven built-in mathematical calculation options: Count, Sum, Average, Lowest, Highest, Std. deviation (standard deviation), and Variance. The calculations allow you to process data from all the detail records and print information such as subtotals for each customer or grand totals at the end of the report.

The value of the Report Variable is primed to the *Initial value* when the report begins. Then, as each record is processed, the *Value to store* expression is evaluated and used in the calculation. When the Report Writer reaches the *reset* point defined for the calculation, the value of the Report Variable is reset to the *Initial value*. Processing then resumes with the next record, building the calculation again. Whenever a calculated Report Variable prints on a report, it's the value of the calculation and *not* the value of the Value to store expression that prints. This fact often confuses developers.

Calculate

The first step in telling the Report Writer to apply an internal calculation to this variable is to select one of the following options from the Calculate option group.

- **Count:** This option counts the number of times this Report Variable is processed—in other words, it counts the number of records processed. The value of the expression defined in the Value to store text box is immaterial to the results of this count. However, the Initial value is very important to the results, as the count begins with this value.

- **Sum:** This option keeps a running total based on the results of the Value to store expression. As each record is processed, the Report Writer evaluates the expression and adds the results to the Report Variable. If the result of the expression does not return a numeric value, this Report Variable is set to .F.

- **Average:** This option performs an *arithmetic mean* (average) based on the Value to store expression. As each record is processed, the Report Writer keeps a separate running total based on the Value to store expression. Then, for the value of this Report Variable, it divides the accumulative total by the number of records processed to obtain the average. If a currency field is used in the Value to store expression, the results are returned with a precision of four decimal places. Otherwise, two decimal places are returned. If the Value to store expression returns a non-numeric value, this Report Variable is set to .F.

- **Lowest:** This option keeps track of what the lowest value of the Value to store expression is for all the records processed so far. However, the *Initial value* is also taken into account and can really skew the results. For example, if the data contains all positive numbers greater than zero, the *initial value* of zero is always less than any of the data. You must remember to set the Initial value to at least one more than the highest value you expect from the Value to store expression of all the records. Note that non-numeric data types (such as character and date) can be returned from the Value to store expression.

- **Highest:** This option keeps track of what the highest value of the Value to store expression is for all the records processed so far. However, as with the Lowest option, the *Initial value* is also taken into account. So, again, you must remember to set the Initial value to something lower than the lowest value that results from the Value to store expression of all the records. And don't be so quick to set it to zero and call it good. If the Value to store expression returns any negative values, you have to set an Initial value to a negative number less than any of the negative numbers returned by the Value to store expression. Note that non-numeric data types (such as character and date) can be returned from the Value to store expression.

- **Std. Deviation:** This option can be used to calculate the square root of the variance (described next). If the Value to store expression returns a non-numeric value, this Report Variable is set to .F.

- **Variance:** This option can be used to measure how spread out a distribution is. It's computed by taking the average squared deviation of each number from its mean. So what does that mean in English? I don't know! How about I explain it in terms we all know—FoxPro. The following code prints the Variance and Standard Deviation for the series of numbers 1-10. The code can be found in a program called Variance.PRG and is included in the source code available with this book. The results are shown in **Figure 2**. If the Value to store expression returns a non-numeric value, this Report Variable is set to .F.

```
*-- Variance and Standard Deviation (calculated manually)

*-- Prime
nTotal = 0

*-- Loop thru the values 1-10
FOR n = 1 to 10

   *-- What's the average so far
   nTotal = nTotal + n
   nAverage = nTotal / n

   *-- Do another loop
   nNewTotal = 0
   FOR x = 1 TO n
     nNewTotal = nNewTotal + (x - nAverage)^2
   ENDFOR

   *-- Calculate the variance and standard deviation
   nVariance = nNewTotal / n
   nDeviation = SQRT(nVariance)

   *-- Print the variance and standard deviation
   ? ' This value: ', n, ;
     '       Variance: ', nVariance, ;
     '       Deviation: ', nDeviation

ENDFOR
```

This value:	1	Variance:	0.0000	Deviation:	0.0000
This value:	2	Variance:	0.2500	Deviation:	0.5000
This value:	3	Variance:	0.6667	Deviation:	0.8165
This value:	4	Variance:	1.2500	Deviation:	1.1180
This value:	5	Variance:	2.0000	Deviation:	1.4142
This value:	6	Variance:	2.9167	Deviation:	1.7078
This value:	7	Variance:	4.0000	Deviation:	2.0000
This value:	8	Variance:	5.2500	Deviation:	2.2913
This value:	9	Variance:	6.6667	Deviation:	2.5820
This value:	10	Variance:	8.2500	Deviation:	2.8723

Figure 2. This example shows the results of the Variance and Standard Deviation of a series of numbers (1-10).

Initial value

The VFP Report Writer evaluates the *Initial value* at the beginning of the report and uses the results to prime the variable. It also resets the Report Variable to the Initial value whenever a *reset* point is reached. The default Initial value is zero.

When using calculations, it's very important to set this value to a meaningful value. As mentioned previously, when using some calculations such as Lowest and Highest, the Initial value is very important to the results of the calculation. Your results might be skewed if you're not careful in choosing an appropriate Initial value.

It's also very important to make sure the results of the Initial value is of the same data type as the results you desire from the calculation. Very strange results can happen when the data type of the Initial value is not as expected, especially when dates are used. For example, if you set the Value to store expression to a numeric data type, set the Initial value expression to a date data type, and set the calculation to Count, the results returned to this Report Variable is the date in the Initial value for *every* record. Or even stranger, change the Value to store expression to a currency field. This time the Julian Day Number of the date in the Initial value is returned to this Report Variable for *every* record. Not exactly the *Count* you were expecting!

Reset at

The Reset at drop-down combo box is used to tell the Report Writer *when* to reset the Report Variable to the Initial value. The default is *End of Report*. The following options are available.

- **End of Report:** The Report Variable is only primed once at the beginning of the report.

- **End of Page:** The Report Variable is reset at the end of each page. The exact point of the reset occurs after all the bands on the current page print and before any bands on the new page print. This means that if you use the Report Variable in the Page Footer band, it still contains the value of the last detail record on the page. If you use the Report Variable in the Page Header band, it contains the value returned by the Initial value.

- **End of Column:** The Report Variable is reset at the end of each column. This option is only available when multiple column sets have been set up for the report. This means that if you use the Report Variable in the Column Footer band, it still contains the value of the last detail record for that column. If you use the Report Variable in the Column Header band, it contains the value returned by the Initial value.

- **<Data Grouping>:** In addition to the three standard options, an additional Reset at option is available for each Data Grouping defined on the report. This allows you to reset the Report Variable each time a new value is encountered for the Data Group. This means that if you use the Report Variable in the Group *Footer* band, it still contains the value of the last detail record for that group. If you use the Report Variable in the Group *Header* band, it contains the value returned by the Initial value.

Using Report Variables

Now that you're able to create Report Variables, you're probably wondering *how* to use them. Well, the answer is, "Just the same as any other variable." You can use the Report Variable by itself as the expression of a Field object. You can also use the Report Variable within another Report Variable or complex expression of a Field object. You can even reference the Report Variable from within UDFs and method calls made by the report. The sample report shown in **Figure 3** uses several different Report Variables. The report definition is included in the source code available with this book, and is called Variables3.FRX.

Order Date	Count	Order #	Country	All Freight	USA Freight
03/17/2002			Order Freight - Summarized by Month		Page 1
05/09/1992	1	1	Italy	0.00	
05/12/1992	2	2	Canada	79.45	
05/13/1992	3	3	Sweden	36.18	
05/14/1992	4	4	Denmark	18.59	
05/15/1992	5	5	Denmark	20.12	
05/19/1992	6	6	Finland	4.13	
05/20/1992	7	7	Italy	3.62	
05/21/1992	8	8	Germany	36.19	
05/22/1992	9	9	Portugal	74.22	
05/23/1992	10	10	UK	49.21	
05/27/1992	11	11	Denmark	3.01	
05/28/1992	12	12	Brazil	31.54	
05/29/1992	13	13	Venezuela	102.59	
05/30/1992	14	14	Switzerland	50.87	
			Subtotal for May 1992:	509.72	0.00
06/02/1992	1	15	Venezuela	17.67	
06/04/1992	2	16	Austria	22.10	
06/05/1992	3	17	France	113.01	
06/06/1992	4	18	France	111.81	
06/09/1992	5	19	USA	65.46	65.46
06/10/1992	6	20	Italy	2.42	
06/12/1992	7	21	France	27.51	
06/13/1992	8	22	Austria	75.17	
06/16/1992	9	23	France	46.00	
06/17/1992	10	24	Germany	66.87	
06/18/1992	11	25	USA	5.19	5.19
06/20/1992	12	26	USA	3.32	3.32
06/23/1992	13	27	Germany	1.34	
06/24/1992	14	28	Austria	100.13	
06/25/1992	15	29	Mexico	46.86	
06/26/1992	16	30	Norway	6.72	
06/30/1992	17	31	Venezuela	26.49	
			Subtotal for June 1992:	738.07	73.97

Report Total	79,202.21	16,032.82

Report includes 1079 orders from 36 different months

Figure 3. This report uses Report Variables to count the orders per month, to print the USA Freight column, to count the total orders for the entire report, and to count the number of months on the report.

Simple Report Variables

The report shown in Figure 3 contains a few simple Report Variables to count the number of orders per month and the total number of orders for the entire report. I started by creating a Report Variable called *nCountMonth* that has a Value to store of *1*, an Initial value of *0*, and the *Count* option selected. I set the Reset at value to my Data Grouping so it resets the count for each different month. I then added a Field object to the report and used *nCountMonth* as the expression as seen in the Count column.

Next, I wanted to count the total number of orders of the entire report. I did this by adding another Report Variable called *nCountAll*, which is similar to *nCountMonth*. The only difference is that I set it to reset at *End of Report*. I then used the *nCountAll* variable in the expression of a Field object in the Report Summary band (along with some text and another variable, which I'll describe in a moment).

Conditional Report Variables

Have you ever needed to create a column that only includes certain records *and* has a summary calculation based on those records (as I did with the *USA Freight* column shown in Figure 3)? At first, you might think, "This is easy. I'll use the Print When expression." But you'd only be half right. Why? The reason is that the Print When expression only controls *when* the object prints. It does *not* have anything to do with whether or not the record participates in the calculation. Each and every record processed by the Report Writer causes the Report Variables to be evaluated, including calculations, regardless of whether or not those Report Variables happen to be used by Field objects with a Print When expression.

So now what? Well, to create the USA Freight column, start by creating a Report Variable called *nUSAFreight*. For the Value to store expression enter *IIF(ship_to_country = 'USA', freight, 0)*. For the Calculation option, select *Nothing*. For each record processed, this variable contains zero if it's not USA; otherwise, it contains the freight amount.

Now that you have a Report Variable that only contains a freight amount if the order is for the USA, add a Field object to the Detail band of the report and enter *nUSAFreight* as the expression.

To add a little more finesse to the report, you can also enter *ship_to_country = 'USA'* as the Print When expression of this object so it suppresses all non-USA orders. This is better than selecting the "Blank if zero" option because it helps the user distinguish between USA orders that don't have any freight vs. non-USA orders.

To add the subtotals and totals for this USA Freight column, copy the Field object from the Detail band into the Group Footer and Summary bands. You could also add a new Field object manually, but hey, why do more work than necessary! Once you have Field objects in the Group Footer and Summary bands with *nUSAFreight* as the expression, edit them to set the Calculation option to SUM and the Reset at option to the Data Group and End of Report, respectively. That's it. Nothing more is needed. Since you already told the Report Variable to include the freight amount *only* if the record is for USA, you don't need to do anything more to the SUM. It's already taken care of.

Counting Data Groups

The final line of the report shown in Figure 3 prints the total number of orders *and* it prints the total number of different months encountered. The total number of orders is easy and I just explained how to do it with a Report Variable using the Count option. So how did I count the total number of months encountered? This takes a little bit of ingenuity, but once you know the secret, it's easy!

The first step is to create a Report Variable (I called mine *nTotalMonths*). Set the Value to store to *0*, the Initial value to *0*, the Calculate option to *Sum*, and the Reset at option to *End of Report*.

Right about now you're saying, "That's stupid. I have a Report Variable that sums nothing. How is that going to work?" Bear with me and it will all make sense. Earlier, I mentioned that Report Variables are public variables. Here's where you can take advantage of this and manipulate the variable yourself with the _VFP.SetVar() function. Just enter the following as the On Exit expression of the Data Group Footer.

```
_VFP.SetVar("nTotalMonths", nTotalMonths + 1)
```

That's it! Whenever the VFP Report Writer encounters a new value for the Data Group, it executes this line of code, which increases the nTotalMonths Report Variable by 1. And remember that you defined the Report Variable as SUM with a Value to store of zero. This means that as each record is processed, the Report Writer does just what you told it to do—it adds zero to the Report Variable and doesn't reset it until the end of the report. Therefore, it maintains your manipulations to the Report Variable without making any of its own.

So, you haven't made the leap to Visual FoxPro and you have no idea what I mean when I say "On Exit expression." Well, once again, FoxPro provides several different ways to do the same thing, so you're not out of luck. Create the following UDF and then add a Field object to the Group Footer band of the report. Enter IncrMonths() *as the expression for the Field object. Problem solved!*

```
FUNCTION IncrMonths
nTotalMonths = nTotalMonths + 1
RETURN ""
```

Note: I consciously put the code to increment the counter in the Group Footer band and not the Group Header band. The reason is that the Data Group can be defined to repeat the Group Header on each page. If this were the case, the variable would get incremented each time the Group Header printed, which may be more than once for each different month.

Understanding the process

To fully understand Report Variables you need to understand exactly when the Report Variable is evaluated, when it's reset, and how it relates to other Report Variables. Otherwise, you may struggle with trying to get them to work the way you want.

Order of Report Variables

When multiple Report Variables are defined on a report, they're processed in the order they appear in the Variables list box. This is important if one Report Variable references another Report Variable. You can use the Mover button to the left of each item in the list box to reposition the Report Variables.

Evaluating a Report Variable

Report Variables are evaluated by the VFP Report Writer just prior to the current record being printed in the Detail band. The sample report shown in **Figure 4** demonstrates exactly when a Report Variable is processed. The first column shows which band is printed. The second column shows the value of a Report Variable (defined as Count). The third column shows the current record number. This report, called Variable1.FRX, is included in the source code available with this book.

	Report Variable (Count reset at End of Report)	RECNO()		
Page Header	0	1		
Group Header	0	1		
Detail	1	1		
Detail	2	2		
Detail	3	3		
Group Footer	3	3		
Group Header	3	4		
Detail	4	4		
Detail	5	5		
Detail	6	6		
Page Footer	6	6	Page	1

Figure 4. This sample report demonstrates when Report Variables are evaluated.

Notice the Report Variable and the RECNO() value don't always match. This is the part that can bite you if you're not expecting it. In Page Header and Group Header bands, the

RECNO() reflects the record that is about to be printed next because the record pointer has already been moved. However, the Report Variable hasn't been processed yet, so it still reflects the value from the previously printed record.

Resetting a Report Variable

You already know that when you define a Report Variable, you tell it what the Reset point is. In other words, you tell it when to reset to its Initial value. But exactly *when* the variable is reset is important, especially when compared to when the Report Variable is evaluated. For example, see the sample report shown in **Figure 5**, which has a Report Variable defined as Count and Reset at Data Group. This report, called Variable2.FRX, is included in the source code available with this book.

```
                  Report Variable
                  (Count reset at
                  Data Group 1)           RECNO()

     Page Header          0                  1
     _____

     Group Header         0                  1
     _____

          Detail          1                  1
          Detail          2                  2
          Detail          3                  3
     _____

     Group Footer         3                  3
     _____

     Group Header         0                  4
     _____

          Detail          1                  4
          Detail          2                  5
          Detail          3                  6
     _____

     Page Footer          3                  6        Page    1
```

Figure 5. This sample report demonstrates when Report Variables are reset.

You should notice that although the Report Variable is reset to zero after it finishes the Data Group, it doesn't get evaluated again until the next Detail band is processed. This means that if you reference the Report Variable in the Page Header or Group Header band, the value it contains is the Initial value. So even though the record pointer is on the next record, the Report Variable hasn't been processed yet.

Mission impossible

As I mentioned at the beginning of this chapter, it's impossible to create an application without using variables, and reports are no different. There are many different situations that warrant the use of Report Variables. Understanding exactly how the Visual FoxPro Report Writer processes these variables helps you write the reports as easily as possible.

Chapter 9
Running Reports

The whole point behind creating reports is to run them. I mean, come on, you don't create a report just for the satisfaction of saying, "I did it!" Well... maybe you do... developers are definitely a different breed of people. That said, I'm pretty sure you'd like to know how to run all those awesome reports you created. This chapter explains how to run reports and warns you about a few different *gotchas* you need to look out for.

Once a report has been created, it's very easy to run using the REPORT command. Enter the following line in the VFP Command Window or as a line of code in a program to run a report called *MyReport*.

```
REPORT FORM MyReport
```

You can also use the question mark (?) instead of a report name to indicate that you don't know what the exact name of the report is and you want VFP to bring up an Open dialog so you can find the report you want to run.

Of course, this is a very simple example. The REPORT command actually has several clauses associated with it, which gives you much more flexibility. The full-blown REPORT command is as follows.

```
REPORT FORM FileName1 | ? [ENVIRONMENT] [Scope] [FOR lExpression1]
   [WHILE lExpression2] [HEADING cHeadingText] [NOCONSOLE]
   [NOOPTIMIZE] [PLAIN] [RANGE nStartPage [, nEndPage]]
   [PREVIEW [[IN] WINDOW WindowName | IN SCREEN] [NOWAIT]]
   [TO PRINTER [PROMPT] | TO FILE FileName2 [ASCII]] [NAME ObjectName]
   [SUMMARY]
```

Throughout the rest of this chapter, I'll discuss the different clauses and how to apply them in a real application.

Where did it go?

If you tried the simple REPORT FORM MyReport example shown earlier, you might be thinking that it was sorely lacking in output. First of all, it didn't print to any printer. And second, even though it displayed on the screen, it just flew by and didn't give you the opportunity to control the scrolling, paging, or much of anything. This isn't exactly the type of output you want to offer your clients.

Well, don't worry. The REPORT command has several clauses that let you control where the output goes.

Preview on the screen

Use the PREVIEW clause to display the report in *Page Preview Mode*. By default, the report is displayed in a new window titled "Report Designer - <reportname> - Page 1". The window is displayed in the current active window (or in the VFP desktop if no window is active). The report window can be minimized, maximized, resized, and moved just like any other window. The following command displays the report shown in **Figure 1**.

```
REPORT FORM reports\pizzazz2 PREVIEW
```

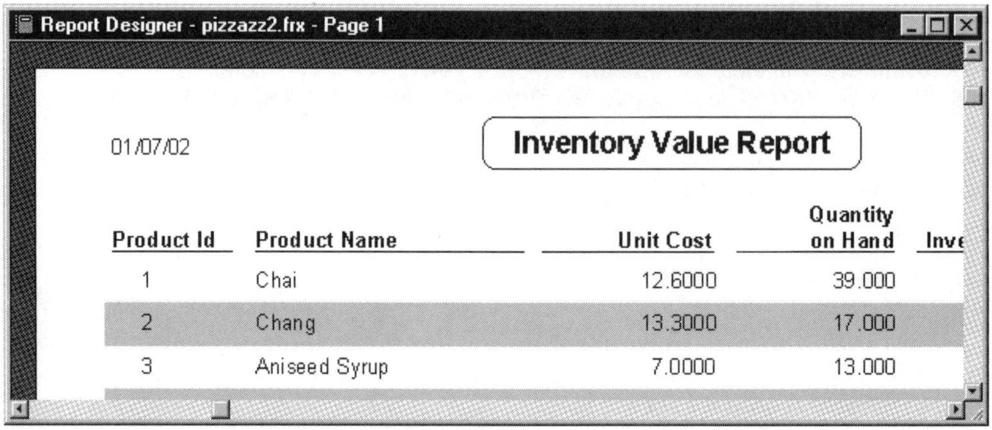

Figure 1. Use the PREVIEW clause to display a report on the screen.

Right off the bat, this doesn't exactly look like what you want. It's pretty unlikely that the user only wants to see the upper left corner of the report. Most likely, they'll maximize the window right away or at least expand the size of the window. Whenever the user changes the window, the settings are stored in the current resource table (if one is in use). Then, each subsequent time the user previews this report, the settings are restored from the resource file and the window takes on the properties it had the last time the user previewed this report.

A window of opportunity
The REPORT command has a few clauses that give you the ability to control the window the report is previewed in, as well as where this window is put.

- Use *WINDOW <windowname>* to tell the Report Writer to use the specified window instead of the default Preview window when displaying this report.

- Use *IN WINDOW <windowname>* to tell the Report Writer to place the Preview window inside of the specified window. This means that either the default Preview window or the window specified with *WINDOW <windowname>* is placed inside of the window specified with *IN WINDOW <windowname>*.

- Use *IN SCREEN* to tell the Report Writer to place the Preview window on the screen and not in the current active window. This means that either the default Preview window or the window specified with *WINDOW <windowname>* is placed on the screen. Note that IN WINDOW and IN SCREEN are mutually exclusive—you may not use them both in the same REPORT command.

The WINDOW, IN WINDOW, and IN SCREEN clauses are not available in FoxPro 2.x.

The following code shows an example of how to use the WINDOW and IN WINDOW clauses to produce the results shown in **Figure 2**. The code can be found in the program called Preview.PRG, in the source code available with this book. The program runs the report called Pizzazz2.FRX, also included with the source code.

```
*-- Define my own Preview window
DEFINE WINDOW MyPreview ;
  FROM 5,5 TO 40,80 ;
  TITLE 'My Preview Window' ;
  CLOSE FLOAT GROW MINIMIZE ZOOM ;
  IN SCREEN

*-- Define and activate a new window
DEFINE WINDOW MySuper ;
  FROM 0,0 TO 50,90 ;
  TITLE 'My Super Duper Window' ;
  CLOSE FLOAT GROW MINIMIZE ZOOM
ACTIVATE WINDOW MySuper

*-- Define and activate the window that will hold the preview window
DEFINE WINDOW MyReport ;
  FROM 5,5 TO 45,85 ;
  TITLE 'My Report Window' ;
  IN WINDOW MySuper ;
  CLOSE FLOAT
ACTIVATE WINDOW MyReport

*-- Go back to the "Super Duper" window just to prove that the "current"
*-- window isn't where the preview goes
ACTIVATE WINDOW MySuper

*-- Preview the report in MyPreview window instead of the default window
*-- and put the MyPreview window inside of the MyReport window.
REPORT FORM reports\pizzazz2 PREVIEW WINDOW MyPreview IN WINDOW MyReport

*-- Restore things
RELEASE WINDOWS MySuper, MyReport, MyPreview
ACTIVATE SCREEN
```

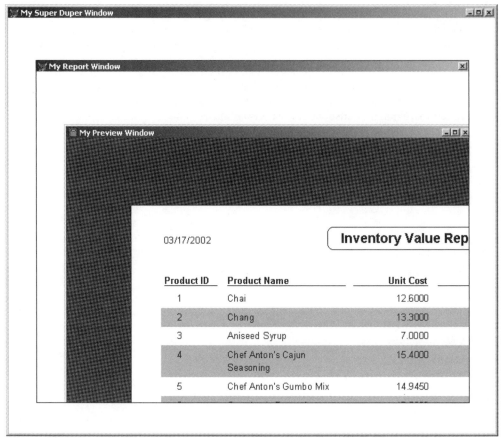

Figure 2. Use the IN WINDOW and the WINDOW clauses to control where the Preview is sent.

Print to a printer

To print the report to a printer, use the TO PRINTER clause, which sends the report to the VFP default printer. To allow the user to choose the printer as well as change the printer settings, include the PROMPT clause. The following code shows how to print a report to the printer with and without the PROMPT clause.

```
*-- Print to the VFP default printer
REPORT FORM MyReport TO PRINTER

*-- Print to a printer chosen by the user
REPORT FORM MyReport TO PRINTER PROMPT
```

If you tried either of the two commands just described, you were probably surprised to see the report printed on the printer *and* displayed on the screen. Only this time, it wasn't near as nice as with the PREVIEW clause because it just scrolled up the screen until the entire report was done. It never stopped and gave you a chance to see each page.

To stop that nasty behavior of scrolling on the screen at the same time it prints to the printer, use the NOCONSOLE clause as shown in the following code. This suppresses the echoing of the report to the screen whenever the PREVIEW clause is not used.

```
*-- Print to the VFP Default Printer
REPORT FORM MyReport NOCONSOLE TO PRINTER

*-- Print to a printer chosen by the user
REPORT FORM MyReport NOCONSOLE TO PRINTER PROMPT
```

What printer?

A little clarification is warranted as to what the *default* printer is. Visual FoxPro has its own default printer, which isn't necessarily the same as the Windows default printer. When VFP is first started, the VFP default printer is set to the Windows default printer. The VFP default printer can be changed through the main VFP Menu bar by selecting File | Page Setup..., by using the SET PRINTER TO NAME command, or by using the SYS(1037) function. The next time VFP is restarted, the VFP default printer is once again set to the Windows default printer.

The following code shows how to send a report to a specific printer without having to prompt the user to pick it. Often, this technique is used to send forms such as invoices or checks to a printer that is dedicated to one specific task.

```
*-- Remember the current VFP default printer
LOCAL lcPrinter
lcPrinter = SET('PRINTER', 3)

*-- Set the Invoice Printer as the VFP default printer
SET Printer TO NAME 'HP DeskJet 660'

*-- Print the report
REPORT FORM reports\pizzazz2 TO PRINTER

*-- Restore the VFP default printer
SET Printer TO NAME "&lcPrinter"
```

> *Notice the SET PRINTER TO NAME command in the previous example uses quotes around the macro substitution. If you forget the quotes and the printer name includes a space, it won't work!*

Now in a real-world application, I wouldn't hard-code the printer. What would happen if that printer happens to break or the client decides to buy a new printer? I wouldn't want to have to build a new executable for them just for this reason. Especially if they're hot-to-trot to get their invoices printed and out the door!

Instead, I would incorporate some type of control file into the application that lets the user assign which printer is the *Check* printer and which printer is the *Invoice* printer. You can use the GETPRINTER() function, which returns a printer name selected by the user, and then save that name in a control file. In your invoice program, grab the printer name from the control file and use macro expansion to set the printer for the report just as I did in the previous code sample to restore the VFP default printer.

Printer "gotcha"

One of the biggest struggles with printing reports from Visual FoxPro has to do with which printer the report goes to and what printer settings it uses. I just explained how to send a report to a specific printer—but it doesn't always work as anticipated and here's why.

Besides the *Windows* default printer and the *Visual FoxPro* default printer, there's a third printer to deal with—the *report-specific* printer. When you create a new report, the VFP Report Designer sets the *report-specific* printer to the same printer as the VFP default printer. As long as that printer happens to be the same printer as the Windows default printer, you won't have any problems. When you save the report, the Report Designer checks to see what the report-specific printer is and compares it against the Windows default printer. If the printers are the same, it doesn't bother to save all the specific settings of the report-specific printer with the report.

However, if the report-specific printer is not the same as the Windows default printer, the Report Designer saves a bunch of information about the report-specific printer with the report definition stored in the FRX file. It's that hard-coded information saved with the report that can cause you headaches down the road. For example, you may try to use the code shown in the previous example to print to a printer that you specify, but no matter how many times you try, the report keeps going to the wrong printer. The reason is that it goes to the report-specific printer saved with the report definition and does not honor the printer you tried to print to with SET PRINTER TO NAME. How's that for a great big "gotcha"?

To avoid falling into this trap, always be sure that the report-specific printer is the same printer as your Windows default printer whenever you save a report in the Report Designer. This includes any time you modify an existing report and save it again—even if you don't change anything. The point is, each time you *save* the report with the Report Designer, the comparison of printers takes place and the subsequent hard-coded printer information gets saved in the report definition if the printers are different.

As mentioned earlier, the current VFP default printer is used as the report-specific printer when you first create a new report. To change the report-specific printer from within the Report Designer, select File | Page Setup... from the main VFP Menu bar to invoke the Page Setup dialog. From this dialog, select the Print Setup... command button to invoke the Print Setup dialog where you can select a printer to assign to the report. Remember, if the printer you select happens to be the same printer as the Windows default printer, the Report Designer won't bother to save any of the special hard-coded printer information with the report.

All this sounds very complex and is a *sleeping giant* waiting to cause major problems. The first time you forget to make sure the report-specific printer matches the Windows default printer will be the same time you build a new executable for your client, deliver it, and then go on a weeklong vacation. By the time you get back from your nice relaxing vacation, all hell has broken loose and you've got one very irate client!

Later, in the section titled "Eliminating printer-specific information," I'll show you a way to comment out any hard-coded printer information saved with a report so you can be assured that your vacation won't come to a screeching halt—at least not because of a printer issue!

Print to a file

Sometimes, there's a need to send a report to a file so you can print it later. The REPORT command offers a clause to do just that. Use the TO FILE clause as shown in the following example to send a report to a file.

```
REPORT FORM reports\pizzazz2 TO FILE MyFile NOCONSOLE
```

By default, the file is created with the TXT extension, but you can override this behavior and create a file with any extension by explicitly setting it as shown in the following example.

```
REPORT FORM reports\pizzazz2 TO FILE MyFile.clp NOCONSOLE
```

> *If the file indicated with the TO FILE clause already exists and SET SAFETY is ON, you're prompted with a dialog telling you the file already exists and it asks whether you want to overwrite the file. If you answer* No, *the Windows Save As dialog is displayed so you can pick a different file name.*

I suppose you'd like to know *what* is actually in this file. If you bring this file up with any text editor, I guarantee it won't make any sense. It contains the ASCII representation of binary code for PostScript and other printer codes, not just text. And believe me, that ASCII representation looks extremely funky. Lucky for you, though, you don't have to worry about that. Just use the RUN command to execute a DOS Copy command to print the saved report as follows.

```
RUN copy /B MyFile.txt LPT1:
```

The /B option of the DOS Copy command indicates the file is a binary file. Using LPT1: as the destination indicates I want the file sent to the LPT1 port instead of copying it to another file. Of course, this is simple when I have a printer plugged directly into the back of my laptop. When you're on a network, it can get a bit trickier copying a file to a network printer. Especially when you send something to the printer and it doesn't come out. So you send it again and it still doesn't come out. Then, 10 minutes later, you have two copies of the report sitting on the printer. Just be aware that the report may be delayed.

> *Note: On some networks, the trailing ":" after LPT1 can cause problems so you may need to omit it.*

Now, keep in mind that just as with printing to a printer, you're going to have to deal with the printer situations. For example, whatever printer driver is used at the time the file is created is the printer driver used when the report is printed later with the DOS Copy command. So it's important that you understand which printer driver is used to create the file. If no specific report information is saved with the report definition, the Visual FoxPro default printer is used to create the file. However, if a specific printer is saved with the report definition, the Report printer is used to create the file.

> *I want to mention that I have one specific printer in my office that gives me trouble when I print TO FILE with that printer set as the default. The reason is that it* always *prompts me for a file name, even though I've already given it a name in the line of code that prints to the file. This means that all my great code to get a unique file name, print to it, and then erase the file when I'm done is useless. Luckily, I've never had a client with this same printer so it hasn't been a major issue for me.*

Print to an ASCII file

You can also send a report to an ASCII text file with the REPORT command as shown in the following example.

```
REPORT FORM reports\pizzazz2 TO FILE MyFile ASCII NOCONSOLE
```

When using the ASCII clause, all PostScript and printer codes are stripped out and only text characters are sent to the file. Any graphics, lines, or boxes are also omitted from the file. What you're left with is a file that contains only text characters. You can use any text editor, including VFP, to open the file and look at it. It won't contain any of the funky characters that the other file contained.

To print a file created with the ASCII clause, simply use the TYPE command or choose File | Print… from the main VFP Menu bar. The file can also be printed from any number of different applications such as Microsoft Word because it is just a regular ASCII text file.

There are two system variables used by the ASCII clause: _ASCIIROWS and _ASCIICOLS. These two variables determine the number of rows and columns per page. By default, _ASCIIROWS is 63 and _ASCIICOLS is 80, but you can change these system variables as needed. The following example shows how the outputted text of a customer report looks with the _ASCIIROWS system variable set to 5.

```
Page Header
   Alfreds Futterkiste
   Ana Trujillo
   Antonio Moreno
Page Header
   Around the Horn
   Berglunds snabbköp
   Blauer See
Page Header
   Blondel père et fils
   Bólido Comidas
   Bon app'
```

Notice that setting the system variable to "5" did not mean that five detail lines print on each page. The Report Writer also counts lines in the Page Header and lines in the Page Footer toward the total rows per page. And even though my report did not have a Page Footer, the Report Writer still counted one line for it.

The ASCII clause is not available in FoxPro 2.x.

Which records?

In Chapter 4, "The Data Source," I discussed the Report Data Environment in great detail. You can open tables, set the index orders, set relations, and even set filters using the Data Environment. You can also do all kinds of special things with custom code in several methods of the Data Environment. But what if you aren't using the Data Environment?

The Data Environment is not required to run reports. You can open tables, set the index orders, set relations, and even set filters yourself with code. As long as the report is not defined with a Private Data Session, it can access any tables already opened at the time the REPORT command is executed. The following code shows an example of how to run a report based on the Customer table without using the Data Environment.

```
*-- Open the table
USE Customer

*-- Set the order
SET ORDER TO TAG customer_I

*-- Run the report
REPORT FORM CustList

*-- Close the table
SELECT Customer
USE
```

Scope

There are four different scope clauses available when running reports. A scope clause determines which records in the table are printed.

- **ALL:** By default, reports have a scope of *all*. This means when the REPORT command is executed, it starts at the beginning of the table and processes all *available* records in the table. Any records filtered out by a SET FILTER or SET DELETED ON command are not *available*, and therefore are not processed by the Report Writer.

- **NEXT:** Use the NEXT clause, followed by a number, to tell the Report Writer to start at the current record position and only process the next *n* records. Any records filtered out with SET FILTER or SET DELETED ON don't count toward the number of records processed.

- **RECORD:** Use the RECORD clause, followed by a number, to tell the Report Writer to only print the one record whose RECNO() matches the number. This clause doesn't care whether the record is actually filtered out by a SET FILTER or SET DELETED ON command—it prints the record regardless.

- **REST:** Use the REST clause to tell the Report Writer to start processing at the current record position and continue until the end of the file is reached. Any records filtered out by a SET FILTER or SET DELETED ON command are not processed.

The following sample code shows how to use each of the different scope clauses.

```
*-- Open the table
Use Customer

*-- ALL
*-- Start at the beginning and process all records
*-- (notice no GOTO TOP is needed)
REPORT FORM CustList ALL && FYI, the ALL clause is optional here

*-- NEXT
*-- Start with record number 10 and process 5 records
*-- (because no index order is set, this prints records 10-14)
GOTO 10
REPORT FORM CustList NEXT 5

*-- RECORD
*-- Process record number 20
REPORT FORM CustList RECORD 20

*-- REST
*-- Start with record number 25 and process the remaining records
GOTO 25
REPORT FORM CustList REST

*-- Close the table
SELECT Customer
USE
```

> Note: The scope clauses only apply when the report is not defined with a Private Data Session and you're printing the report from a table that is not opened by the Data Environment of the report.

For <expression>

In addition to the scope, you can add a filter by using the FOR clause. Any records not matching the FOR expression are skipped. Also keep in mind that any records already filtered out with SET FILTER or SET DELETED ON are skipped too. The following code sample shows how to print the report for only those customers in the United States.

```
*-- Open the table
USE Customer

*-- Set the order
SET ORDER TO TAG 'customer_I'

*-- Run the report
REPORT FORM CustList FOR country = "USA"

*-- Close the table
```

```
SELECT Customer
USE
```

When using the FOR clause, remember that the scope also applies. In the previous example, I didn't explicitly set any scope; therefore, the default of ALL is in place. This means processing begins at the beginning of the table and continues to the end, only printing those records that match the FOR expression.

Rushmore optimizes the REPORT FOR command if the expression is optimizable. For best performance, use an optimizable expression.

While <expression>

Just as with a DO WHILE command loop, the WHILE clause tells the Report Writer to process records as long as the expression is true. If no scope has been explicitly set, using the WHILE clause changes the default scope to REST. The following code sample shows how to print all the customers whose name starts with the letter *B*.

```
*-- Open the table
USE Customer

*-- Set the order
SET ORDER TO TAG 'company_na'

*-- Prime the table
SET EXACT OFF
SEEK 'B'

*-- Run the report
REPORT FORM CustList WHILE company_name = 'B'

*-- Close the table
SELECT Customer
USE
```

Miscellaneous clauses

Wow! I've covered several different clauses of the REPORT command. Would you believe I'm not done yet? There's still another handful of clauses left to cover.

Heading

The HEADING clause is used to tell the Report Writer to print an extra line of text in the Page Header band. This can be useful when you want to print something in the header that could change at run time. For example, you could use it to print a description of the criteria the user entered when running the report. Use it as shown in the following example.

```
REPORT FORM CustList PREVIEW HEADING 'My Special Heading'
```

The extra *heading* is printed using the Default Font defined with the report. It's positioned at the bottom of the Page Header band and centered within the left and right margins of the report. You must be sure to leave some extra room at the bottom of the Page Header band or else the extra heading text prints on top of other information as shown in **Figure 3**.

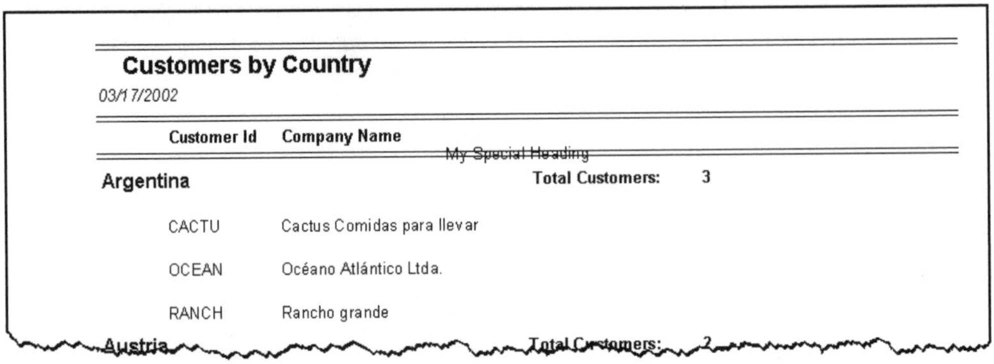

Figure 3. *Be sure to leave room at the bottom of the Page Header when using the HEADING clause to avoid overwriting other information.*

Plain

The PLAIN clause tells the VFP Report Writer to not print the Page Header band on any page. The main reason for using this clause is when you're printing to an ASCII text file and you don't want any headings printed. The PLAIN clause only suppresses the Page Header band and not the Page Footer band.

> *The PLAIN clause is incorrectly documented in the Visual FoxPro Help file.*

Range

The RANGE clause lets you print the report starting at a specific page instead of the first page. It also lets you optionally stop the report at a specific page. The following sample code shows how to do both.

```
*-- Print the report starting with page 10
REPORT FORM CustList TO PRINTER NOCONSOLE RANGE 10

*-- Print pages 10-20
REPORT FORM CustList TO PRINTER NOCONSOLE RANGE 10,20
```

If no ending range is specified, the report continues until either the end is reached or page 65,534 is reached (hopefully your report has finished by then!). To use the ending range, you must enter a starting page number, even if it's 1. The RANGE clause is ignored when previewing the report. However, if the report is being previewed and printed, the RANGE clause is honored for the printed report.

> I've been told that printing a report without the range clause stops printing at 9,999 pages. Personally, I haven't sat down and tested this theory, nor do I plan to. But in any event, the workaround to this problem is to use the RANGE clause to print pages 1 through 9,999, then run the report again printing pages 10,000 through 19,999, then run the report again printing pages 20,000 through 29,999, and so on.

 The RANGE clause is not available in FoxPro 2.x.

Summary

The SUMMARY clause is used to suppress the detail lines of a report. This feature is nice when you've defined a report with Data Groups that have information in the Group Header and Group Footer bands. If you only want to see the information in the Group Headers and Group Footers and don't care to see all the details, use the SUMMARY clause. **Figure 4** shows an example of how the same report looks when printed with and without the SUMMARY clause.

Customers by Country
03/17/2002   **Without SUMMARY**

Customer Id	Company Name

Argentina   Total Customers: 3

    CACTU   Cactus Comidas para llevar

    OCEAN   Océano Atlántico Ltda.

    RANCH   Rancho grande

Austria   Total Customers: 2

    ERNSH   Ernst Handel

    PICCO   Piccolo und mehr

Customers by Country
03/17/2002   **With SUMMARY**

Customer Id	Company Name

Argentina	Total Customers:	3
Austria	Total Customers:	2
Belgium	Total Customers:	2
Brazil	Total Customers:	9
Canada	Total Customers:	3
Denmark	Total Customers:	2
Finland	Total Customers:	2
France	Total Customers:	11
Germany	Total Customers:	11

***Figure 4**. Use the SUMMARY clause to suppress the Detail band of a report.*

NoOptimize

As mentioned earlier, Rushmore optimizes REPORT FOR if the expression is optimizable. Use the NOOPTIMIZE clause to tell the Report Writer to prevent Rushmore optimization.

NoWait

When using the PREVIEW clause to display a report on the screen, execution of the program stops and waits for the Preview window to be closed. Use the NOWAIT clause to tell Visual FoxPro to leave the Preview window open and continue execution.

 The NOWAIT clause is not available in FoxPro 2.x.

Name

One of the biggest complaints about the VFP Report Writer is that it's not object-oriented. While this is true 99.9% of the time, there is one tiny little bit that is object-oriented. When a report is being run, an object reference to the Data Environment is created. By default, the name of the object reference is the same name as the report itself. For example, if my report was called *MyReport,* I could use *MyReport.InitialSelectedAlias* to find out what the InitialSelectedAlias is for the report.

You can use the NAME clause to tell the Report Writer to use a different name as shown in the following example. Now, instead of using *MyReport* to access the PEMs of the Data Environment, I have to use *MySuperRpt;* thus, the reference to the InitialSelectedAlias property becomes *MySuperRpt.InitialSelectedAlias.*

```
REPORT FORM MyReport Preview NAME MySuperRpt
```

 The NAME clause is not available in FoxPro 2.x.

Environment

The ENVIRONMENT clause only applies to reports that were created in FoxPro 2.x and converted to Visual FoxPro. Using this clause tells the VFP Report Writer to ignore the settings of the AutoOpenTables and AutoCloseTables properties and treat them both as if they're set to .T.

Special preview issues

There are a few issues that you need to be aware of when dealing with previewing a report.

The Print Preview toolbar

When previewing the report, the Print Preview toolbar (see **Figure 5**) appears on the screen as a separate window or on a toolbar docked somewhere on the screen, depending on how it was last used in VFP. This toolbar allows you to navigate through the report, change the size of the display, and print the report to a printer.

Figure 5*. The Print Preview toolbar can appear as a window by itself or within a toolbar docked somewhere on the screen.*

 In FoxPro 2.x there is no such thing as a Print Preview toolbar. Buttons to the right of the Preview window are used to navigate through the report displayed on the screen.

Accessing the Print Preview toolbar

You *must* be sure the Print Preview toolbar is available to the user. I already said that the toolbar comes up automatically when a report is previewed, but what if the user closes the toolbar? Now what? Without this toolbar, the user can't navigate through the report.

Make sure your application has the Toolbars… option available on the menu so the user can reopen the toolbar if necessary. See the section titled "The View menu" later in this chapter for more information about how to do this.

Using the Print Preview toolbar

The default Print Preview toolbar consists of the following eight buttons (from left to right).

- **First Page:** This option displays the first page of the report on the screen. If you're already on the first page, this option is disabled.

- **Previous Page:** This option displays the previous page of the report on the screen. If you're already on the first page, this option is disabled.

- **Go to Page**: This option displays the dialog shown in **Figure 6**. Enter the page number you wish to jump to and select OK. If you enter a page number greater than the number of pages in the report, the last page is displayed. Selecting Cancel from this dialog returns to the preview and does not move to a different page.

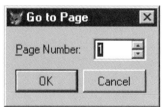

Figure 6*. Use the Go to Page dialog to jump to any page in the report.*

- **Next Page:** This option displays the next page of the report on the screen. If you're already on the last page, this option is disabled.

- **Last Page:** The option displays the last page of the report on the screen. If you're already on the last page, this option is disabled.

- **Zoom:** This option allows you to choose how big or small the report should be on the screen (see **Figure 7**). You may choose 100%, 75%, 50%, 25%, 10%, or Zoom. Zoom shrinks the report so the entire page displays on the screen. The percentages are relative to some abstract size chosen by Microsoft—they are not relative to the actual paper size chosen for the report.

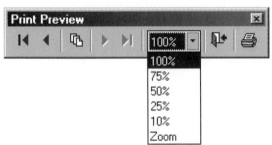

Figure 7. The Zoom drop-down combo box allows you to select the size of the report displayed on the screen.

- **Close Preview:** This option clears the report from the screen and closes the Print Preview dialog.

- **Print Report:** This option sends the report to the printer, and then closes the Print Preview.

Printing from the Print Preview toolbar

When the user chooses the Print button from the Print Preview toolbar, the report goes to the Report printer, if one has been saved with the report. Otherwise, the report goes to the VFP default printer. If you'd rather have the Print button prompt the user for a printer, use a combination of the TO PRINTER PROMPT and PREVIEW clauses as follows.

```
REPORT FORM MyReport TO PRINTER PROMPT PREVIEW
```

Using these clauses together causes the Print button to display the Print dialog, from which the user can choose a printer, set some printer properties, select the range of pages, and select the number of copies. When combining these clauses, you *must* place the PREVIEW clause after the TO PRINTER PROMPT clauses. If you attempt to reverse the order, you'll get an error.

Customizing the Print Preview toolbar

The default Print Preview toolbar, shown earlier in Figure 5, can be customized. One of the most common reasons for customizing the toolbar is to remove the Print button so the user can only preview the report. You may have some special processing that goes on when the report is printed; therefore, you want more control over when the user prints. So how do you remove the Print button from the Print Preview toolbar?

The solution to this dilemma involves the Visual FoxPro resource file, which saves all kinds of information about the positioning and makeup of toolbars, forms, reports, and lots of other things. So… you just need to create a special resource file with the special Print Preview toolbar and then use the special resource file when calling the report.

Create the resource file

To create the special resource file, you need to start with an empty resource file. You can create this by entering the following in the Command Window:

```
SET RESOURCE ON
cFox=SET('RESOURCE',1)
SET RESOURCE OFF
USE (cFox)
COPY TO MyUser
USE MyUser EXCLUSIVE
ZAP
USE
SET RESOURCE TO MyUser
```

Now that you have an empty resource file set as the current resource file, modify a dummy report so you can begin manipulating the toolbar.

```
MODIFY REPORT MyReport
```

Next, select View | Toolbars… from the main VFP Menu bar. Make sure the Print Preview toolbar is checked and then select the Customize… button. This puts you into a special mode that allows you to manipulate any of the displayed toolbars. Click and drag the Print button from the Print Preview toolbar (*not* the Customize Toolbar dialog) to somewhere off of the toolbar. This removes the button from the toolbar. Now select Close to end the customization session. You should also set the resource file back to the original file with the following command so you don't record any more information in your new special resource file.

```
SET Resource TO (cFox)
```

Printing the report

Now that you have a special resource file saved, you can temporarily use this resource file when printing the report as follows:

```
* Set the resource file to the special printer resource file
LOCAL lcResourceTo, lcResourceOnOff
lcResourceOnOff = SET('RESOURCE')
lcResourceTo = SET('RESOURCE',1)
SET Resource ON
SET Resource TO MyUser
```

```
* Print the report
REPORT FORM MyReport PREVIEW

* Restore the resource file
IF EMPTY(lcResourceTo)
   SET Resource TO
ELSE
   SET Resource TO (lcResourceTo)
ENDIF
SET Resource &lcResourceOnOff
```

The report displays on the screen along with the special *No Print Button* toolbar you've created. The user is not given the choice to print the report, yet all other reports can still be printed with the standard resource file in place, which has the standard Print Preview toolbar with the Print button still on it.

Maximize the Print Preview window

As seen in Figure 1 at the beginning of this chapter, the Print Preview window does not come up maximized. The first thing a user is going to do is maximize the window. If you have a read/write resource file in use during the execution of your application, the user's change to the window is recorded so the next time the user runs the same report, the window appears maximized. If you really want to be a hero, you could always run the report, maximize it, and then include *your* resource file with the application so the user doesn't have to maximize each report the first time each one is run.

However, if you don't have a read/write resource file in use during the execution of your application, you can use the KEYBOARD command to fudge the key combination that maximizes a window. This is a lot easier than running each report in the entire application. Use the following code to call the report.

```
KEYBOARD '{CTRL+F10}'
REPORT FORM MyReport PREVIEW
```

The reason this trick doesn't work when a read/write resource file is in use is because Ctrl-F10 is a toggle that switches between maximizing the window and restoring the window. The first time the user runs the report, the KEYBOARD command does as you expected and maximizes the window. However, the maximized state of the window gets saved in the resource file. The next time the user runs the report, it automatically comes up maximized so when the KEYBOARD command is executed, it ends up restoring the normal size of the window instead of maximizing as you intended.

Another method you can use to force the Print Preview window to maximize is to use the following line of code in the Init method of the Data Environment of the report.

```
ZOOM WINDOW "Report Designer" MAX
```

Of course, this means you have to put this same line of code in *every* report you write.

Preview multiple reports at once

The introduction of the NOWAIT clause to the REPORT command opened up the ability to preview more than one report at the same time. Use the following code to preview two reports at the same time.

```
REPORT FORM MyReport1 PREVIEW NOWAIT
REPORT FORM MyReport2 PREVIEW NOWAIT
```

Of course, the first time you do this, the two reports are going to display on top of each other. Just grab the top one and move it down to expose the first report. You can also use the WINDOW and IN WINDOW clauses to define exactly where you want each of the windows positioned on the screen instead of letting the default Print Preview window display.

There are two caveats to using the NOWAIT clause with reports. First, you can't display the same report—not even if you use two different window names. Visual FoxPro can't access the same report definition at the same time. If you need to do this, you'll have to copy one of the report definitions to a temporary file and report from that file (see "Modifying reports within an application," later in this chapter, for more information on how to do this).

The second caveat is that unless you use a Private Data Session for the report, you could inadvertently close the table out from under the report. Consider the following code.

```
*-- Open the table
USE Customer

*-- Preview the report
REPORT FORM MyReport PREVIEW NOWAIT

*-- Close the table
USE
```

When the REPORT command is executed, the report is displayed along with the Print Preview toolbar. Execution is then continued with the next statement, which closes the table. Now, when you attempt to navigate to the next page, the Report Writer won't be able to access the table anymore so it displays the Open dialog. To avoid this *major* problem, be sure to use Private Data Sessions whenever you plan to use the NOWAIT clause.

Seeing ghosts

There's a very annoying bug that sometimes occurs when previewing a report, and it has *bugged* me for a long time because I wasn't able to figure out what triggered it. A few months ago I sat down and was bound and determined to figure it out. Well, I'm happy to report that I was finally able to figure it out and I can sleep much better these days. Oh wait, I haven't even told you what the bug is yet.

When previewing a report, the Preview window has a dark gray background to help with the illusion of showing the report as white paper. On some occasions, the report is displayed in the Preview window, yet the entire background is white with no distinction between the background and the *paper*. You're probably thinking, "Big deal, Cathy. I certainly don't consider this a show stopper!"

Well, I agree with you on this point, but I'm not done explaining the bug yet. It gets better. Click on the report to zoom out and what you see is not what you expected, as shown in **Figure 8**. When the report is displayed in full-page mode, the VFP Report Writer only repaints the printable area of the page. The non-printable margins of the page don't get repainted so you end up seeing what was on the screen before you zoomed.

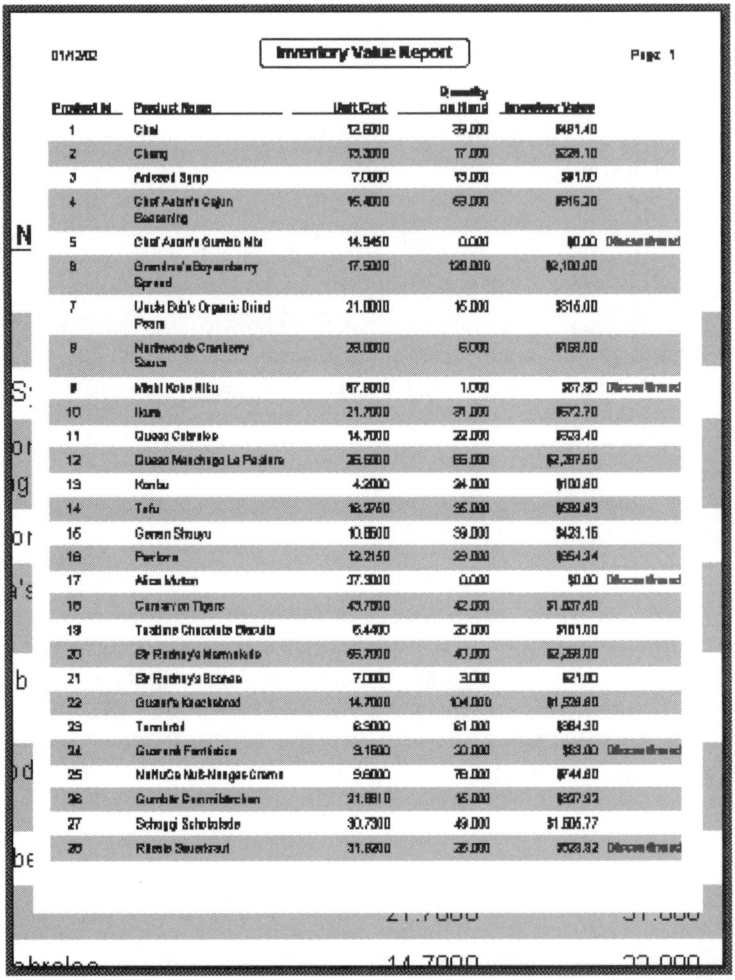

Figure 8. The non-printable margins of the page don't get repainted under certain circumstances.

Bug Alert! *There's a very annoying bug in the VFP Report that causes the Preview window to not paint correctly whenever a UDF is used in the report.*

To force the Report Writer to repaint, just click on the report once to zoom in and then again to zoom back out. Or, for a good laugh, grab the Print Preview toolbar and move it on top of one of the non-printable margins. Then move it again to another spot. Each time you move the toolbar, the Report Writer correctly repaints the area underneath it.

As harmless as this bug is, it's still very annoying to always have to click twice to get rid of the ghosting. I can't offer you any solution to correct it, but I can tell you what causes it. It happens when you call a UDF from within the report, such as from the expression of a Field object or from the expression of the Print When of an object. Ironically, if the UDF does nothing—in other words, it consists of a FUNCTION statement followed by a RETURN statement—the bug does not happen. The function actually has to do something for the bug to happen.

Special printing issues
There are a few issues that you need to be aware of when printing reports.

The Printing dialog
When printing a report to the printer, the dialog shown in **Figure 9** appears on the screen. It shows the name of the report being printing as well as the current page number. It also contains a Cancel button so the user can stop the printing.

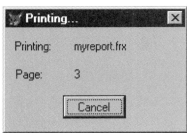

Figure 9. *The Printing… dialog automatically appears when printing a report to a printer.*

Suppressing the Printing… dialog
In some situations, you may want to suppress the standard Printing… dialog. The bad news— you can't suppress it. The good news—you can fake it out!

The Printing… dialog box always appears when you print to the printer. This, you can't stop. But you can move the window off the screen so it *appears* as if you've suppressed it. Place the following code in a UDF or class method that's accessible from the report.

```
IF WEXIST("Printing...")
  MOVE WINDOW "Printing..." TO -1000, -1000
ENDIF
```

In the Title band of the report, use the On Entry expression to call the UDF or class method you just created. If you don't really need a Title band, create one anyway and change the band height to zero.

When the user prints the report, the dialog flashes for a brief moment and then *disappears*. However, realize that it really hasn't disappeared. It's still there. You just can't see it. So if you had a glimmer of hope thinking that this would allow you to print reports from COM objects—no such luck!

Display your own dialog

I just showed you how to *suppress* the standard Printing… dialog. This, in itself, is a cool trick. However, it also paves the way for you to create and display your own dialog box. Use the following code to call the report and define two UDFs for creating and releasing your own dialog. This code can be found in the program called PrintDialog.PRG, included in the source code available with this book. The program runs the report called PrintDialog.FRX, which is also included in the source code.

```
*-- Call the report
REPORT FORM reports\printdialog TO PRINTER PROMPT PREVIEW

*---------------------
FUNCTION MyPrintDialog
*---------------------
* Use my custom print dialog instead of the default print dialog

LPARAMETERS tcReportName

*-- Only do this if the report is being printed
IF WEXIST('Printing...')

  *-- Move the old window out of the way
  MOVE WINDOW "Printing..." TO -1000, -1000

  *-- Create a new window
  DEFINE WINDOW MyPrintDialog ;
    FROM 0,0 TO 10,50 ;
    SYSTEM ;
    TITLE 'Printing...' ;
    MINIMIZE ZOOM FLOAT CLOSE ;

  *-- Center the window
  MOVE WINDOW MyPrintDialog CENTER

  *-- Display the Report Info
  ACTIVATE WINDOW MyPrintDialog
  @ 2,0 SAY PADC("Cathy's Super Duper Application", WCOLS('MyPrintDialog'))
  @ 5,0 SAY PADC(tcReportName, WCOLS('MyPrintDialog'))

ENDIF

*---------------------
FUNCTION ReleaseDialog
*---------------------
* Release the custom print dialog

IF WEXIST('MyPrintDialog')
  RELEASE WINDOWS MyPrintDialog
ENDIF
```

Place the following expression in the On Entry expression of the Report Title band.

```
MyPrintDialog('Inventory Value Report')
```

Now place the following expression in the On Exit expression of the Report Summary band.

```
ReleaseDialog()
```

That's it! When the report is printed, the standard dialog is moved off the screen and my custom dialog, as shown in **Figure 10**, is displayed.

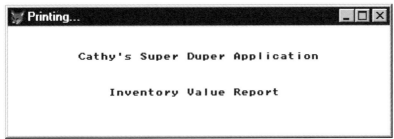

Figure 10. You can display your own Printing… dialog by calling a UDF from the Title band of a report.

Now, this dialog certainly won't win any awards for appearance, but that's only because I wanted to keep the sample code as simple as possible. In a live application, I'd probably change the font, change the background color, and even use my own icon instead of the Fox head. And with a few simple modifications, I could even get fancier and call the UDF from the Page Header band instead of the Report Title band so I could display the current page being printed by referencing the _PAGENO system variable.

The one downfall to using your own Printing… dialog is that you can't include a Cancel button to allow the user to stop the printing. Or can you? Remember, this is FoxPro and you can do *anything* with FoxPro. The original Printing… window you moved out of the way is still there and *it* has a Cancel button on it. Put a Cancel button on your custom Printing… dialog that executes the following code.

```
ACTIVATE WINDOW 'Printing...'
KEYBOARD "{ENTER}"
DOEVENTS
```

This code brings up the original Printing… dialog and simulates the user pressing the Cancel button with the Enter key. Slick, huh?

Chaining reports

Have you ever wanted to offer one menu option for the user to select, yet have it run several reports back to back? What I'd like to be able to do is the following.

```
REPORT FORM report1 NOCONSOLE TO PRINTER PROMPT
REPORT FORM report2 NOCONSOLE TO PRINTER ADDITIVE
REPORT FORM report3 NOCONSOLE TO PRINTER ADDITIVE
```

Unfortunately, the ADDITIVE clause isn't part of the REPORT command. However, you can pull off this scenario by using the SYS(1037) command. This command prompts the user with a printer dialog box and sets that printer as the VFP default printer so you can call each of your reports, one after the other, as shown in the following example.

```
=SYS(1037)
REPORT FORM report1 NOCONSOLE TO PRINTER
REPORT FORM report2 NOCONSOLE TO PRINTER
REPORT FORM report3 NOCONSOLE TO PRINTER
```

But wait—there's more! Besides printing all three reports as one, you can also have the page numbers continue from one report to the next. For example, if each report consisted of three pages, *report1* needs to show pages 1-3, *report2* needs to show pages 4-6, and *report3* needs to show pages 7-9 in the footer. To do this, use a memory variable to offset the _PAGENO system variable as shown in the following code.

```
PRIVATE nOffset
nOffset = 0
=SYS(1037)
REPORT FORM test1 NOCONSOLE TO PRINTER
nOffset = nOffset + _PAGENO
REPORT FORM test2 NOCONSOLE TO PRINTER
nOffset = nOffset + _PAGENO
REPORT FORM test3 NOCONSOLE TO PRINTER
```

In each of the report definitions, use *_PAGENO + nOffset,* instead of *_PAGENO* to print the page number in the footer.

 This approach causes three print jobs to be sent to the printer. There's a way to do this with one print job, but it has a cost. The following code can be found in a program called OnePrintJob.PRG, included in the source code available with this book.

```
*-- Initialize
PRIVATE nOffset, cFile1, cFile2, cFile3, nRow, aPrt, cPrinter
nOffset = 0

*-- Create a unique name in the DOS 8.3 format
cFile1 = '_' + SUBSTR(SYS(2015), 4,7) + '.prn'
cFile2 = '_' + SUBSTR(SYS(2015), 4,7) + '.prn'
cFile3 = '_' + SUBSTR(SYS(2015), 4,7) + '.prn'

*-- Get the printer
IF APRINTERS(aPrt) = 0
  RETURN
ENDIF
=SYS(1037)
nRow = ASCAN(aPrt, SET('PRINTER',3), -1, -1, 1, 15)
IF nRow = 0
  RETURN
```

```
ENDIF

*-- Strip out any trailing ":" as a preventative measure
cPrinter = aPrt[nRow,2]
cPrinter = SUBSTR(cPrinter, 1, (LEN(ALLTRIM(cPrinter)) -1))

*-- Print the reports to files
REPORT FORM test1 NOCONSOLE TO FILE &cFile1
nOffset = nOffset + _PAGENO
REPORT FORM test2 NOCONSOLE TO FILE &cFile2
nOffset = nOffset + _PAGENO
REPORT FORM test3 NOCONSOLE TO FILE &cFile3

*-- Run the reports as one print job
RUN Copy /B &cFile1 + &cFile2 + &cFile3 &cPrinter

*-- Clean up
ERASE &cFile1
ERASE &cFile2
ERASE &cFile3
```

The cost of this method is that you take a performance hit. Instead of going directly to the printer, you first send the report to three files and then send the files to the printer.

> When printing through the DOS Copy command on a network, you may have to check with your Network Administrator to see whether the printers are set up to handle this.

Number of copies
Depending on which printer is chosen by the user, they may or may not be allowed to choose the number of copies on the Print dialog. And if you're not using the PROMPT clause to let the user choose the printer, they definitely can't choose the number of copies to print. So what do you tell them if they need to print several copies? Do you say, "Just print the report 10 different times"? I don't know about your clients, but mine certainly wouldn't like that answer.

The solution is actually quite simple. You really do print the report 10 times, but *you* are doing it and not making *them* do it. Create a common form class that prompts the user for the number of copies and saves that value to the memory variable *lnCopies*. Then, to print multiple copies of the report, use the following code.

```
LOCAL ln
FOR ln = 1 to lnCopies
  REPORT FORM MyReport TO PRINTER
ENDFOR
```

That's it! Sometimes the simple solutions are just as effective as the complex ones.

Distribution
Now that you have a ton of reports designed, you need to know how to get them into your project file and how to distribute them with your application. The metadata for each report you

create is stored in two files, the first being an FRX file and the second being an FRT file. These files are really nothing more than a VFP table where the FRX file is really just a DBF file and the FRT file is really just an FPT file.

To be or not to be (excluded, that is)

Adding reports to the Project Manager is no different from adding other types of files. I'm assuming you're already familiar with the Project Manager so I'm not going to explain the 20 different ways to add files. I will, however, tell you that reports are stored in the Reports section of the Documents tab in the Project Manager.

Now that I've said I'm not going to explain how to add reports to the Project Manager, I'm going to take that statement back and show you one, lesser-known method that many developers aren't aware of. This applies to all types of files, not just reports. You can use Windows Explorer to add multiple reports to the Project Manager quickly and easily. First, open up the Project Manager in Visual FoxPro. Next, use Windows Explorer and highlight the report files you want to add to the project. Now just *drag and drop* them from Windows Explorer to the tree-view portion of the VFP Project Manager. That's it. Visual FoxPro looks at the extension of each file and determines which section it belongs to. When it sees an FRX extension, it assumes the file is a report and adds it to the Reports section of the Documents tab. When using drag and drop, you can select either the FRX or the FRT file and Visual FoxPro realizes you want a report added. You can even select both files and Visual FoxPro correctly adds the report to the Project Manager.

Once the report is added to the Project Manager, you need to decide whether you're going to leave it as is or whether you're going to *exclude* it. If you leave the reports as is, they're built directly into the EXE when you build the application and you don't have to distribute the actual reports to your client. However, this also means the reports are read-only and can never be changed by the user. This may or may not be what you want to do. We all know that end-users' computer knowledge ranges from illiterate to expert. You have to make the judgment call as to whether or not you're going to give the users access to the report definitions.

On the other side of the coin, you can choose to *exclude* the reports in the Project Manager. This doesn't mean you don't add the reports to the Project Manager. Excluding a file means you still add it to the Project Manager, but you mark it as *excluded.* You can do this by right-clicking on the file in the Project Manager and either selecting Exclude from the right-click menu or selecting Project | Exclude from the main VFP Menu bar.

Marking a file as *excluded* means it's not built into the EXE when the application is built. When you distribute the application to the client, you have to give them the actual FRX and FRT files for each report in the system. The advantage of this method is that the users can modify the reports themselves. Of course, this can also be a disadvantage if a user ends up trashing the reports beyond recognition and has to make a support call to you.

Modifying reports within an application

In today's world, users want more control over everything they do and reports are no exception. Often times, users want to have the ability to modify even *canned* reports included in an application. The easiest way to give them this ability is to exclude the reports from the application, distribute the report files separately, install the full-blown version of Visual

FoxPro on their system, and hope like hell they know enough about VFP to modify the reports without screwing up the rest of the system.

This, of course, isn't the *best* solution to offer most clients. A better solution is to allow the users access to the VFP Report Designer from within your application. This means they don't have to have a licensed copy of Visual FoxPro on their system, nor do you have to worry that the *wanna-be programmers* will… ahem… screw up the rest of the system. You can easily access the Report Designer from a menu option by defining it as *Command* and entering the following as the command to execute.

```
MODIFY REPORT ?
```

Of course, this is awfully simplistic and assumes the user knows what the report file is and can find it on the system. It also doesn't deal with making sure the right toolbars are accessible to the user. And even more importantly, it doesn't offer any way for the users to restore the report if they really muck it up (except to restore from a backup, which we all know they do faithfully every night).

A more forgiving approach to take is to write a small Report Manager to interface between your application and the Report Designer. The concept is this…

- The Distribution

    - The *original* reports are included in the application and are *not* marked as excluded.

    - The application includes a Report table that holds one record for each customizable report in the application. At a minimum, the table should include fields to store the name of the report file and a descriptive name for the user to recognize.

- Modifying a Report

    - A user interface is used to display the list of reports from the Report table and lets the users choose which report they want to modify.

    - The chosen report is *copied* from the original report stored in the EXE to a special custom report directory on the system.

    - The Report Designer is invoked with the new custom report ready to modify.

    - The user modifies the customized version of the report as he or she sees fit.

- Running a Report

    - The user picks a report from the menu or whatever UI you have implemented.

    - The program checks to see whether a custom version of the report exists in the special custom report directory and runs it if found. Otherwise, the original report in the application is run.

- Restoring a Report

    - A user interface is used to display the list of reports from the Report table and lets the users choose which report they want to restore.

    - The chosen report is removed from the special custom report directory.

You can modify this scenario as much as you want to fit your needs. For example, you can add another level of complexity by allowing *each* user to have his or her own customized version of each report. I'm sure you can think of other things to do as well, but this should be enough information to get you started on creating your own report interface.

Copying the report
At first thought, you might be asking how in the world you can copy a report that is stored in the EXE. Remember, earlier I said a report definition is stored in a standard VFP table that happens to have a different extension. You can take advantage of this as follows.

```
USE MyOrigReport.frx
COPY TO MyNewReport.frx
```

Even though the table is stored in the EXE, the USE command can find it and open it just like any other table. The only difference is that it's opened with read-only access, which is fine for this situation. You don't want to write back to the original file.

Modifying the report
The MODIFY REPORT command has several clauses available, some of which are only applicable when executing the command from within an application.

Windows
Three of the clauses, *WINDOW, IN WINDOW,* and *IN SCREEN,* are the same three clauses used when running a report with the REPORT command. See the sectioned titled "A window of opportunity" earlier in this chapter for a description of each of these clauses.

NoWait
By default, program execution stops until the Report Designer is closed. Use the NOWAIT clause to tell Visual FoxPro to leave the Report Designer open and continue execution with the next command.

Save
By default, the Report Designer is closed when another window is activated. Use the SAVE clause to tell Visual FoxPro to leave the Report Designer open even after other windows are activated.

NoEnvironment
The NOENVIRONMENT clause is only applicable to FoxPro 2.x. It prevents the environment information from being saved with the report.

The View menu
Another very important aspect to letting users modify reports from within the application is making sure the appropriate menu options are available. It's extremely important to be sure the View menu is accessible and contains a Toolbars… option when the user is modifying a report. Otherwise, the user's ability to design reports is severely crippled.

Edit your application's menu with the Menu Designer. Add an option called \<*View* to the Menu Bar level, setting its result to *Submenu*. Now, select *Create* to drill down to the View menu. Next, add an option to the view menu with \<*Toolbars…* as the prompt. Set the result to *Bar #* and enter *_mvi_toolb* as the bar name.

Eliminating printer-specific information
As mentioned earlier, VFP may save specific information about the printer associated with a report in the report definition itself. This printer-specific information has the potential for causing problems when a user runs a report and doesn't have the same printer you used to design the report. In fact, under certain conditions the dreaded C0000005 error can occur—yikes!

For peace of mind, the best thing you can do is strip out any printer-specific information from each report. The only way to do this is to hack the FRX file and manually strip out the offending information for each report. Although Chapter 11, "Hacking the FRX," goes into more detail about where the information is and how to hack it, I couldn't wait until then to describe how to do this because it's really important to the distribution of your application. Besides, I'm going to show you how to do this through a Project Hook so you don't even have to know how to hack the file.

 Sorry! Project Hooks are not available in FoxPro 2.x.

Start by creating a class based on VFP's base ProjectHook class with the following code.

```
CREATE CLASS MyProjHook OF MyLib AS ProjectHook
```

Next, add the following code to the BeforeBuild method of the Project Hook class you just created.

```
LOCAL ln, lcFileName, loProject, loFile, lcExpr
loProject = Application.ActiveProject

* Loop through the project files
FOR ln = 1 TO loProject.Files.Count
  loFile = loProject.Files(ln)

* Is this a Report?
  IF loFile.Type = 'R'

    * Open the report file
    lcFileName = loFile.Name
    WAIT WINDOW 'Clearing printer-specific information from ' + ;
      lcFileName NOWAIT
    SELECT 0
```

```
      USE (lcFileName) EXCLUSIVE
      GOTO TOP

      * Strip some information from EXPR
      lcExpr = expr
      lcExpr = STRTRAN(lcExpr, 'DEVICE=', '*DEVICE*=')
      lcExpr = STRTRAN(lcExpr, 'DRIVER=', '*DRIVER*=')
      lcExpr = STRTRAN(lcExpr, 'OUTPUT=', '*OUTPUT*=')
      lcExpr = STRTRAN(lcExpr, 'DEFAULT=', '*DEFAULT*=')
      lcExpr = STRTRAN(lcExpr, 'PRINTQUALITY=', '*PRINTQUALITY*=')
      lcExpr = STRTRAN(lcExpr, 'YRESOLUTION=', '*YRESOLUTION*=')
      lcExpr = STRTRAN(lcExpr, 'TTOPTION=', '*TTOPTION*=')
      lcExpr = STRTRAN(lcExpr, 'DUPLEX=', '*DUPLEX*=')

      * Replace TAG, TAG2 and EXPR
      REPLACE TAG WITH '', TAG2 WITH '', EXPR WITH lcExpr

      * Clean up and continue
      PACK && Avoid memo bloat
      USE
   ENDIF
ENDFOR

* Clean up
loProject = NULL
WAIT CLEAR
```

This code scans through the project looking for reports. For each report it finds, it strips the *potentially* offending printer-specific information from the report's metadata, while leaving other settings, such as Orientation, untouched.

Okay, so now that you have the Project Hook class defined, how do you *hook* it up to your project? Start by opening up your project. Next, select Project | Project Info... from the main VFP Menu bar to display the Project Information dialog shown in **Figure 11**.

If you're looking for the word *hook* on this dialog, you won't find it. Instead, check the Project Class check box at the bottom of the dialog. Next, use the ellipse button (...) to the right of the Project Class check box to invoke a dialog that lets you navigate to the project class you defined and select it. You have now defined a Project Hook for your project.

Using a Project Hook is the easiest way to remove all the printer-specific information from reports because once implemented, it happens automatically without you having to remember to do anything. I don't know about you, but my memory isn't quite the same as it used to be so I like anything that can be automated!

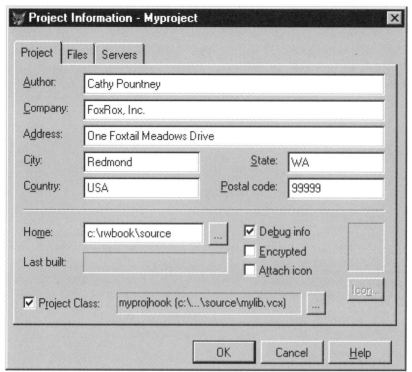

***Figure 11**. Use the Project Information dialog to set a Project Hook for your application.*

Debugging

There's one last thing I want to say about running reports and that has to do with debugging. I know… your code *never* has bugs in it… but mine does. Every once in a while I do make a mistake (although I won't always admit to it).

Invalid report

Error 50, "Report file <name> is invalid," occurs when something is severely wrong with the report metadata. So much so, the VFP Report Writer can't figure out how to print the report. Unless you have a lot of time on your hands and are very skilled at hacking the report file, your best bet is to restore the report definition from a backup.

Nesting error

Error 1645, "Report contains a nesting error," occurs when the report contains a UDF that has a REPORT FORM command in it. You can't invoke one report from within another report.

Variable not found

The "Variable not found" error and several other common VFP errors are usually caused by typos, unexpected data, or simple mistakes by the developer. Unfortunately, you can't call the Debugger when running a report so tracking these down becomes very difficult.

The trick to tracking these down is to preview or run the report from within the Report Designer and not from the Command Window or from within your application. If you run a report from the Report Designer and an error occurs, as soon as you acknowledge the error and return to the Report Designer, it brings up the offending object's dialog so you can edit it.

So what do you do if the report relies on data prepared by your application, variables defined in your application, PEMs in your application, and so on? Add the following code immediately before the REPORT command.

```
SUSPEND
```

This temporarily suspends execution of the program, yet all the tables are still opened, the variables are still accessible, and so on. Now modify the report by entering MODIFY REPORT <name> in the Command Window (use Ctrl-F2 to display the Command Window if it isn't active). Once the Report Designer is open, preview or print the report and *voilà!* After the error occurs, the Report Designer displays the offending object's dialog so you can correct it.

Run with it

This chapter has shown you many aspects of running reports, including how to avoid some problems. The next chapter, Chapter 10, "Solutions to Real-World Problems," explains how to design reports that solve many of the real situations you might encounter. Fasten your seatbelt, stow all your belongings, and keep your hands inside the ride at all times. Oh, yeah—enjoy the ride!

Chapter 10
Solutions to Real-World
Problems

By far, this is my favorite chapter in the whole book because it's so full of information that even the most experienced Visual FoxPro developer is bound to learn something. This chapter gives you answers to some of the most frequently, and even some not so frequently, asked questions on how to provide solutions to real-world reporting problems. I'm guessing that's the whole reason you bought this book—you want answers to your questions. Well, read on!

If you just bought this book, looked at the Table of Contents, and immediately jumped to this chapter—I don't blame you. I probably would've done the same thing. However, if you're not experienced with the Visual FoxPro Report Writer, I urge you to start from the beginning of this book. You're certainly welcome to skim this chapter right now, but a lot of things might not make sense yet. For example, I may say, "Add a Report Variable..." and not explain *how* to add the Report Variable. That's because I'm assuming you've already read Chapter 8, "Report Variables."

So, you're ready to read on. Great! Get ready to learn how to solve many real-world reporting problems through the use of *Print When* expressions, UDFs, Report Variables, and pre-processing the data in just the right manner. You'll also learn how to solve some graphical issues and a slew of miscellaneous problems.

Using Print When expressions

Many real-world reporting problems can be solved by using Print When expressions. This section explains how to know whether the user is previewing or printing, how to print ledger-style shading, how to simulate greenbar paper, and a few ideas for keeping Group Footers where you want them.

How do I know whether the user is previewing or printing?

Many times you need to know whether the user is previewing the report on the screen or printing the report to the printer. For example, if the report is for producing invoices that are printed on preprinted forms, you wouldn't include the company name, address, logo, or graphical lines on the report. However, omitting this information makes it difficult to read when the report is previewed on the screen.

The solution is to include the company name, address, logo, and graphical lines on the report, but only print them when the user is previewing the report. Simply place the following code in the Print When expression of each object.

```
NOT WEXIST('Printing...')
```

The Printing… dialog only appears when the report is printed to the printer, so checking for the existence of this window determines whether the user is previewing or printing.

 In FoxPro 2.x, the name of the Preview window is "Page Preview" instead of "Printing…".

How do I print ledger-style shading?

Accountants like the look of ledger paper where every other row is shaded (see **Figure 1**). It helps them keep their eyes from crossing when they're looking at rows and rows of numbers. So give them what they want and make them happy. Remember, if they're happy, they're more likely to leave you alone.

Invoice Number	Invoice Date	PO#	Due Date	Invoice Amt	Line
1001	11/01/2000	5301	12/01/2000	100.25	1
1002	11/02/2000	9872	12/02/2000	422.35	2
1003	11/02/2000	5305	12/02/2000	234.33	3
1004	11/02/2000	5307	12/02/2000	395.99	4
1005	11/02/2000	9874	12/02/2000	878.99	5
1006	11/03/2000	9876	12/03/2000	509.90	6
1007	11/04/2000	5311	12/04/2000	988.00	7
1008	11/05/2000	5315	12/05/2000	765.32	8
1009	11/10/2000	9387	12/10/2000	9387.00	9
1010	11/12/2000	9732	12/12/2000	987.00	10
1011	11/15/2000	2342	12/15/2000	435.00	11
1012	11/16/2000	9587	12/16/2000	872.20	12
1013	11/13/2000	9723	12/13/2000	876.00	13
1014	11/20/2000	9472	12/20/2000	9234.40	14

Figure 1. *Use a Report Variable, a Rectangle object, and a Print When expression to achieve ledger-style shading.*

Start by creating a Report Variable called *nLine*. Select the *Count* option and set the *Reset at* value to *End of Page*. If you have a Data Group defined on the report, you may wish to set the *Reset at* value to the Data Group instead.

Next, place a Rectangle object on the report. Make it the same height as your Detail band and as wide as you need. Change the background and foreground colors to gray. The final step is to put the following code in the Print When expression of the Rectangle object.

```
MOD(nLine,2) = 0
```

When the report is printed, every other row is shaded gray. Now the accountants are happy and you have some spare time on your hands. Well, it's wishful thinking anyway. The report definition to produce a ledger report is included in the source code available with this book, and is called Ledger.FRX.

> *Instead of gray, you can also use yellow Rectangle objects—as long as the report is only printed on a black and white printer. When yellow is converted to black and white, it comes out a lighter shade of gray than the standard light gray color you can select with the Color dialog. When your users need to fax reports, the lighter shade of gray faxes much better than the regular gray.*

How do I simulate greenbar paper?

A twist to *ledger-style shading* is *multi-line shading*, just like the old greenbar paper where three lines are white and three lines are green (see **Figure 2**). The report definition to produce this sample is included in the source code available with this book, and is called Ledger3.FRX. This can be accomplished in the same manner as the ledger-style shading by substituting the following for the Print When expression of the Rectangle object.

```
INLIST(MOD(nLine,6),4,5,0)
```

Invoice Number	Invoice Date	PO#	Due Date	Invoice Amt	Line
1001	11/01/2000	5301	12/01/2000	100.25	1
1002	11/02/2000	9872	12/02/2000	422.35	2
1003	11/02/2000	5305	12/02/2000	234.33	3
1004	11/02/2000	5307	12/02/2000	395.99	4
1005	11/02/2000	9874	12/02/2000	878.99	5
1006	11/03/2000	9876	12/03/2000	509.90	6
1007	11/04/2000	5311	12/04/2000	988.00	7
1008	11/05/2000	5315	12/05/2000	765.32	8
1009	11/10/2000	9387	12/10/2000	9387.00	9
1010	11/12/2000	9732	12/12/2000	987.00	10
1011	11/15/2000	2342	12/15/2000	435.00	11
1012	11/16/2000	9587	12/16/2000	872.20	12
1013	11/13/2000	9723	12/13/2000	876.00	13
1014	11/20/2000	9473	12/20/2000	9234.40	14

Figure 2. Change the Print When expression to achieve multi-line ledger shading, commonly known as the greenbar effect.

How do I keep a stretchable Group Footer together without wasting space all the time?

With Group Headers, you have the ability to tell the Report Writer to start a new page if there's less than a certain amount of room on the page. However, it only applies to the Group *Header* and not to the Group *Footer*. So how do you tell the Group Footer to start a new page if there's less than a certain amount of room?

Here's the scenario: You have a memo field that prints in the Group Footer band. It can contain anywhere from 0-10 lines of text. You create a Field object that's one line tall and place it in the Group Footer band, which is also one line tall. You also mark the Field object as Stretch with overflow so it can accommodate the 10 lines of text, when necessary. The only problem is, before printing the Group Footer band the VFP Report Writer only thinks it needs one line, so it may print one or two lines of the memo at the bottom of the page and then overflow to the next page.

If you increase the height of the Group Footer band and the Field object to accommodate all 10 lines, the Report Writer correctly goes to the next page before printing. However, now it uses up all 10 lines, whether it needs it or not, before printing the next Group Header band. So you've solved one problem, but created another.

The solution is to trick the Report Writer. Make the height of the Group Footer band tall enough to accommodate 10 lines, but keep the Field object only as tall as one line. Next, add one more Field object to the very bottom of the Group Footer band. Use " " as the expression and mark the "Remove line when blank" option under the Print When options. Now when the Report Writer gets ready to print the Group Footer, it checks to see that there's enough room for 10 lines and goes to the next page if necessary. However, this time as it evaluates the last object at the bottom of the band, it realizes it has a *blank* value. And because you've marked it as *Remove line when blank*, it removes the line *and* all the extra white space between it and the object directly above it. Now the next Group Header band prints directly underneath the last line of your memo field.

How do I prevent an orphaned Group Footer?

The same technique just described to keep a stretchable footer together without wasting space can also be used to prevent orphaned Group Footers. An *orphaned* Group Footer occurs when the last detail line is too far down the page and there's not enough room for the Group Footer band to print. The Group Footer band ends up on the next page, but it's all by itself without any detail lines above it.

If you want to ensure that there's always at least one detail line at the top of a page along with the Group Footer, follow these steps. Expand the height of the Detail band so that the final height of the Detail band is equal to the height of the Group Footer band plus the height of the original Detail band. Place a new Field object at the very bottom of the Detail band and use " " as the expression. Check the "Remove line when blank" check box on the Print When dialog for this object. Now, before printing each Detail record, the Report Writer checks to see whether there's enough room for the band, which is fudged to the height of the Detail band plus the Group Footer band.

Using UDFs and Report Variables

Many real-world reporting problems can be solved by using a combination of UDFs and native Report Variables. This section explains how to know if the user canceled the report, how to print "continued" at the top and bottom of the page, and how to print subtotals and totals in the Page Footer band.

How do I know if the user canceled?

Often, you need to update some type of *printed* flag in the data or do some special processing once the user has printed a particular report. To accomplish this, you need to make sure the user really did *print* the report. You wouldn't want to update the flag if the user only previewed the report. In addition, you need to make sure the user didn't cancel the report before it finished.

To solve this problem, use the following code to call the report.

```
*-- Initialize variable
PRIVATE plPrinted
plPrinted = .f.

*-- Print the report
REPORT FORM MyReport NOCONSOLE TO PRINTER PROMPT PREVIEW

*-- Check to see if the user printed
IF plPrinted
   * Do your update code here
ENDIF

*-- Get out
RETURN

*----------------
FUNCTION Rpt_Done
*----------------

*-- Set the printed flag
IF WEXIST("Printing...")
   plPrinted = .t.
ENDIF
```

As the final step, use the following expression in the *On Exit* portion of the Summary band.

```
Rpt_Done()
```

Because the Summary band is the last thing processed by the Report Writer, calling the UDF in the *On Exit* section of the Summary band ensures the *plPrinted* flag isn't set until the entire report has finished. Of course, you can't be sure it physically printed, but that's out of your control.

How do I print "continued"?

Whenever Data Groups are involved in a report, you run the risk of having a Data Group span across two or more pages. Sometimes, this can be confusing to someone reading the report, especially if the Group Header is repeated on each page. When looking at the second page of a Data Group, the reader might not realize that it's continued from the previous page. So because you're such a conscientious developer, you'd like to provide the reader with a signal that the report is continued from the previous page. Heck, you even want a signal at the bottom of the first page when a Data Group is about to continue on the next page—being the conscientious developer that you are.

Print "continued" at the top of the page

The first part, signaling when a Data Group is continued from a previous page, is quite easy to do. Create a Report Variable called *nGrpLines,* set the Calculate option to *Count*, and change the *Reset at* value to the Data Group. Next, add a Field object to the Group Header band with the following expression.

```
IIF(nGrpLines = 0, '', ' ...continued from previous page')
```

The final step is to check the "Reprint Group Header on each page" check box in the Data Grouping dialog. That's it! Run the report and you'll see "continued" at the top of each continued page as shown in **Figure 3**. The report definition to produce this sample is included in the source code available with this book, and is called Continued.FRX.

03/17/2002	**Tasmanian Traders**	Page	1
	Customer Directory		

Company Name	City	Country
S ...continued from previous page		
Spécialités du monde	Paris	France
Suprêmes délices	Charleroi	Belgium
T		
The Big Cheese	Portland	USA

Figure 3. Use a Report Variable to easily print "continued", at the top of a page.

You may be wondering why I used a Field object with an *IIF()* function instead of a Label object with a *Print When* expression. Well, there's a really good reason for this—the *Print When* expression won't work! The Report Writer evaluates the Print When expressions in the Group Header *before* it resets any Report Variables designated to reset at the Data Group. So, when the Print When expression is evaluated, the value of the Report Variable is still left over from the last detail record of the previous Data Group. You can save yourself a lot of grief and aggravation by remembering this little tidbit.

Print "continued" at the bottom of the page

Printing "continued" at the bottom of a page when a Data Group is about to overflow to the next page isn't quite as intuitive as you might think. Start by adding a Field object to the Page Footer using the following expression.

```
IIF(nGrpLines > 0 , 'continued on next page ...', '')
```

However, Report Variables designated to *Reset at* a Data Group aren't really reset at the end of the Data Group. They're actually reset when the Group Header of the next Data Group is processed. This means that at the time the Page Footer is processed, the Report Variable of a Data Group that has just ended hasn't been reset yet. So even though the Data Group is done, the Report Variable is not zero. And if that's not bad enough, if left like this, the last page of the report always prints "continued," sending the reader on a wild goose chase looking for one more page that doesn't exist.

Luckily, adding the following expression to the On Exit area of the Group Footer band solves these problems.

```
_VFP.SetVar('nGrpLines', 0)
```

This line of code forces the Report Writer to reset the Report Variable to zero as soon as the Data Group is finished instead of waiting until the Group Header of the next Data Group is processed. Problem solved! Now, when you run the report you see "continued" at the bottom of each appropriate page as shown in **Figure 4**. The report definition to produce this sample is included in the source code available with this book, and is called Ledger.FRX.

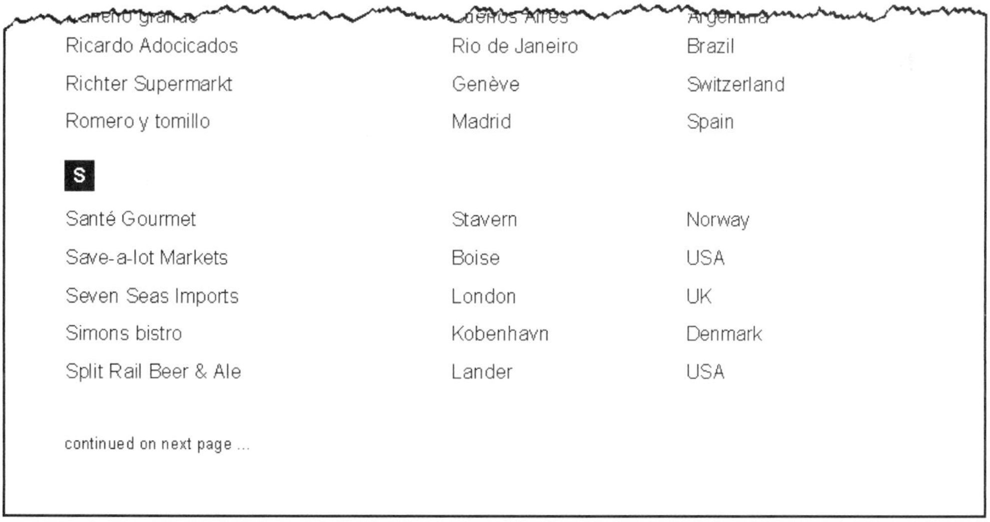

Ricardo Adocicados	Rio de Janeiro	Brazil
Richter Supermarkt	Genève	Switzerland
Romero y tomillo	Madrid	Spain
S		
Santé Gourmet	Stavern	Norway
Save-a-lot Markets	Boise	USA
Seven Seas Imports	London	UK
Simons bistro	Kobenhavn	Denmark
Split Rail Beer & Ale	Lander	USA

continued on next page ...

Figure 4. *Use the On Exit expression of the Group Footer band to force the Report Variable to reset sooner than normal.*

Incidentally, resetting the Report Variable in this manner also solves the problem of the *Print When* logic being processed prior to the Report Variable being reset. Therefore, if you prefer, you can use *Print When* expressions instead of the IIF() functions to control the printing of "continued" at the top and bottom of the page—six of one, half a dozen of the other.

 The On Exit expression is not available in FoxPro 2.x. To simulate this feature, add a Field object to the Group Footer band, setting the expression as a call to a UDF that resets the variable. Also, be sure to use the Bring to Front *option to ensure the new object is the last thing processed in the band.*

How do I print subtotals in the Page Footer band at the end of each Data Group?

This question is commonly asked when printing preprinted forms, such as orders, where the bottom of the form has a shaded area or box for printing the total as shown in **Figure 5**. As described in the previous section, the order in which the Report Writer processes Report Variables and Data Groups works for you and against you in this situation. At the time the Page Footer is processed, you *want* the value of the *total* Report Variable to still contain the value from the Data Group just finished. However, you want the *count* Report Variable already reset so that you know you're done with a Data Group.

To create the Order shown in Figure 5, start by creating a Data Group with *Order_ID* as the expression and check the "Start each group on a new page" check box. Add all the objects you want at the top of the order form to the *Page Header* band—not the *Group Header* band. Next, add all the necessary objects to the Detail band.

Now you can focus on the Page Footer band and add the shaded box, the words *Total Amount*, and a Field object for the dollar amount. The expression for the Field object should be the same expression as the object in the Detail band that you're totaling. However, the object in the Page Footer needs to have the Calculate option set to *Sum*. Now set the *Print When* expression of all of the objects in the Page Footer to *nLines = 0*.

To create the rectangle that stretches the entire length of the page, add a Rectangle object to the Page Header band. Change the height of the Rectangle object so it stretches into the Page Footer band. Incidentally, the only reason I had you use the Page Header band for all the objects at the top of the page is because it's the only way to stretch the Rectangle object from the top of the page to the bottom of the page. If you do not need this effect, you can place those objects in the Group Header band instead of the Page Header band.

The final trick to this solution is the same trick used in the last few sections. Add the following expression to the On Exit area of the Group Footer band.

```
_VFP.SetVar('nLines', 0)
```

 The complete report definition to produce the Order shown in Figure 5 is included in the source code available with this book, and is called Orders.FRX.

Order Number	Order Date	Customer	Ship-To			
16	06/04/1992	PICCO	Piccole und mehr			

Product	Product Name	Unit Price	Quantity	Extended Price
11	Queso Cabrales	14.7000	60.000	882.00
24	Guaraná Fantástica	3.0000	25.000	75.00
41	Jack's New England Clam Chowder	6.7000	20.000	134.00
73	Röd Kaviar	10.5000	15.000	157.50
74	Longlife Tofu	7.0000	25.000	175.00

Total Amount	1,423.50

Figure 5. Use Report Variables and Print When expressions to print totals in the Page Footer only at the end of each Data Group.

How do I print totals in the Page Footer band of only the last page?

With FoxPro, there are always several different ways to accomplish the same thing. In this case, there are three different methods that I'm going to explain. The first method is to follow the steps just described in the section titled "How do I print subtotals in the Page Footer band at the end of each Data Group?" The only difference is that you use *EOF()* as the expression of the Data Group.

The second method can be used if you don't want to use a Data Group. Use the following code to do some pre-processing and to call the report.

```
*-- Find the last record
PRIVATE pnLastRec
USE DATA\orditems
SET ORDER TO Order_ID
GOTO BOTTOM
pnLastRec = RECNO()
USE

*-- Print the report
REPORT FORM reports\orders PREVIEW
```

The private variable called *pnLastRec* contains the record number of the last record to be processed. Therefore, set the Print When expression of the objects in the Page Footer band to the following.

```
RECNO() = pnLastRec
```

Now, the objects in the Page Footer only print after the last record has been processed. And just in case you were wondering why I closed the table before calling the report, it's because the Data Environment of that particular report is set up to open all the tables.

The third method is probably the simplest method because you don't have to create a Data Group for EOF() and you don't have to do any pre-processing of the data. Start by creating a Report Variable called *lLastPage*. Set the value to *.f.* and leave the Calculation option at *Nothing*. Next, create a Summary band and place the following expression in the On Exit portion of that band.

```
_VFP.SetVar('lLastPage', .t.)
```

As the final step, set the Print When expression of all the objects in the Page Footer to *lLastPage*. That's it. After the summary band is processed (even if there aren't any objects in it), it processes the On Exit expression, which sets the Report Variable to .t. Now when the Page Footer is printed for the final page, it knows that it's at the end so it prints the totals.

There is, however, one problem with this last method. It assumes you don't print the Summary band on its own page, and it also assumes you don't run into the bug that occurs when the last Detail band fills up the page and the Summary band is forced to the next page, but it forgets to print the Page Footer. So even though this is the *easiest* solution, it might not be the best.

Building the right cursor

Some real-world report problems seem just about impossible to solve. However, by pre-processing the data and building just the right cursor, you can get the Report Writer to do what you want. This section explains how to print multiple Detail bands, how to span one detail record across several pages, and how to print laser style checks with the dreaded stub-check-stub format.

How do I print multiple Detail bands?

Often times, you're faced with the situation where you have to create multiple Detail bands on a report (see **Figure 6**). In this example, there are two tables involved in the report. The first table is a list of invoices for the clients. The second table is a list of payments from the clients. In the real world, you'd probably have three tables because you'd also have a separate client table. However, for the sake of making this example simple, I included the client information in each table so I wouldn't have to introduce a third table. Enough said!

The report you're creating needs to sort by client, listing the invoices for client A, followed by the payments for client A, followed by the invoices for client B, followed by the payments for client B, and so on. I think you get the picture.

Unfortunately, the native Report Writer does *not* allow multiple Detail bands. You get one Detail band per report—and that's Microsoft's final answer! So what do you do? Give up and tell your client it can't be done? Although this might sound like a good idea to you right now, I don't think your client will be happy with that answer. In fact, they might decide to phone a friend or ask the audience.

The solution is to put all the records from both tables into one temporary table, and then use a special group combined with a lot of Print When expressions to control the printing of each desired Detail band.

Start by creating a temporary cursor or table that contains all the fields from the Invoice table and all the fields from the Payment table. You also need an additional field for tracking the source of each record. The following code creates a temporary cursor and includes a character field called *rec_type*. This field is populated with "1" (character, not numeric) for all records originating from the Invoice table and "2" for all records originating from the Payment table.

Client Invoices & Payments

Client: ABC Industries

*** Invoices ***

Invoice Number	Invoice Date	PO#	Due Date	Invoice Amt
1001	11/01/2000	5301	12/01/2000	100.25
1003	11/02/2000	5305	12/02/2000	234.33
1004	11/02/2000	5307	12/02/2000	395.99
1007	11/04/2000	5311	12/04/2000	988.00
1008	11/05/2000	5315	12/05/2000	765.32

*** Payments ***

Invoice Number	Check Number	Date Received	Amt Paid
1001	5650	11/23/2000	100.25
1003	5652	11/24/2000	234.33
1004	5653	11/28/2000	395.99
1007	5659	12/02/2000	988.00
1008	690	12/05/2000	765.32

Client: Duffy Duct

*** Invoices ***

Invoice Number	Invoice Date	PO#	Due Date	Invoice Amt
1002	11/02/2000	9872	12/02/2000	422.35
1005	11/02/2000	9874	12/02/2000	878.99
1009	11/10/2000	9387	12/10/2000	9387.00
1014	11/20/2000	9472	12/20/2000	9234.40

*** Payments ***

Invoice Number	Check Number	Date Received	Amt Paid
1002	685	11/24/2000	422.35
1005	687	11/29/2000	878.99

Figure 6. Build a cursor with combined data to simulate multiple Detail bands.

Notice the cursor also has a compound index on *client + rec_type + inv_no*, which ensures the correct sequence when the report is printed. Using a "character" field for *rec_type* makes it much easier to include it in the compound index. Using "1" and "2"

as opposed to "INV" and "PAY" gives me the flexibility to force the Detail bands to print in the order I want. In my example, the Invoices for the first client are printed, followed by the payments for that client, followed by the invoices for the second client, followed by the payments for the second client, and so on. If I had wanted payments to appear first and I had used "INV" and "PAY", I would've been out of luck because "P" comes before "I". So out of habit, I've found it best to always use numbers instead of descriptive codes for controlling the sort order. The following code can be found in the program called MultiDtl.PRG, included in the source code available with this book.

```
*-- Create a temporary cursor
CREATE CURSOR tmpcurs ;
  (rec_type C(1), inv_no C(4), client C(30), po_no C(4), inv_date D(8), ;
  due_date D(8), inv_amt N(10,2), chk_no C(4), date_rcvd D(8), ;
  amt_paid N(10,2))
INDEX ON client + rec_type + inv_no TAG PrimaryKey

*-- Add the invoices to the cursor
SELECT tmpcurs
SCATTER MEMVAR MEMO BLANK
SELECT 0
USE datacustom\invoice
SCAN
  SCATTER MEMVAR MEMO
  m.rec_type = '1' && Invoices
  INSERT INTO tmpcurs FROM MEMVAR
ENDSCAN
USE IN INVOICE

*-- Add the payments to the cursor
SELECT tmpcurs
SCATTER MEMVAR MEMO BLANK
SELECT 0
USE datacustom\payment
SCAN
  SCATTER MEMVAR MEMO
  m.rec_type = '2' && Payments
  INSERT INTO tmpcurs FROM MEMVAR
ENDSCAN
USE IN PAYMENT
```

Now that you have all the data in one cursor, you can focus on creating the report itself. Start by creating a report that contains two Data Groups. Use *client* as the expression for the first Data Group and use *rec_type* as the expression for the second Data Group.

In the Detail band, place all the fields from the Invoice table on the report. Move them around and arrange them however you want. Also, place the column headings for the Invoice fields in the *rec_type* Group Header band. Now change the Print When expression of every object in the Detail Band and the Group Header band to the following.

```
rec_type = '1'
```

To make future maintenance easier, select all the objects relating to the invoice and *group* them together (select Format | Group from the main VFP Menu bar).

Now that the Invoice objects are in place, you need to do the same for all the fields in the Payment table. This starts to get real ugly (see **Figure 7**) because you need to place the Payment fields on top of all the Invoice fields, which makes it hard to see which fields belong to which column headings. This report definition is included in the source code available with this book, and is called MultiDtl.FRX.

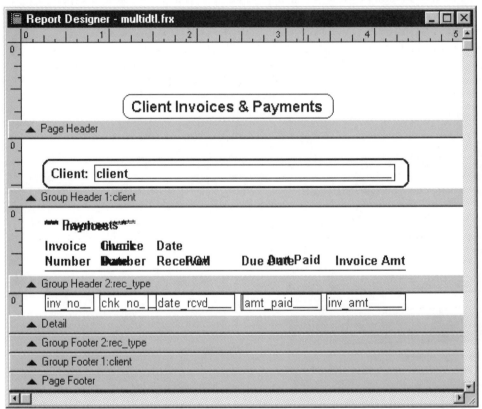

Figure 7. Simulating multiple Detail bands gets real ugly in the Report Designer.

I've found that it works best to create a dummy report and place all the Payment fields and headings on the dummy report. Move them around and get them arranged exactly how you want. Then, change the Print When expression of all the Payment objects to *rec_type* = '2'. Once you have them laid out nicely, group them together just as you did with the Invoice objects. Now cut and paste the entire Payment section from the dummy report into the real report you're working on. Place it right on top of the fields from the Invoice table.

That's all there is to it! Now use the following code to run the report.

```
*-- Print the report
SELECT tmpcurs
GOTO TOP
REPORT FORM reports\multidtl NOCONSOLE TO PRINTER PROMPT PREVIEW
USE
```

Easy, right? Okay, so it's not so easy, but it *is* doable. And by *grouping* the Invoice objects together and the Payment objects together, future maintenance is much easier. If and when the client asks for a change, you can move the entire group of Payment objects away from the Invoice objects so you can see them without going crazy. *Ungroup* the section you need to change, make the changes, *group* the objects again, and then move the Payment objects back on top of the Invoice objects.

How do I span a single record across multiple pages?

In the section titled "Spanning multiple pages" in Chapter 7, "Data Grouping," I described one method for accomplishing this through the use of a Data Group with an expression of *RECNO()*. I joked that because you're limited to 20 Data Groups, the solution is limited to 41 pages per record. In this section, I describe another method for spanning a single record across multiple pages—and there's no limit to the number of pages per record!

The trick to this method is very similar to what was just described in the section titled "How do I print multiple Detail bands?" Begin by creating a temporary table or cursor that contains multiple records for each record in the source table. For example, if you want to print two Detail pages for each record and the source table contains six records, the new table should have 12 records in it (2 x 6) to achieve the final result of 12 printed pages. The new cursor should have an additional field called *rec_type* added to the structure and the sort order should be the desired sort field plus the *rec_type* field. The following code shows an example of how to create the new cursor (assuming the first field in the table is what you want to sort on).

```
*-- Create the temporary cursor
SELECT '1' AS rec_type, * FROM MyData ;
  UNION ;
    SELECT '2' AS rec_type, * FROM MyData ;
  INTO CURSOR tmpcurs ;
  ORDER BY 2, 1
```

You can, of course, create the temporary data a number of different ways. The bottom line is to create a cursor that has one record for each *page* you want printed.

Next, you need to turn your attention to the Report Designer and create a report that has the height of the Detail band increased to accommodate almost a full page. I say *almost*, because you have to leave room for any Title, Header, Footer, Data Group Header, Data Group Footer, and Summary bands that also exist on the report.

Now add all the fields you want on the *first* page to the Detail band, making sure to set the Print When expression to *rec_type = '1'*. Then add all the fields you want on the *second* page to the Detail band, making sure to set the Print When expression to *rec_type = '2'*. Again, I suggest you use the same *dummy report* technique previously described to save yourself from going cross-eyed and pulling all your hair out. Once this is done, you're ready to go. Run the report and for each record in the original table, two pages are printed.

How do I print laser checks (stub/check/stub)?

Printing laser checks with a stub at the top, followed by the actual check and ending with another stub (as shown in **Figure 8**) can be a bit of a dilemma. You need to print the same set of detail lines at the top of the page and at the bottom of the page. And even more confusing, how are you going to get the check portion to print right in the middle of all those detail lines?

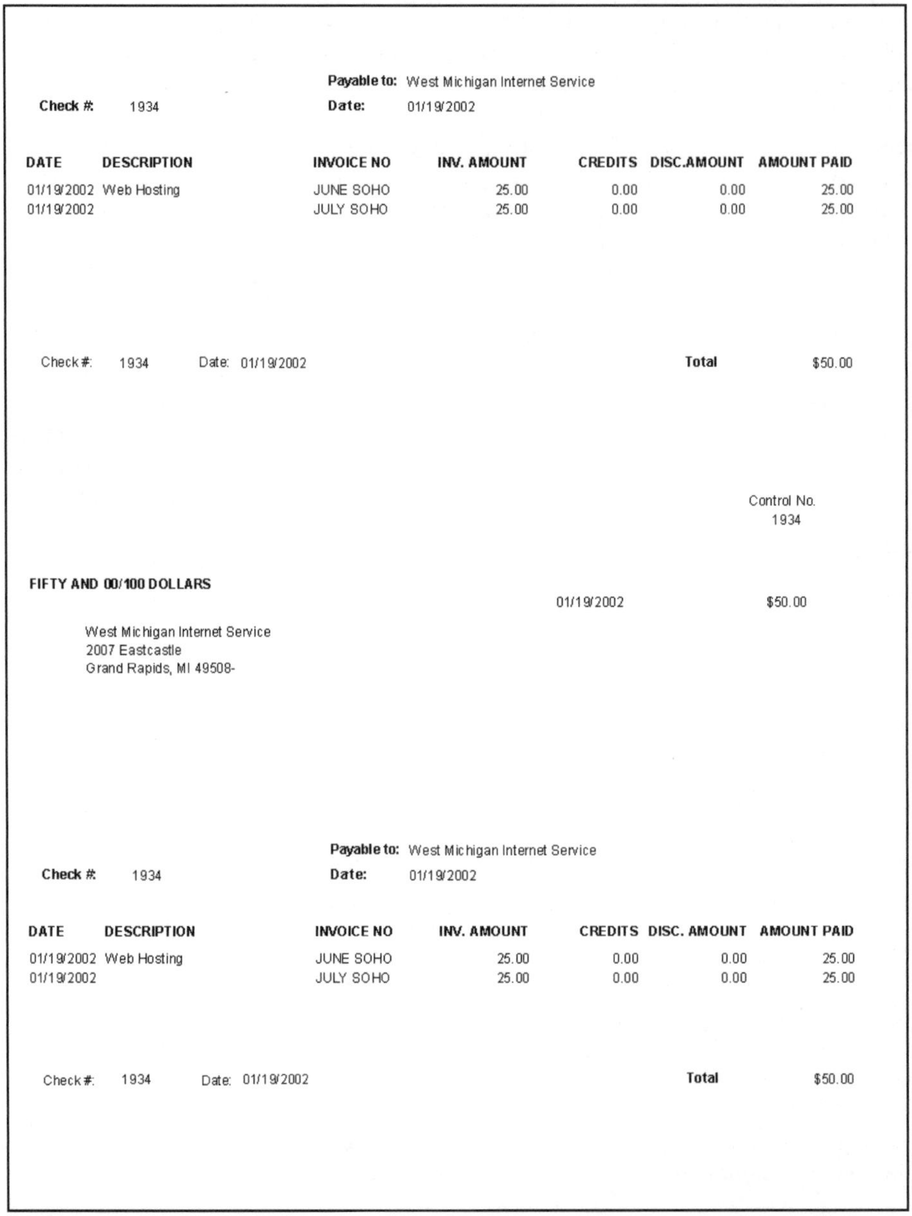

		Payable to:	West Michigan Internet Service				
Check #:	1934	**Date:**	01/19/2002				
DATE	**DESCRIPTION**	**INVOICE NO**	**INV. AMOUNT**	**CREDITS**	**DISC.AMOUNT**	**AMOUNT PAID**
01/19/2002	Web Hosting	JUNE SOHO	25.00	0.00	0.00	25.00
01/19/2002		JULY SOHO	25.00	0.00	0.00	25.00

Check #:	1934	Date: 01/19/2002	**Total**	$50.00

Control No.
1934

FIFTY AND 00/100 DOLLARS

01/19/2002 $50.00

West Michigan Internet Service
2007 Eastcastle
Grand Rapids, MI 49508-

		Payable to:	West Michigan Internet Service				
Check #:	1934	**Date:**	01/19/2002				
DATE	**DESCRIPTION**	**INVOICE NO**	**INV. AMOUNT**	**CREDITS**	**DISC. AMOUNT**	**AMOUNT PAID**
01/19/2002	Web Hosting	JUNE SOHO	25.00	0.00	0.00	25.00
01/19/2002		JULY SOHO	25.00	0.00	0.00	25.00

Check #:	1934	Date: 01/19/2002	**Total**	$50.00

Figure 8. Laser checks in the format of stub/check/stub can be accomplished by pre-processing the data.

The solution to this dilemma is to pre-process the data, building one giant record for each individual check. Then, create a report with a Detail band that spans the entire height of the printable page. Now you can place all the objects for the check in the Detail band. You need to add separate Field objects for each column of each detail line as well as Field objects for the basic check information. **Figure 9** shows how the report looks in the Report Designer. The report definition is included in the source code available with this book, and is called Check.FRX.

When creating the temporary check cursor, the structure needs to contain a field for each item printed on the *check* portion of the page (check number, check date, dollar amount, and so on). It also needs to contain a field for each item printed on the *stub* portion of the check, which you can do one of two ways. One way is to add one field for each column of each detail line. For example, if a stub can contain up to 15 detail lines, you would add fields for InvNo1, InvNo2, InvNo3, and on up to InvNo15. Then you'd need to add 15 more fields for the next column (InvDate1, InvDate2, InvDate3, and on up to InvDate15). In other words, the temporary cursor has a lot of fields in it!

A second way you can build the *stub* portion of the temporary cursor is to add one memo field for each column on the stub. As you're processing each detail record, add the contents to a string, followed by a CHR(13), and write the entire string to the record when you're done. The following code shows an example of how to do this.

```
*-- Initialize variables
m.InvNo = ''
m.InvDate = ''
m.InvAmt = ''
nLines = 0
nMaxLines = 15

*-- Scan through detail records
SCAN FOR checkno == cThisCheck
  m.InvNo = m.InvNo + MyTable.InvNo + CHR(13)
  m.InvDate = m.InvDate + DTOC(MyTable.InvDate) + CHR(13)
  m.InvAmt = m.InvAmt + TRANSFORM(MyTable.InvAmt, '$999,999,999.99') + CHR(13)
  nLines = nLines + 1
ENDSCAN

*-- Pad the memo fields to the correct number of detail lines
IF nLines < nMaxLines
  m.InvNo = m.InvNo + REPLICATE(CHR(13), nMaxLines-nLines)
  m.InvDate = m.InvDate + REPLICATE(CHR(13), nMaxLines-nLines)
  m.InvAmt = m.InvAmt + RELICATE(CHR(13), nMaxLines-nLines)
ENDIF

*-- Write the check record
SELECT tmpCursor
APPEND BLANK
GATHER MEMVAR MEMO
```

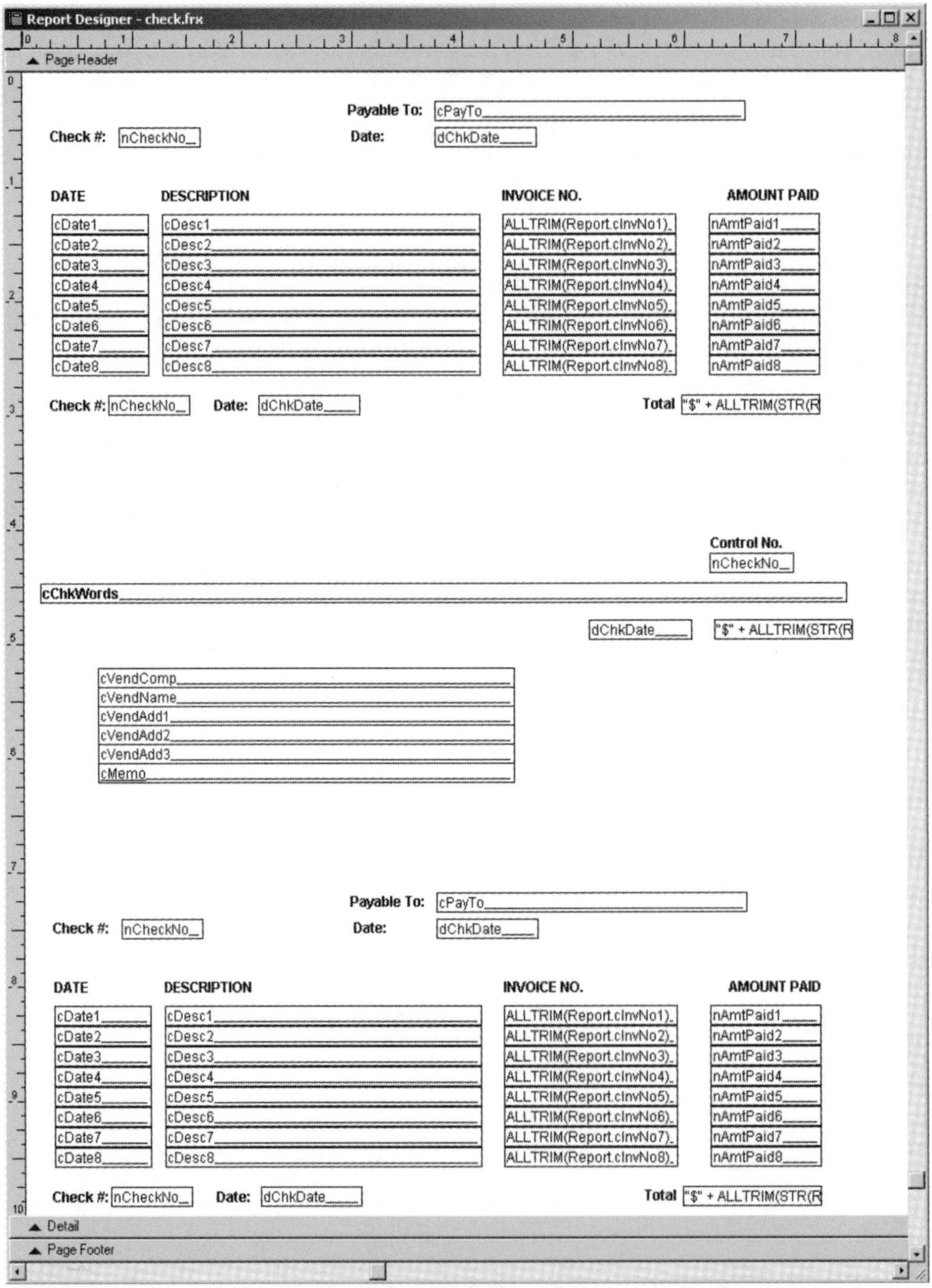

Figure 9. Use one large Detail band to hold all the information for the stubs and the check.

Now that the information is stored in memo fields, you need to get it back out for the report. This can be done by calling a UDF from the On Entry expression of the Detail band. The UDF should do the following.

```
*-- Extract the detail lines from the memo fields
=ALINES(aInvNo, tmpCursor.InvNo)
=ALINES(aInvDate, tmpCursor.InvDate)
=ALINES(aInvAmt, tmpCursor.InvAmt)
```

The sample code just shown extracts the information from each memo field and puts it into an array, with each line in the memo field corresponding to one row in the array. Now, instead of adding Field objects to the report with expressions of InvNo1, InvNo2, InvNo3, and on up to InvNo15, you use aInvNo[1], aInvNo[2], aInvNo[3], and on up to aInvNo[15].

This second method is a little more work up front, but I tend to favor it over the first method because I can change the number of detail lines without having to change the structure of the cursor. This means it's more flexible and lends itself to having one set of code that can handle checks of different sizes.

Printing graphics

Many real-world report problems arise when graphics have to be included in reports. This section explains how to print dynamic graphic images, how to print detail lines beside a graphic image for a Data Group, how to print Rich Text, and how to print bar codes.

How do I print dynamic graphic images in FoxPro 2.x?

In the section titled "Picture from File" of Chapter 5, "Report Objects," I explained how to dynamically print pictures by using an expression in the *Picture from File* area of the Report Picture dialog. This works great for Visual FoxPro, but it doesn't work in FoxPro 2.x. So is there a way to simulate that functionality in FoxPro 2.x? Of course there is!

The trick here is to stuff a general field with the picture that needs to be printed for each record. However, you don't have to pre-process an entire table of 100,000 inventory items because you can do it on the fly. Create a report that has a Picture object on it. Set the *Picture from Field* value to *tmpCursor.MyPicture*. Next, create a Report Variable that has *FillPict()* as the expression (it doesn't matter what you call the variable). Now use the following code to run the report.

```
*-- Create a temporary cursor and add one dummy record
CREATE CURSOR tmpCursor (MyPicture G)
APPEND BLANK

*-- Run the report
SELECT 0
USE MyTable
REPORT FORM MyReport PREVIEW
USE
RETURN

*-- Create a function to fill the cursor with this record's picture
FUNCTION FillPict
```

```
* Get the name of the picture that's associated with this record
LOCAL lcFile
lcFile = MyTable.PictName

* Add the picture to the temporary cursor
SELECT tmpCursor
APPEND GENERAL MyPicture FROM &lcFile

* Restore the report table and return
SELECT MyTable
RETURN ''
```

As each record in the table (MyTable) is processed by the Report Writer, it calls the FillPict function in an attempt to assign a value to the dummy Report Variable. Once inside the UDF, it updates the temporary cursor with the picture associated with this record. When the Detail band is printed, the contents of tmpCursor.MyPicture always reflects the appropriate picture for the current record. Problem solved! You've just created dynamic graphic images in FoxPro 2.x.

How do I print several detail lines to the right of one image?

Have you ever needed to print one graphic image for the entire Data Group, yet have the Detail lines print next to it as shown in **Figure 10**? At first, this might seem impossible because Group Headers and Group Footers print above and below the Detail band, not beside it. So how did I pull off this trick?

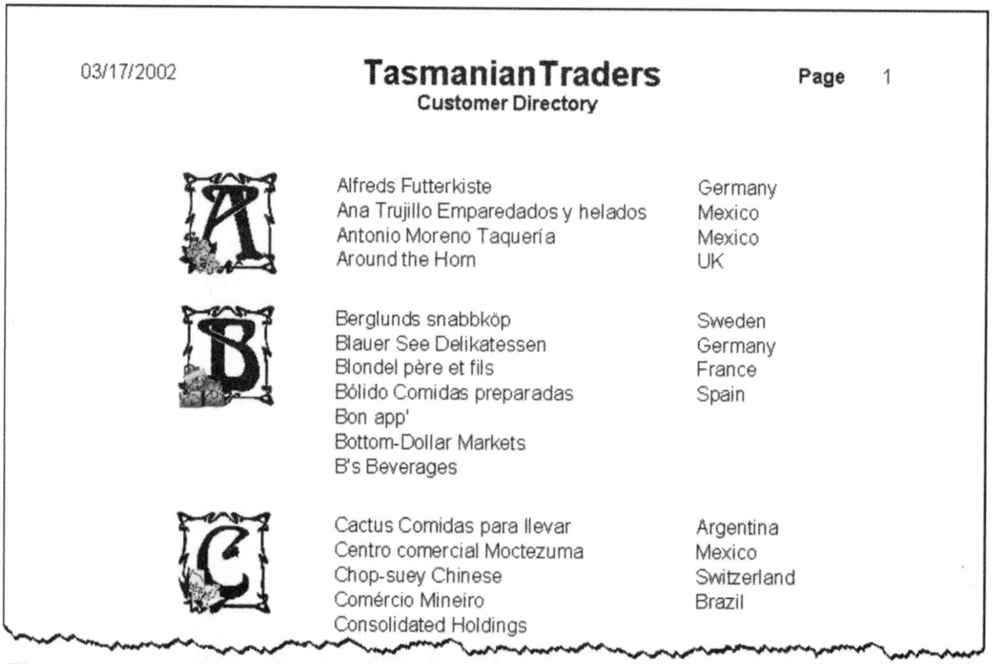

03/17/2002	**TasmanianTraders**		Page	1
	Customer Directory			

	Alfreds Futterkiste	Germany
	Ana Trujillo Emparedados y helados	Mexico
	Antonio Moreno Taquería	Mexico
	Around the Horn	UK
	Berglunds snabbköp	Sweden
	Blauer See Delikatessen	Germany
	Blondel père et fils	France
	Bólido Comidas preparadas	Spain
	Bon app'	
	Bottom-Dollar Markets	
	B's Beverages	
	Cactus Comidas para llevar	Argentina
	Centro comercial Moctezuma	Mexico
	Chop-suey Chinese	Switzerland
	Comércio Mineiro	Brazil
	Consolidated Holdings	

Figure 10. Printing multiple detail lines next to a single graphic image takes a little ingenuity.

It's actually really cool once you know the secret. The trick is I didn't print anything in the Detail band. All the printing was done in the Group Footer band as shown in **Figure 11**. The report definition, called Letters.FRX, is included with the source code available with this book.

I started by creating three Report Variables.

- cNames has an expression of *cNames + alltrim(comp_name) + CHR(13)*, an initial value of "", and a Reset at value of the Data Group.

- cCountries has an expression of *cCountries + alltrim(country) + CHR(13)*, an initial value of "", and a Reset at value of the Data Group.

- cFile has an expression of 'GRAPHICS\LETTER' + LEFT(COMP_NAME,1) + '.JPG' and a Reset at value of End of Report.

Once the Report Variables were set up, I focused on adding the objects to the Group Footer band of the report—not the Detail band.

- Add a Picture object with the Picture from File expression set to *cFile*. I also selected the "Scale picture, retain shape" option.

- Add a Field object with the expression set to *cNames* and check the "Stretch with overflow" option. Make the height of this object the same height as the Picture object.

- Add a Field object with the expression set to *cCountries* and check the "Stretch with overflow" option. Make the height of this object the same height as the Picture object.

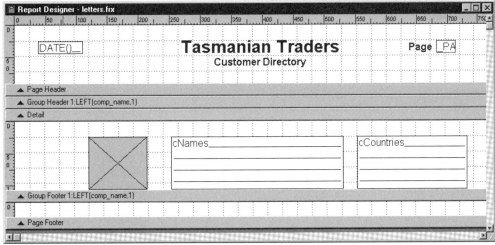

Figure 11. *Add the objects to the Group Footer band instead of the Detail band to have them wrap around the graphic image.*

See, I told you this was a pretty cool trick!

How do I print Rich Text on a report?

Rich Text is a term used to describe text that has formatting codes embedded in it. For example, this is **bold**, this is *italic*, and this is <u>underlined</u>. On occasion, it would be nice to print a string of text on a report that has certain words highlighted. This is done by using the RichTX32.OCX ActiveX control shipped with most versions of Visual FoxPro (VFP 3 did not ship with this control).

Start by storing the text you want to print in a *general* field of a table with the special codes already embedded in the string. The following sample code shows how this can be done.

```
*-- Create a temporary table
CREATE TABLE MyTable (MyGen G)

*-- Create the RTF file
LOCAL cRTFString
cRTFString = "{\rtf1\ansi\ansicpg1252\uc1 \deff0\deflang1033\deflangfe1033" + ;
  "{\fonttbl{\f0\froman\fcharset0\fprq2" + ;
  "{\*\panose 02020603050405020304}Times New Roman;}" + ;
  "}"
cRTFString = cRTFString + ;
  "\pard\plain \ql " + ;
  "\li0\ri0\widctlpar\aspalpha\aspnum\faauto\adjustright\rin0\lin0\itap0 " + ;
  "\fs24\lang1033\langfe1033\cgrid\langnp1033\langfenp1033 "
cRTFString = cRTFString + "{This is a test to see if }{\b bold}" + ;
  "{ and }{\i italics}{ works." + ;
  "\par }}"

*-- Create the RTF file (you MUST use an RTF extension)
STRTOFILE(cRTFString, 'MyRTF.RTF')

*-- Add the RTF file to the temporary cursor
SELECT MyTable
APPEND BLANK
APPEND GENERAL MyGen FROM myrtf.rtf CLASS "RICHTEXT.RICHTEXTCTRL.1"
```

Once the formatted string is embedded in a general field, you can print it using a Picture/ActiveX Bound control on the report. Add this control to the report and set the *Picture from field* expression to MyTable.MyGen. That's it. Print the report and the string comes out formatted with bold and italics or whatever formatting you used.

So how in the world did I come up with all the special formatting codes? Well, I'm no genius—I cheated! I used Microsoft Word, entered the string exactly as I wanted to see it on my report, and then saved the document as an RTF file. Then, from Visual FoxPro, I opened the RTF file and did a little cut and paste of the huge string into my program, followed by a little parsing to separate the string into several readable lines. Once you understand which codes you need, you can design some classes or UDFs that contain the special formatting codes so your application can call them to concoct any string you want to print.

How do I print bar codes?

More and more, we're being asked to create reports with bar-coded information. You'd pretty much have to be living under a rock to not know what bar codes are, but just because you've seen them doesn't mean you understand them. There are a handful of different *types* of bar codes (3 or 9, UPC, and so on) and they all have their own rules. Some require check digits, some require start and stop characters, and I'm sure there are a bunch of rules that I'm not aware of. I'm not going to explain the different rules; I'm only going to explain how to print them. It's up to you to make sure that *what* you print is really a valid bar code.

For the most part, printing bar codes is nothing more than using the correct font. **Figure 12** shows a sample of four different Field objects, all with "1234567890" as the expression, but each one uses a different font (keep in mind that these probably aren't *valid* bar codes).

Figure 12. Use fonts to print bar codes.

Simple, right? Okay, so there are a few issues that you'll probably have to deal with. One of which is the fact that you may need the bar code to print taller than what the font prints. The easiest way to accomplish this is to copy the Field object several times, butting each one right up underneath the previous one. In fact, I'd suggest you overlap them to avoid having any horizontal gap between them.

Bar-coding fonts are available from numerous sources, some free, some not. Search the Internet and I'm sure you can find exactly what you're looking for.

Miscellaneous

This section is chock-full of many more solutions to real-world reporting problems, including an answer to the age-old question, "How do I print 'Page x of y'?"

How do I print "Page x of y"?

This has to be one of the most, if not *the* most, frequently asked question by Fox developers. Unfortunately, there isn't any special variable created by VFP to hold the total number of pages. You have to create a memory variable yourself by printing the report twice—once as a phantom print to determine the total number of pages and once to actually print the report for the user.

First, declare a memory variable for holding the page count, *nPages*. Next, print the report to a file. When the report is done, the *_PAGENO* system variable contains the page number of the last page. Save it to your memory variable (*nPages = _PAGENO*) and print the report again, this time to the printer. In the Report Designer, use the following expression to print the page number.

```
'Page ' + ALLTRIM(STR(_PAGENO)) + ' of ' + ALLTRIM(STR(_nPages))
```

Although this might sound easy at first, the final solution isn't quite so simple. There are a few issues you need to deal with. First, you need to prompt the user for the printer *before* you print the phantom report. Otherwise, you could end up with an incorrect page count. When printing to a file, the default printer driver is used. It's possible that the user would choose a different printer that has a printable area different from the default printer's. This means that the phantom report might break at different points than the actual report, thus causing the final page count to be different.

Another issue you need to deal with is getting a unique file name to print the phantom report to and then erasing that file when you're done. You wouldn't want a bunch of temporary files to build up on your user's system. And you might be tempted to avoid printing to a file by using *REPORT FORM MyReport NOCONSOLE*. Although this *might* work, it doesn't *always* work. I'm not sure why, but sometimes this method doesn't always return the correct page count. You're better off sticking with printing to a file even though it means more work for you.

The last issue you need to deal with is determining whether the user canceled the first phantom print. There's no point in printing the real report if the user canceled the phantom report. Here's the complete code to print the report.

```
*-- Initialize variables
PRIVATE plPhantom, plPrinted, pnPages, pcTemp
plPrinted = .f.
pnPages = 0
pcTemp = SUBSTR(SYS(2015), 3, 10) + '.txt'

*-- Prompt for the printer
=SYS(1037)

*-- Print the Phantom report
WAIT WINDOW 'Calculating Page Count...' NOWAIT
plPhantom = .t.
REPORT FORM MyReport NOCONSOLE TO FILE &pcTemp
pnPages = _PAGENO
ERASE (pcTemp)
plPhantom = .f.
WAIT CLEAR

*-- Print the real report
IF plPrinted
   REPORT FORM MyReport TO PRINTER PROMPT PREVIEW
ENDIF

*---------------
FUNCTION Printed
*---------------

*-- Update the printed flag
IF plPhantom
   plPrinted = .t.
ENDIF
RETURN
```

Because you're printing the report to a file on a hard disk before printing the actual hard copy, it takes much longer to print the final report for the user. If the report is only expected to be a few pages, the user is probably willing to live with the performance hit. In fact, he or she might not even notice it. However, if the report is expected to be several hundred pages long, the user might not be willing to wait for the double processing. Be sure your users understand the penalty for printing the total page count.

How do I force a Data Group to start on an odd page?

When printing double-sided reports, it's quite common to want to start each Data Group on the *front* of a page. This means you need to have a blank page inserted in the report whenever a Data Group ends on an odd-numbered page so the next Data Group doesn't start on an even-numbered page.

It's actually quite simple to do this. Start by making sure the "Start each group on a new page" check box is checked for the Data Group. Next, add a Field object to the very bottom of the Group Footer band. Check the "Stretch with overflow" check box, check the "Remove line if blank" check box in the Print When dialog, and set the expression to the following.

```
IIF(MOD(_PAGENO, 2) = 0, '', REPLICATE(CHR(13), 40))
```

This forces the Report Writer to print 40 blank lines in the Group Footer only if it's an odd page. And since 40 lines won't fit on the page, the Report Writer overflows to the next page to print the rest of the *blank* lines. You may have to adjust the number *40* up or down for your particular report depending on the size of the other bands such as the Page Header, Group Header, Group Detail, and the Page Footer.

Keep in mind that this solution always prints a blank page if the Data Group ends on an odd-numbered page. This means that even the last Data Group is followed by a blank page. Depending on your situation, you may or may not want this to happen. If you don't want a blank page at the very end of the report, use the following code to run the report.

```
*-- Find the last record
PRIVATE pnLastRec
USE MyData
GOTO BOTTOM
pnLastRec = RECNO()
USE

*-- Print the report
REPORT FORM MyReport TO PRINTER PROMPT PREVIEW
```

Now simply add a check for the last record to the expression of the dummy Field object in the Group Footer as follows.

```
IIF(MOD(_PAGENO, 2) = 0 OR RECNO() = pnLastRec, '', REPLICATE(CHR(13), 40))
```

That's it. Now, each new Data Group starts on an odd-numbered page.

How do I print vertical text?

Unfortunately, the VFP Report Designer does not allow you to rotate text. You can, however, print *vertical* text as shown in **Figure 13**.

Figure 13. Use vertical text instead of rotated text.

To print vertical text, you can use Field objects with an expression or Label objects with the static text. Regardless of which type of object you use, make the object only as wide as one character and make it tall enough to accommodate all the letters. Also, set the text alignment to *center* so each letter is centered along the vertical axis.

Occasionally, you may run into a situation where you have two skinny letters, like "I", next to each other and they end up not wrapping. To force them to wrap you can just enter spaces between the letters like this: "ABC I I I DEF".

Incidentally, the reverse text was created by first adding a Rectangle object with a black background. Then I added the text and changed the foreground color to white and placed it on top of the black rectangle.

How do I print check boxes, check marks, and so on?

We programmers all know that *.t.* means true and *.f.* means false, but our customers don't appreciate seeing that on a report. They'd rather see *Y* and *N* printed on the report. This can easily be done by using a Field expression with a logical value and using *Y* as the format character.

You can even go a step further and print *Yes* and *No* by using the following expression in the Field object.

```
IIF(MyField, 'Yes', 'No')
```

Well, why not go two steps further and print check boxes or check marks to indicate yes and no. The trick is to use the Wingdings font and find the right character that represents the graphic you want to see. To get the results shown in **Figure 14**, I used the following expressions for the eight different Field objects: 'o', 'x', 'o', CHR(251), 'o', CHR(252), CHR(253), CHR(254), respectively.

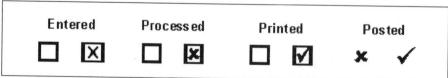

Figure 14. Use the Wingdings font to print check boxes and check marks.

> *Note: If the Wingdings font is not available, you can use the Marlett font to print check marks and x's.*

More than likely, you want to print either an empty box or a checked box depending on the value of the field. For example, to print one or the other boxes shown in the *Printed* column in Figure 14, use the following expression for the Field object.

```
IIF(MyField, CHR(252), 'o')
```

To easily figure out which characters you need, select the Start button and then select Programs | Accessories | System Tools | Character Map. This invokes a utility that is great for finding what you need. Select the Wingdings (or Marlett) font and then navigate through the grid until you find what you're looking for.

How do I print captions from the database container?

The database container is great because it allows you to enter extended properties about each field in a table, like a caption. Unfortunately, the VFP Report Writer doesn't use those extended properties in any way. So how do you take advantage of all the hard work you put into building the database container?

The trick is to use the DBGETPROP() function. Instead of using Label objects for all the column headings in your report, use Field objects with expressions such as the following.

```
DBGETPROP('customer.company_name', 'FIELD', 'CAPTION')
```

Not only does this take advantage of all the hard work you put into setting up the tables, it makes your reports less hard-coded. If you change a caption in the database container, all reports using it automatically inherit the new caption. This can save a ton of time if the field has been used in several different reports.

> *The database container is not available in FoxPro 2.x; therefore, neither is DBGetProp().*

How do I create a Report template?

In the words of Ted Roche, "Repetition, repetition, repetition!" I'm taking Ted's word out of context here, but the point here is that doing the same thing over and over again is just not an acceptable practice to us developers. Whenever we find ourselves repeating the same steps, we do something to automate it.

When creating a new report, I have some personal preferences that I like to follow. I center the title in the Page Header band. I take the date and page number out of the Page Footer band and put them in the Page Header band. I also change the default font to Arial. So why am I doing this same thing over and over again for each report I create? The answer is, I don't. I use one of the following three methods to create a template, from which the rest of my reports are created.

Cop & Mod

One of the easiest methods for creating a report template is to simply set up a report with everything the way you want it and then save it (use a name such as *template*). In fact, you might want to create a few templates, one for portrait reports and one for landscape reports. Or take it a step further and create a portrait and landscape template for each of the commonly used paper sizes.

Each time you need to create a new report, don't start from scratch. Using the Report Designer, open one of the *template* reports and then select *Save as* to save it with a new name. Now you can begin designing the new report without having to reset all your preferences.

> *Whenever I use this method, it's inevitable that at least once during the life of the project, I open the template report, start making changes, and then save it—forgetting to use* Save as *to give it another name. Doh! To avoid having to re-create my template, I always have two copies of each template lying around. For added protection, you can mark the templates as* Read-Only *so you can't accidentally overwrite them; however, it means you have to take the extra steps of resetting the flags if you really do want to change the templates.*

Untitled

In older versions of FoxPro you can take advantage of the naming convention used by the Report Designer. Have you ever noticed that when you create a brand-new report, it's called *untitled* and the first time you save it, FoxPro prompts you to give it a new name? You really have to go out of your way to actually save the report with the name *untitled*. So, set up a report exactly as you want it and then go out of your way to save it with the name *untitled*. Now, each time you create a new unnamed report, FoxPro uses the report called *untitled* as the starting point.

Unfortunately, this behavior was changed in Visual FoxPro. Now, for each new report created in a session, the name is numbered sequentially. And even if you try to save several templates named Report1, Report2, and so on, creating a new unnamed report does not use the templates you created.

The wizard

In Chapter 2, "The Report Wizard," I explained in great detail how to create reports with the Report Wizard. One of the options in the wizard allows you to choose the *style*. There are five built-in styles: Executive, Ledger, Presentation, Banded, and Casual. Wouldn't it be nice if you could tweak these styles to satisfy your preferences? Or even better, wouldn't it be nice if you could add *your* very own style to the list? Well, guess what—you can!

The first three styles (Executive, Ledger, and Presentation) are hard-coded and cannot be changed. However, the last two styles (Banded and Casual) are saved as regular VFP reports and can be modified by you. For each customizable style, there are three versions of the report. One is for One-to-Many reports, another is for reports with groups and totals, and the third is for plain-Jane reports. These reports can be found in the Wizards subdirectory of your VFP Home directory (HOME() + 'WIZARDS'). You can edit these reports and tweak them as you see fit.

So how do you add your own new styles to the Report Wizard? Well, start by creating three different versions of the template you want. I *strongly* suggest you copy the three Banded or Casual reports to use as your starting points. The Report Wizard makes many assumptions about how things are named and if you don't set things up as it's expecting, the wizard can't successfully create a report.

Now that you have the new *styles* created, you have to tell the Report Wizard about them so it can list them along with the five it already knows about. In the same *Wizards* directory that you found the Banded and Casual reports, you should also find a table called *rptstyle.dbf*. Open this table and you'll soon discover how easy it is to add your own styles to the Report Wizard. Each record in this table represents a different style listed in the Report Wizard, so all you have to do is add a new record to the table and *voilà!* A new style appears in the Report Wizard. The seven fields in the table are as follows.

- **Stylename:** This is the descriptive name that appears in the Style list box of the Report Wizard.

- **Stylehbmp:** This is the name of BMP that is displayed on the Style dialog of the Report Wizard when this style is chosen with a Data Group.

- **Stylevbmp:** This is the name of the BMP that is displayed on the Style dialog of the Report Wizard when this style is chosen for a non-One-to-Many report without Data Groups.

- **Stylembmp:** This is the name of the BMP that is displayed on the Style dialog of the Report Wizard when this style is chosen for a One-to-Many report.

- **Stylehfile:** This is the name of the report file used when this style is chosen for a report with a Data Group.

- **Stylevfile:** This is the name of the report file used when this style is chosen for a non-One-to-Many report.

- **Stylemfile:** This is the name of the report file used when this style is chosen for a One-to-Many report.

Once you add a record to this table, the Report Wizard lists your new style as one of the choices in the appropriate dialog. This can be a real time-saver for creating brand-new reports because not only can you have the basics, such as date, time, page number, and default font set the way you like it, you can quickly have the wizard add fields to the report as well. How's that for cutting down on repetition?

 The FoxPro 2.x Report Wizard cannot be customized.

How do I print preprinted forms?

A preprinted form poses an interesting problem, especially when it has tiny check boxes and is unforgiving on alignment. Every printer has its own quirks about what the nonprintable margins are and these variances can give you lots of headaches.

The first step in ensuring that the printed page isn't subject to the margins of the particular printer is to set the report up as *Whole* page and not *Printable* page. This can be done by selecting File | Page Setup... from the main VFP Menu bar to invoke the Page Setup dialog. In the middle of this dialog, check the *Printable page* option and then save the report.

The next step is to make sure that no hard-coded printer information is stored with the report. See "Eliminating printer-specific information" in Chapter 9, "Running Reports," for more information on how to do this.

Now, if you're lucky, this is all you have to do and the report prints as expected on every printer in your office. If you're not lucky, you may have to take it one step further and provide a mechanism in your application for setting up a top and left offset value for each printer. This gets more complicated and has to be done by hacking the report file, so I'll cover it in the next chapter, Chapter 11, "Hacking the FRX."

If all else fails, another alternative is to ignore the VFP Report Writer and print directly to the printer with "?", "??", and "???" commands. This is discussed in greater detail in Chapter 13, "Beyond the VFP Report Writer."

How do I print from two different paper trays?

Printing from one specific paper tray is hard enough, but two different trays—impossible! At least that's how it seems. To design a report to print to one specific tray, it's just a matter of using the Print Setup dialog to select the desired paper tray and then save that setting with the report. You can also dynamically change paper trays by hacking the FRX file just before running the report (see Chapter 11, "Hacking the FRX," for more information on how to do this).

So how do you print the first page of a report to one paper tray and the rest of the report to a different paper tray? Well, I'm sorry to say that the answer is you have to do some finagling. The VFP Report Writer cannot switch to a different paper tray in the middle of printing. To pull off this feat, you can employ one of the following scenarios.

Create two separate reports

This method works well when the first page of the report is a Title page designated to print on its own page.

For the first page, create a report and use the Print Setup dialog to set the paper tray to the desired tray. Next, instead of using the Title band, put all the information in the Detail band. For the rest of the pages, create another report and use the Print Setup dialog to set the paper tray to the desired tray. Then continue designing the report as you normally would.

To run the reports, you first create a temporary cursor with one record and print the first report. Then, run the second report as you normally would. The following code shows how to do this.

```
*-- Print the first report
CREATE CURSOR TmpFirst (Junk C(10))
APPEND BLANK
REPORT FORM Report1 TO PRINTER

*-- Print the second report
SELECT MyData
REPORT FORM Report2 TO PRINTER
```

Print the same report twice

When the first page of the report isn't a special title page, it doesn't lend itself to solving this problem by creating two reports. One interesting solution is to print the report twice, using the RANGE clause to only get the desired pages. This solution also means you have to hack the FRX to change the printer tray between printing the first copy and the second copy. Again, refer to Chapter 11, "Hacking the FRX," for more information on how to do this. But the general concept is shown in the following code.

```
*-- Print the first page
<<Call a UDF or method to hack the FRX and change the paper tray to #1>>
REPORT FORM MyReport TO PRINTER RANGE 1,1

*-- Print the rest of the pages
<<Call a UDF or method to hack the FRX and change the paper tray to #2>>
REPORT FORM MyReport TO PRINTER RANGE 2
```

Use Word Automation

Another slick solution to this problem is to send the report to Microsoft Word (using John Koziol's FRX2Word utility, which is discussed in Chapter 13, "Beyond the VFP Report Writer"). Then use Word Automation to modify the document to select the correct paper trays. Word Automation is definitely beyond the scope of this book, but I suggest you read *Microsoft Office Automation with Visual FoxPro* by Tamar E. Granor and Della Martin, edited by Ted Roche (Hentzenwerke Publishing), for more information on this topic.

Conclusion

Wow! If you sat down and read this entire chapter without taking a break, my hat's off to you. I'm even more impressed if you were able to read the entire chapter without saying "I didn't know that" at least once. Heck, I'm even willing to bet that at least once, you *had* to run to the keyboard and try out one of the ideas. This chapter was chock-full of so many ideas that you might just have to go back and read it again to make sure you didn't miss anything.

Chapter 11
Hacking the FRX

I've been saying all along that the Visual FoxPro Report Writer is a very powerful tool. You just have to understand how it works so you can make it work *for* you instead of *against* you. In fact, the Visual FoxPro *Report Writer* is even more powerful than the Visual FoxPro *Report Designer*. Huh? What do I mean by this? I mean that the Report Writer can do some things at run time that the Report Designer doesn't let you do when you're creating the report. The only way to get the Report Writer to do these *extra* things is to hack the report definition once you're done using the Visual FoxPro Report Designer. This chapter guides you through doing just that… Yeah! We *all* love hacking!

Visual FoxPro is a *special* tool in that it uses itself, Visual FoxPro, for many of its own features. The core product is written in Visual C++, but many of the wizards and other user interface portions of the product are actually written in Visual FoxPro. In addition to the Xbase coding, VFP also uses Visual FoxPro tables to store its own metadata.

Where's the report?

Usually, Visual FoxPro tables are named using a DBF extension. In addition to the main DBF file, there can be two additional files associated with the DBF file. A file with an FPT extension contains all the data of any MEMO and GENERAL fields of the same-named DBF file. A file with a CDX extension contains the index of the same-named DBF file.

So what does all this have to do with reports? Well, Visual FoxPro stores report definitions in VFP tables. The main portion of the table is stored in a file with an FRX extension, instead of a DBF extension. The memo portion of the table is stored in a file with an FRT extension, instead of an FPT extension. In other words, each VFP report definition is stored in two files, *MyReport.FRX* and *MyReport.FRT*. Collectively, these two files are referred to as the *Report Metadata*. However, you'll often hear developers refer to report definitions as *the FRX file*, *the report file*, *the report definition*, and so on.

No matter what you call it—the bottom line is that report definitions are stored in Visual FoxPro tables. Whether you realize it yet or not, this is a very, very, very big feature! I'm sure you already know how to use VFP tables, how to browse them, how to manipulate the data, how to add records to them, and how to delete records from them. Well… don't you get it yet? If you haven't figured it out by now, this means you have a back-door mechanism for manipulating report definitions! Enter the following line of code into the Command Window to open up a report called MyReport (don't forget the FRX extension).

```
USE MyReport.frx
```

Now, you can browse the table, add and delete records, change existing data, and do anything else you can do with regular Visual FoxPro tables. Very cool!

> *Note: Although labels aren't discussed until Chapter 12, "Labels," I want to point out that Label definitions can be hacked in the same way as report definitions. Just substitute an LBX extension for the FRX extension when USEing the table.*

Understanding the report table

The first step in hacking a report definition is to understand exactly how the data is stored in the table. Otherwise, you don't know what to hack, when to hack, or where to hack. Oh, hack, er, I mean heck!

Before continuing, I want to take a moment and thank John Koziol for his outstanding article, "Demystifying Visual FoxPro Report Files," in the August 2000 issue of *FoxTalk*. It was this article that really helped to shed some light on what is happening behind the scenes. Without this article it would have taken me a lot longer to dig into the FRX file and fully understand it. Thanks, John!

Taking the praise one step further, in John's article, he thanks Markus Egger for his work in exploring this topic in conjunction with EPS Software's GenRepoX freeware utility. John says he doubts he would have gotten very far without the *jumpstart* research provided by Markus. So this means I owe one more person some praise. Thanks, Markus!

The records

There are several different *types* of records stored in the report metadata. The *objtype* field identifies what type each record is and the rest of the information in the record varies greatly, depending on the *objtype*. In other words, the fields in the table have multiple purposes and you need to know the objtype to decipher the meaning of the rest of the record. The valid types are as follows:

- **Report definition (objtype = 1):** The first record in the table is a *report definition* record. It contains general information about the overall report, such as printer information and page setup information. There's one report definition record per table—no more, no less.

- **Report objects:** Several different types of objects are used to portray text, data, and graphics on a report. Collectively, these objects are referred to as *Report objects* and they consist of the following five types.

    - **Label (objtype = 5):** A Label object is *not* a sticky tag you put on an envelope. It's the term used to describe a static piece of text put on a report. It's commonly used for report titles, column titles, company name, and other information that does not change each time the report is printed. Each Label object on a report is represented by one record.

    - **Line (objtype = 6):** A Line object is used to represent horizontal and vertical lines on a report. Each Line object on a report is represented by one record.

- **Shape (objtype = 7):** A Shape object is used to represent rectangles and rounded rectangles on a report. Each Shape object on a report is represented by one record.

- **Field (objtype = 8):** A Field object is one of the most commonly used objects on a report. It's used to print data on a report. The data can be a field from a table or the results of an expression. It can even use the internal calculations provided by the VFP Report Writer to obtain the results. Each Field object on a report is represented by one record.

- **Picture (objtype = 17):** A Picture object is used to represent a Picture/ActiveX Bound control on a report. Each Picture/ActiveX object on a report is represented by one record.

- **Band (objtype = 9):** A Band object is used to represent an individual band on a report. As a minimum, all reports have three Band objects: Page Header, Detail, and Page Footer. A report can also contain several optional bands: Title, Column Header, Data Group Header, Column Footer, Data Group Footer, and Summary.

- **Group (objtype = 10):** A Group object is used to represent a *group* of Report objects that have been grouped together using the Format | Group option from the main VFP Menu bar from within the Report Designer (don't confuse this with Data Groups).

- **Variable (objtype = 18):** A Variable object is used to represent an individual Report Variable. Each Report Variable on a report is represented by one record.

- **Font (objtype = 23):** A Font object is used to represent a unique font used somewhere on the report. Each different font used on the report is represented by one Font object record. At a minimum, one Font object exists (for the Default Font).

- **Data Environment (objtype = 25):** A Data Environment object is used to represent the Data Environment of a report. All properties and method code of the Data Environment is stored in this record. There's one Data Environment record per table—no more, no less.

- **Data (objtype = 26):** A Data object is used to represent either a Cursor object or a Relation object. Each Cursor or Relation defined in the Data Environment of a report is represented by one record.

The records are placed in the table in a specific physical order and it's important to honor that order if you programmatically add new records. You can use the SORT command to copy the records to a temporary table and then back to the report table in the correct order, which is as follows.

1. The Report Definition record (objtype = 1)

2. The Band records (objtype = 9). The bands are added to the table in ascending order of the OBJCODE field. When multiple Data Groups are defined on the report…

- • …the Group Header bands (objcode = 3) are added in the same order they appear on the Data Grouping dialog.

- • …the Group Footer bands (objcode = 5) are added in the opposite order they appear on the Data Grouping dialog.

3. The Report objects (objtype = 5, 6, 7, 8 and 17) are added in the order of their Z-order, with the bottommost object added first.

4. Group records (objtype = 10)

5. Report Variable records (objtype = 18). The Report Variable records are added to the table in the same order as they appear on the Report Variable dialog.

6. Font records (objtype = 23)

7. The Data Environment record (objtype = 25)

8. The Data records (objtype = 26) are added in the order they're added to the Data Environment.

The unit of measure

Visual FoxPro uses its own unit of measure when referring to the size and placement of objects on the report. If your system is set up with inches, the unit of measure is 1/10,000 of an inch. If your system is set up with centimeters, the unit of measure is 1/1,000 of a centimeter. Throughout the rest of this chapter, I'll refer to these *FoxPro Report Units* as FRUs.

The position

It may seem strange, but there's no field in the table that represents what *band* an object belongs to. Instead, Visual FoxPro determines the band by doing some math. It looks at the defined height of each band, and then it looks at the VPOS of the object and figures out which band that particular VPOS falls into.

However, there's one *gotcha* you have to be aware of. When looking at the height of each band, VFP also takes into account the height of the horizontal gray bar that represents each band when displayed on the screen by the Report Designer. This *magic* number is 1979.16666666 when using inches and 502.7083333 when using centimeters. Be sure to remember this when calculating the position of objects.

The fields

Describing what each field represents is difficult because fields can be used for different things, depending on what the *objtype* is of the particular record. It's even more difficult because the documentation provided by Microsoft is pretty limited and not always correct. **Table 1** lists each field in the table and what the meaning is for the different types of objects— at least as much as I can figure out based on the documentation, John Koziol's article, and my research. In other words, your mileage may vary!

Table 1. The FRX file in all its glory.

Field	ObjType	Description
PLATFORM	All	Always "WINDOWS" (FYI, many fields in the table are left over from the early DOS, UNIX, and Mac days of Fox. This is obviously one of them.)
UNIQUEID	All	This is a unique identifier for each record. You can use SYS(2015) to create your own unique value when adding records.
TIMESTAMP	All	A timestamp of when this record was last changed
OBJTYPE		1 = Report Definition 5 = Label 6 = Line 7 = Shape 8 = Field 9 = Band 10 = Grouped objects (not Data Groups) 17 = Picture 18 = Variable 23 = Font 25 = Data Environment 26 = Data (Cursor or Relation)
OBJCODE		When the OBJTYPE field alone is not enough to identify a type of record, the OBJCODE field is used to further identify a type of record.
	1-Report Definition	Always 53
	5-Label 6-Line 8-Field 10-Group 17-Picture	Always 0
	7-Shape	Always 4
	9-Band	Describes the type of band: 0 = Title 1 = Page Header 2 = Column Header 3 = Group Header 4 = Detail 5 = Group Footer 6 = Column Footer 7 = Page Footer 8 = Summary
NAME	18-Variables	Variable name
	25-Data Environment	"dataenvironment"
	26-Data	"cursor" for cursors "relation" for relations
EXPR	1-Report Definition	Printer driver and printer setup information
	5-Label	The text of the Label object
	8-Field	The expression of the Field object
	9-Band/Group Header	The Data Group expression
	18-Variables	The Value to store expression
	25-Data Environment 26-Data	The properties of the Data Environment or Data object

Table 1*. Continued.*

Field	ObjType	Description
VPOS	1-Report Definition	Number of column sets
	10-Group	This number represents the first object included in this group. It's based on the Z-order of the Report objects. However, *grouped* objects can belong to other *grouped* objects. When this occurs, the entire group of objects is only counted once when determining this number.
	23-Font	Character height in pixels, FONTMETRIC(1)
	Report objects	The vertical position of the object, in FRUs
HPOS	1-Report Definition	Left margin, in FRUs Relative to the printable margin if Printable page is chosen. Relative to the physical edge of the paper if Whole page is chosen.
	10-Group	This number represents the total number of Report objects in this group. However, if *grouped* objects are included in another group, the entire group is only counted as *one* object.
	23-Font	The average character width in pixels, FONTMETRIC(6)
	Report objects	The horizontal position of the object, in FRUs
HEIGHT	1-Report Definition	For reports: Always 0 For labels: Spacing between the labels, in FRUs
	9-Band	Height of the band, in FRUs
	23-Font	Character ascent in pixels, FONTMETRIC(2)
	Report objects	Height of the object, in FRUs
WIDTH	1-Report Definition	Width of each column on the report, in FRUs
	9-Band/Group Header	Corresponds to the *Start group on new page when less than* value on the Data Grouping dialog, in FRUs
	23-Font	Maximum character width in pixels, FONTMETRIC(7)
	Report objects	Width of the object, in FRUs
STYLE	All	Not used
PICTURE	8-Field	Corresponds to the expression entered into the *Format* text box on the Report Expression dialog
	17-Picture	If defined as Picture from File: Contains the relative path name for the file. If defined as Picture from Field: Contains the "General" field name containing the image.
ORDER	All	Not used
UNIQUE	18-Variable	Corresponds to the *Release after report* check box on the Report Variables dialog
COMMENT	Report objects	Corresponds to the *Comments* edit box
ENVIRON	25-Data Environment	.T. = Private Data Session .F. = Default Data Session
BOXCHAR	All	Not used
FILLCHAR	8-Field	"C" for character fields "N" for numeric fields "D" for date fields
TAG	1-Report Definition	Binary printer driver information
	9-Band	The On Entry expression
	18-Variable	The Initial value
TAG2	1-Report Definition	Binary printer driver information
	9-Band	The On Exit expression

Table 1. *Continued.*

Field	ObjType	Description
PENRED	23-Font	The character descent in pixels, FONTMETRIC(3)
	Report objects	The foreground "Red" value, as in RGB()
PENGREEN	23-Font	Extra leading in pixels, FONTMETRIC(5)
	Report objects	The foreground "Green" value, as in RGB()
PENBLUE	Report objects	The foreground "Blue" value, as in RGB()
FILLRED	Report objects	The background "Red" value, as in RGB()
FILLGREEN	Report objects	The background "Green" value, as in RGB()
FILLBLUE	Report objects	The background "Blue" value, as in RGB()
PENSIZE	6-Line 7-Shape	Pen size (set when you select Format | Pen from the main VFP Menu bar and choose one of the solid-lined pens) 0 = Hairline 1 = 1 Point 2 = 2 Point 4 = 4 Point 6 = 6 Point
PENPAT	6-Line 7-Shape	Pen pattern (set when you select Format | Pen from the main VFP Menu bar and choose one of the non-solid-lined pens) 0 = None 1 = Dotted 2 = Dashed 3 = DashDot 4 = DashDotDot
FILLPAT	7-Shape	Fill pattern (Format | Fill from the main VFP Menu bar) 0 = None 1 = Solid 2 = Horizontal lines 3 = Vertical lines 4 = Diagonal lines, leaning left 5 = Diagonal lines, leaning right 6 = Grid (horizontal and vertical lines) 7 = Hatch (left and right diagonal lines)
FONTFACE	1-Report Definition	The font name of the Default Font
	5-Label 8-Field 23-Font	The font name
FONTSTYLE	1-Report Definition 5-Label 8-Field 23-Font	0 = Normal 1 = Bold 2 = Italic 4 = Underlined 128 = Strikethrough The above numbers can be combined together to achieve multiple font styles
FONTSIZE	1-Report Definition 5-Label 8-Field 23-Font	The font size
MODE	Report objects	0 = Opaque 1 = Transparent
RULER	1-Report Definition	1 = Ruler measurement is determined by the System Default 3 = Ruler measurement is in pixels

Table 1. *Continued.*

Field	ObjType	Description
RULERLINES	1-Report Definition	0 = Do not show the grid lines in the Report Designer 1 = Show the grid lines in the Report Designer
GRID	1-Report Definition	.T. = Snap to Grid is on .F. = Snap to Grid is off
GRIDV	1-Report Definition	Vertical spacing of grid lines, in pixels
GRIDH	1-Report Definition	Horizontal spacing of grid lines, in pixels
FLOAT	Report objects	Corresponds to the *Float* option on the object's property dialog
STRETCH	Report objects	Corresponds to the *Stretch with overflow* check box on the object's property dialog
STRETCHTOP	7-Shape	Corresponds to the *Stretch relative to height of band* option on the object's property dialog
TOP	1-Report Definition	Always .T.
	Report objects	Corresponds to the *Fix relative to top of band* option on the object's property dialog
BOTTOM	1-Report Definition	.T. = Multiple column sets are printed in left-to-right order .F. = Multiple column sets are printed in top-to-bottom order
	Report objects	Corresponds to the *Fix relative to bottom of band* option on the object's property dialog
SUPTYPE	All	Not used
SUPREST	All	Not used
NOREPEAT	Report objects	Corresponds to the *Remove line if blank* check box on the Print When dialog
RESETRPT	All	Not used
PAGEBREAK	9-Band/Title	Title page is printed on its own page
	9-Band/Group Header	Corresponds to the *Start each group on a new page* check box on the Data Grouping dialog
	9-Band/Group Footer	Matches the corresponding Group Header record
	9-Band/Summary	Summary page is printed on its own page
COLBREAK	9-Band/Group Header	Corresponds to the *Start group on new column* check box on the Data Grouping dialog
	9-Band/Group Footer	Matches the corresponding Group Header record
RESETPAGE	9-Band/Group Header	Corresponds to the *Reset page number to 1 for each group* check box on the Data Grouping dialog
	9-Band/Group Footer	Matches the corresponding Group Header record
GENERAL	17-Pictures	1 = Picture from Field 2 = Picture from File
SPACING	8-Field	Always set to 2 (although it's never used)
DOUBLE	17-Pictures	Corresponds to the *Center picture* check box on the object's property dialog
SWAPHEADER	All	Not used
SWAPFOOTER	All	Not used
EJECTBEFOR	All	Not used
EJECTAFTER	All	Not used
PLAIN	9-Band/Summary	Always .T.
SUMMARY	All	Not used
ADDALIAS	1-Report Definition	Always .T.

Table 1. Continued.

Field	ObjType	Description
OFFSET	6-Line	Always 1
	7-Shape	The radius used on Rounded Rectangle objects
	8-Field	0 = Align left 1 = Align right 2 = Align center
TOPMARGIN	All	Not used
BOTMARGIN	All	Not used
TOTALTYPE	8-Field 18-Variable	Type of calculation: 0 = Nothing 1 = Count 2 = Sum 3 = Average 4 = Lowest 5 = Highest 6 = Standard deviation 7 = Variance
RESETTOTAL	8-Field 18-Variable	Determines when calculations are reset: 1 = At end of report 2 = At end of page 3 = At end of column 5+# = At end of Data Group where # is the Data Group number (for example, a 6 resets the calculation at Data Group 1, a 7 resets the calculation at Data Group 2, and so on)
RESOID	All	Not used
CURPOS	1-Report Definition	.T. = Show position is ON .F. = Show position is OFF
SUPALWAYS	7-Shape	Corresponds to the *Print repeated values* option group on the Print When dialog, but it's backwards (note that this field *and* the SUPVALCHG field are set for shapes) .T. = No .F. = Yes
SUPOVFLOW	Report objects	Corresponds to the *When detail overflows to new page/column* check box on the Print When dialog
SUPRCOL	Report objects	Corresponds to the *In first whole band of new page/column* check box on the Print When dialog (0 = unchecked, 3 = checked)
SUPGROUP	Report objects	Corresponds to the *When this group changes* drop-down combo box. The number is 5+ the group number (for example, a 6 reprints at Data Group 1, a 7 reprints at Data Group 2, and so on)
SUPVALCHG	Report objects	Corresponds to the *Print repeated values* option group on the Print When dialog, but it's backwards .T. = No .F. = Yes
SUPEXPR	Report objects	Corresponds to the *Print only when expression is true* text box on the Print When dialog
USER	All	Available for the developer to use

Let's start hacking!

By now you're saying, "Great, Cathy. You've told me way more than I ever wanted to know about the FRX report file. So what! Why should I care?"

The reason you should care about all of this is so when you run up against a limitation of the Report Designer, you don't throw your hands up in the air and give up. If you truly understand the intricacies of how the report definition is stored in the FRX file, you may be able to solve the problem at hand by hacking the file. I'm not saying that *all* problems can be solved this way, but there are some situations where hacking *is* the solution.

> DISCLAIMER: It should go without saying, but I'm going to say it anyway. Before you hack any file, make a backup!

Printer-specific information

In the section titled "Eliminating printer-specific information" in Chapter 9, "Running Reports," I explained how to use a Project Hook to remove printer-specific information stored in a report definition. However, I didn't give any explanation behind *what* I was doing and just made you blindly follow along. Well, now I'm going to explain what I was actually doing.

The first record in the FRX file is a Report Definition record, which contains printer information. Some of the information is necessary and some of the information can be a real P.I.T.A. By hacking the FRX, you can remove the *bad* stuff, while still leaving the *good* stuff.

Two of the fields, TAG and TAG2, contain binary printer information and there's absolutely nothing worth saving in these fields. You can clear these two fields and not worry about any repercussions. Use the following code to do this.

```
USE MyReport.frx
GOTO TOP
REPLACE TAG WITH '', TAG2 WITH ''
USE
```

A third field, EXPR, isn't quite so cut-and-dried. It contains *bad* stuff and *good* stuff. The trick is to only remove the bad, while still keeping the good. Unfortunately, unlike good and bad cholesterol, there isn't a pill you can take to solve this problem.

The EXPR field is a memo field that contains one piece of information per line as shown in the following example taken from a report I created. It completely depends on which printer is used as to which lines are contained in this field. Only information that applies to the specific printer is saved. For example, my printer doesn't do duplex printing; therefore, there isn't a line saved in the EXPR field for duplex printing.

```
DRIVER=winspool
DEVICE=HP DeskJet 660
OUTPUT=LPT1:
ORIENTATION=0
PAPERSIZE=1
DEFAULTSOURCE=7
PRINTQUALITY=300
COLOR=2
YRESOLUTION=300
TTOPTION=1
```

The trick to hacking this field is to only remove the lines that can cause problems, such as the DEVICE= line, while still leaving the necessary lines, such as the ORIENTATION= line. The first three lines (DRIVER=, DEVICE=, and OUTPUT=) are all *bad* lines because they point to a specific printer, so go ahead and remove these.

The rest of the lines in the EXPR field correspond to the settings that can be obtained through the PRTINFO() function as shown in **Table 2**. See Visual FoxPro's Help file for a complete list of valid values for each setting.

Table 2. PRTINFO() information in the EXPR field of the Report Definition record.

EXPR	PRTINFO()
ORIENTATION=	1
PAPERSIZE=	2
PAPERLENGTH=	3
PAPERWIDTH=	4
SCALE=	5
COPIES=	6
DEFAULTSOURCE=	7
PRINTQUALITY=	8
COLOR=	9
DUPLEX=	10
YRESOLUTION=	11
TTOPTION=	12
COLLATE=	13

Changing information at run time

At this point, you may be having an epiphany (or a coronary!). There's one piece of information stored in the EXPR field of the Report Definition record that the users commonly want to change on-the-fly, which is the COPIES= setting. Another piece of information that you might need to change is the DEFAULTSOURCE=, which controls the *Paper Tray*. Here's where you say, "Ohhhh, now I see where you're going with this!"

Prior to running a report, you can open the FRX table, manipulate the information in the EXPR field, save it, and then run the report as usual. This concept can be handled a few different ways. One method is to directly manipulate the FRX file. The other method is to copy the FRX file to a new file, manipulate the new file, and then run the report from the new file—thus, you never manipulate the original report. For simplicity's sake, in the following examples, I'm just going to manipulate the original FRX file. (Of course, I have already made my backup.)

Controlling the number of copies

A common practice by developers is to display a simple dialog to the users to allow them to select the number of copies and choose whether they want to preview or print the report as shown in **Figure 1**.

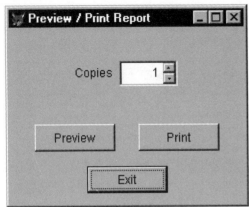

Figure 1. *Use a simple dialog to prompt the user for the number of copies.*

 The following code is behind the scenes of this simple dialog and can be found in the form called PrintPreview.SCX, included in the source code available with this book.

```
*-- Init method of the form
LPARAMETERS pcReportName
ThisForm.cReportName = pcReportName

*-- Click method of the Preview button
ThisForm.RunReport("PREVIEW")

*-- Click method of the Print button
ThisForm.RunReport("NOCONSOLE TO PRINTER PROMPT")

*-- Click method of the Exit button
ThisForm.Release()

*-- RunReport method
LPARAMETERS pcWhere

LOCAL lcReportName, laExpr, lnLen, ln, lcExpr
lcReportName = ThisForm.cReportName
DIMENSION laExpr[1]

*-- Manipulate the copies .. if not previewing
IF NOT pcWhere == 'PREVIEW' && Notice there are TWO equal signs

  *-- Put EXPR in an array
  USE (lcReportName + '.frx')
  GOTO TOP
  lnLen = ALINES(laExpr, expr)

  *-- Find the COPIES= line and change it
  FOR ln = 1 TO lnLen
    IF LEFT(laExpr[ln], 7) = 'COPIES='
      laExpr[ln] = LEFT(laExpr[ln], 7) + TRANSFORM(ThisForm.nCopies)
      EXIT
    ENDIF
  ENDFOR
```

```
*-- Convert the array back to a string and save it in EXPR
lcExpr = ''
FOR ln = 1 TO lnLen
  lcExpr = lcExpr + laExpr[ln] + CHR(13)
ENDFOR
REPLACE expr WITH lcExpr

  *-- Close the table
  USE
ENDIF

*-- Print the report
REPORT FORM &lcReportName &pcWhere RANGE 1,1
```

Of course, this assumes the printer has the ability to print multiple copies, which not all printers do. Use the PRTINFO(6) function to check the printer's abilities. If the function returns a positive number, go ahead and hack the FRX file as just described. Otherwise, use the method described in the section titled "Number of copies" in Chapter 9, "Running Reports," to print multiple copies.

Controlling the paper tray

Changing the paper tray of a report can be done in much the same way as I just described for changing the number of copies. The following code shows how you can send the first page of a report to one tray and the rest of the report to another tray (assuming the printer *has* multiple trays). This sample code can be found in the program called ChangeTray.PRG, included in the source code available with this book.

```
*-- Print the first page
DO ChangeTray WITH 'MyReport', 1
REPORT FORM MyReport TO PRINTER RANGE 1,1

*-- Print the rest of the pages
DO ChangeTray WITH 'MyReport', 2
REPORT FORM MyReport TO PRINTER RANGE 2


*-------------------
PROCEDURE ChangeTray
*-------------------

LPARAMETERS pcReportName, pnTray

LOCAL laExpr, lnLen, ln, lcExpr
DIMENSION laExpr[1]

*-- Put EXPR in an array
USE (pcReportName + '.frx')
GOTO TOP
lnLen = ALINES(laExpr, expr)

*-- Find the DEFAULTSOURCE= line and change it
FOR ln = 1 TO lnLen
  IF LEFT(laExpr[ln], 14) = 'DEFAULTSOURCE='
    laExpr[ln] = LEFT(laExpr[ln], 14) + TRANSFORM(pnTray)
    EXIT
  ENDIF
```

```
ENDFOR

*-- Convert the array back to a string and save it in EXPR
lcExpr = ''
FOR ln = 1 TO lnLen
  lcExpr = lcExpr + laExpr[ln] + CHR(13)
ENDFOR
REPLACE expr WITH lcExpr

*-- Close the table
USE
RETURN
```

Controlling the margins

Often times, preprinted forms are a real hassle to deal with. Let's say you design a great report that is perfectly aligned to the check stock. Everyone's happy—until they order a new box of checks. This time, Joe Blow's Printing Company didn't align the checks exactly the same and they're off 1/8" from the first batch.

Now what? Do you modify the report and adjust everything? Well, you *could*, but then what happens when the next box of checks arrives and they're aligned the same as the first box? You'd have to change it back again.

To overcome alignment issues, design the report to match the first box of checks. Next, create a dialog that allows users to enter a top and left margin offset number. This can be done as a system setup dialog in your application, or you can let them change this information each time they print checks. The way you implement this concept is up to you—I'm just describing the general concept. However, I suggest that you allow the user to enter inches or centimeters, positive or negative, and then convert the number to the appropriate FRU.

The left margin can be offset by adjusting the HPOS field of the Report Definition record. Adjusting the top margin isn't quite as easy. First, you have to adjust the height of the Page Header band. Once that's changed, you need to adjust the position of all the objects on the report. And because you certainly wouldn't want to have the report *creep* each time the user prints it, this is one of those times when you should copy the FRX file, manipulate the copied file, and then print from the newly manipulated file and not the original.

The following code shows how you can call a UDF or method to adjust all the appropriate records of a given report. The code returns the name of the temporary report file created so the calling program can run it. Also, don't forget to remove the temporary FRX and FRT files when you're done printing. This sample code can be found in the Margin.PRG program, included in the source code available with this book.

```
LPARAMETERS pcReportName, pnTopOffset, pnLeftOffset

LOCAL lcTempFile

*-- Copy the file
lcTempFile = FORCEEXT(SYS(2015), '.frx')
USE (pcReportName + '.frx')
COPY TO &lcTempFile WITH CDX
USE

*-- Open the new file
```

```
USE &lcTempFile

*-- Adjust the left margin
GOTO TOP
REPLACE hpos WITH hpos + pnLeftOffset

*-- Adjust the height of the top margin
GOTO TOP
LOCATE FOR objtype = 9 AND objcode = 1 && Find the Page Header band
REPLACE height WITH height + pnTopOffset

*-- Adjust the position of all report objects
GOTO TOP
SCAN FOR INLIST(objtype, 5, 6, 7, 8, 17)
  REPLACE vpos WITH vpos + pnTopOffset
ENDSCAN

*-- Close the file
USE

*-- Return the name of the new file
RETURN lcTempFile
```

It's up to you to have some limitations in the amount you allow the users to offset the margins and it can vary per report. For example, it wouldn't make sense to let the user adjust the left margin of the checks by 5" when the entire check is 8-1/2" wide. It's a pretty good bet much of the information would be lost off the right edge of the check.

Custom paper sizes

The method you use to print a Visual FoxPro report on a non-standard paper size depends on which operating system you're using. On older operating systems, such as Windows 98, you select the paper size when defining the report in the Report Designer. Select File | Page Setup… from the main VFP Menu bar to invoke the Page Setup dialog. From this dialog, select Print Setup… to invoke the Print Setup dialog. On the Print Setup dialog, select *Custom* or *User-defined* from the Size drop-down combo box. Once you've told it to use a custom paper size, you can select the Properties button to define a custom paper size; however, the instructions vary depending on the printer you're working with, so I'm going to assume you can take it from here.

When you save a report with a custom paper size, the PAPERSIZE= entry in the Report Definition record is set to 256 to indicate custom. In addition, two lines are added to the EXPR field. One is PAPERLENGTH= and the other is PAPERWIDTH=. I think you can figure out what these mean. You can manually adjust the custom size by hacking the FRX file and adjusting these values.

Unfortunately, it isn't so easy on all operating systems. In more recent operating systems, you have to predefine custom paper sizes and it gets very complicated. The Microsoft Knowledge Base has two articles that can help you with this: #Q157172 and #Q304639.

Watermarks

Watermarks are nothing more than a graphic image placed on a page (see **Figure 2**). The tricky part with doing this in the Visual FoxPro Report Writer is stretching the image across the entire page. Give it a try and you'll see what I mean. Put an image on a report and stretch it from the top of the Page Header band to the bottom of the Page Footer band. Check the "Scale picture, fill frame" check box, save it, and then run the report. If you were expecting the image to stretch like lines and rectangles do, you're going to be disappointed. That's not what happened. The image stayed the same size as it appears in the Report Designer.

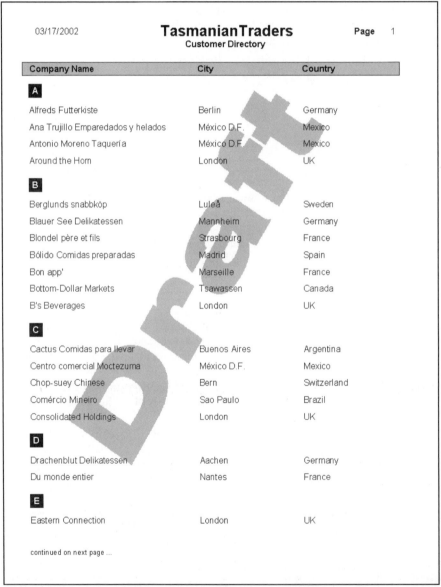

Figure 2. Hack the VPOS, HPOS, HEIGHT, and WIDTH of a Picture object to create a watermark.

So how did I create the report shown in Figure 2? Well, I did it by hacking the FRX file. All I did was change the VPOS, HPOS, HEIGHT, and WIDTH of the Picture object and *voilà!* The report has a watermark. The source code available with this book includes the hacked report called WaterMark.FRX.

Picture objects have an OBJTYPE of 17, so open the FRX table and locate the picture record. If you have more than one picture on the report, look at the PICTURE field to find the one you want. Change the VPOS and HPOS values (in FRUs) to represent the upper right corner of where you want the picture to begin. Next, change the HEIGHT and WIDTH fields to represent the height and width of the picture. You do, however, have to keep in mind the unprintable margins for the printers. If you choose a height and width that is beyond the means of the printer, the entire picture doesn't print.

Two things are worth noting with this technique. First, the *Front-to-back* order of the image in relation to the other Report objects is important. If you place the image on the report after you've placed other Report objects on the report, the image appears on top of the Report objects. This probably isn't what you're looking for, so select the image and then select Format | Send to Back from the main VFP Menu bar. This places the image behind all the other Report objects. The other thing worth noting is that if you make any changes in the Report Designer (especially to the image), the hacked size of the image may revert back to a size that VFP considers within its acceptable range. So you have to remember to re-hack the size again.

Leading

When designing a report with Field objects that can stretch with overflow, you don't have easy control over the *leading*, which is the height of one single line plus the blank space between it and the next line. The Report Writer uses a complex formula for determining the leading, which is based on the defined height of the object and the particular font selected for the object. Making the object taller doesn't necessarily mean the leading is increased. In fact, sometimes the opposite is true and a taller object has less leading as shown in **Figure 3** and **Figure 4**.

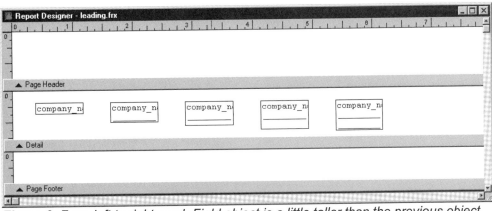

***Figure 3.** From left to right, each Field object is a little taller than the previous object.*

```
    Alfreds        Alfreds        Alfreds        Alfreds        Alfreds
    Futterkis      Futterkis      Futterkis      Futterkis      Futterkis
    te             te             te                            te
                                                 Futterkis
                                                 te



    Ana            Ana            Ana            Ana            Ana
    Trujillo       Trujillo       Trujillo       Trujillo       Trujillo
    Emparedad      Emparedad      Emparedad                     Emparedad
    os y           os y           os y           Emparedad      os y
    helados        helados        helados        os y           helados
                                                 helados
```

Figure 4. *A taller Report object doesn't necessarily mean more leading.*

In Figure 3, the objects are progressively taller, from left to right. Yet as shown in Figure 4, the leading doesn't directly correlate with the height of the object. Even though the fifth object is the tallest in the Report Designer, it has the least leading of all the objects on the printed report. And even though the first object is the shortest of all objects, it's not the one with the least amount of leading.

This may seem a bit strange at first, but once you understand the formula used for calculating the leading, it all makes sense. In layman's terms, the Report Writer figures out how many lines it thinks can fit within the height of the object. It then figures out how much extra space is left over and equally distributes the space between the lines. However, explaining the actual formula isn't as easy as explaining it in layman's terms.

I've done a lot of playing around with this issue and I've come up with two different formulas. The VFP Report Writer uses the first formula *most* of the time and the second formula occasionally. What I haven't been able to figure out yet is what condition triggers the second formula. The following two formulas, written in VFP code, are included in the source code available with this book as the program called Leading.PRG.

```
#DEFINE dObjectHeight 1875
#DEFINE dObjectFontName "Arial"
#DEFINE dObjectFontSize 10
#DEFINE dObjectFontStyle "N"

#DEFINE dDisplayUnits 96 && 96 for Windows, 72 for MAC, 300 for printers
#DEFINE dReportUnits 10000

LOCAL lnLineHeight, lnLines, lnLeading

*-- How tall is one line
lnLineHeight = ;
   FONTMETRIC(1, dObjectFontName, dObjectFontSize, dObjectFontStyle)


*-------------------------------------------
*-- The first and most commonly used formula
*-------------------------------------------

* How many lines will fit in this object
```

```
lnLines = (dObjectHeight + (1 / dDisplayUnits * dReportUnits)) / ;
   (lnLineHeight / dDisplayUnits * dReportUnits)

* Calculate the leading
lnLeading = lnLineHeight / dDisplayUnits * dReportUnits * lnLines / ;
   IIF(lnLines < 1, 1, INT(lnLines))
? 'Leading is:', lnLeading


*-----------------------------------
*-- The second and rarely used formula
*-----------------------------------

* How many lines will fit in this object
lnLines = ((dObjectHeight + (1 / dDisplayUnits * dReportUnits)) + ;
   (1 / dDisplayUnits * dReportUnits)) / ;
   (lnLineHeight / dDisplayUnits * dReportUnits)

* Calculate the leading
lnLeading = lnLineHeight / dDisplayUnits * dReportUnits * lnLines / ;
   IIF(lnLines < 1, 1, INT(lnLines))
? 'Leading is:', lnLeading
```

As you can see by the code, the only difference between the two formulas is the calculation of the *lnLines* variable, but like I said earlier, I can't figure out what condition triggers the use of the second formula. If you can figure it out, please let me know. It's driving me crazy!

So why am I describing all of this in a chapter about hacking? Well, once you know the formula, theoretically, you can reverse engineer it. If you ever have a need to fine-tune the leading of a Report object, come back to this chapter and bring your calculator. Once you've calculated the required height of the object, hack the FRX file and change the HEIGHT field to the magical number you've arrived at.

A certified hacker

You have now successfully completed *Hacking 101* and I consider you a certified hacker. If you're ever asked to call upon these skills, you can confidently say, "I can do that." Then run back to your office, grab this book, and open it up to this chapter.

Chapter 12
Labels

Labels are used everywhere these days. You see them on envelopes, magazines, diskettes, prescription bottles, products in the grocery store, and so many other places. This means that you may need to print labels in your Visual FoxPro application using data from FoxPro tables. Well, don't worry, because Visual FoxPro can handle it and it's not as *sticky* as it may first seem (sorry, it's late, I'm close to a deadline and I couldn't help myself).

Labels are nothing more than a report—on tiny paper. All you have to do is tell Visual FoxPro what size the label is, and from there, it's practically the same as designing a report. This chapter walks you through creating labels and points out the few differences between reports and labels.

The first time

When Visual FoxPro is installed, it does not install the label formats. The first time you try to create a label, you get an error message that says, "No label layouts found."

There are two ways you can install the label formats. The easiest way is to run the Label Wizard. When the Label Wizard is run for the first time, and you have specified the table to use, you're automatically prompted to install the label formats as shown in **Figure 1**.

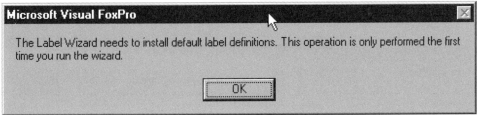

Figure 1. The Label Wizard prompts you to install the label formats the first time it's run.

You can also install the label formats yourself by using Windows Explorer to locate the *labels.reg* file, which should be in the tools\addlabel subdirectory underneath your VFP Home directory. Once you locate this file, double-click it.

Regardless of which method you used to invoke the registration, you're prompted to confirm the installation (see **Figure 2**). Although, you *could* select No, you really have no choice but to choose *Yes*. Without the label formats, you can't very well define labels.

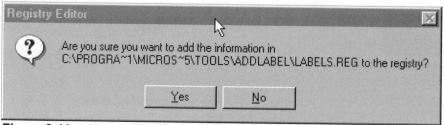

Figure 2. *You must confirm the installation of the label formats.*

And as if you're not already annoyed enough by having to do this in the first place—and having to answer the dialogs—there's one more dialog to get beyond (see **Figure 3**). This dialog tells you the label formats have been installed successfully.

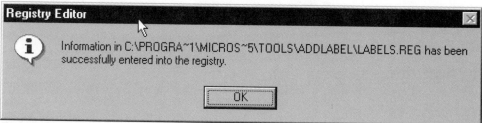

Figure 3. *If you don't see this dialog, something went wrong.*

Whew, that was sure annoying. Personally, I wish the label formats would get installed automatically right along with Visual FoxPro, but they don't. Okay, enough griping. Now it's time to learn how to create labels.

The Label Wizard

Similar to the Report Wizard, Visual FoxPro also offers a Label Wizard. Select Tools | Wizards | Label from the main VFP Menu bar to invoke the Label Wizard, which walks you through a five-step process of creating labels.

Step 1—Select Tables

Upon selecting the Label Wizard from the main VFP Menu bar, the first dialog is shown (see **Figure 4**). This dialog is used to select the table that contains the data you want to print on the labels. If a database is currently opened, it's displayed in the Databases and tables drop-down combo box. Otherwise, *Free Tables* appears in the drop-down combo box. Select the database of your choice to display the tables in the table list box. You can also use the ellipse button (...) to the right of the drop-down combo box to select an unopened database or select free tables to list in the table list box.

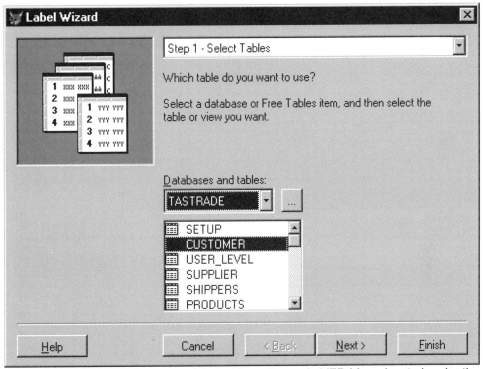

Figure 4. *Select Tools | Wizards | Label from the main VFP Menu bar to invoke the Visual FoxPro Label Wizard.*

Once you see the table you're looking for listed in the table list box, highlight it and select the Next button to move on to the next step.

Step 2—Choose Label Type

The next step is where you tell the VFP Label Wizard what type of label you want (see **Figure 5**). The available label formats are listed in the multi-column list box in the middle of the dialog. You can select the *English* or *Metric* option group buttons to switch between English and Metric label formats.

Luckily, you're not limited to the predefined label formats. You can define your own label formats by selecting the New Label... button. The Custom Labels dialog shown in **Figure 6** shows the two custom label formats I created on my system.

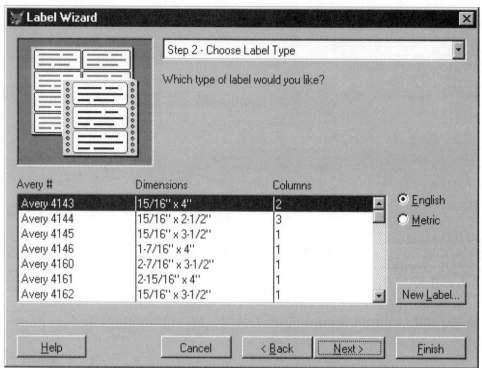

Figure 5. Use Step 2 to choose the type of label you want.

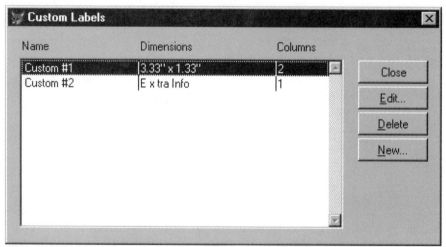

Figure 6. Use the Custom Labels dialog to create your own label formats.

Bug Alert! *There's a very annoying bug that occurs if SET STATUS BAR is OFF at the time you create custom labels. It appears that SET TALK is ON and a slew of values keep getting displayed on the Label Wizard dialog and the Custom Labels dialog, which completely obstructs your view of the dialogs. Therefore, make sure you have SET STATUS BAR ON before creating custom labels.*

To add a new label format, select the New… button, which displays the New Label Definition dialog as shown in **Figure 7**.

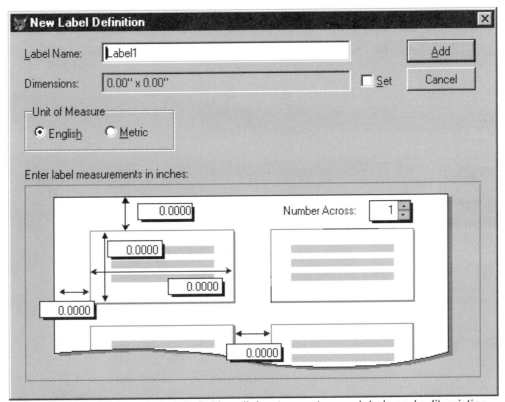

Figure 7. *Use the New Label Definition dialog to create new labels and edit existing custom labels.*

Enter a name for this label in the Label Name text box. Select either English or Metric from the option group to control how the dimensions are displayed. Next, you need to define all the dimensions of the label. The bottom half of the New Label Definition dialog is laid out to help you do just that. You need to enter the margin between the top of the page and the first label as well as the margin between the left edge of the page and the first label. You also need to enter the height and width of the label itself.

If the page contains more than one label per row, use the Number Across spinner to enter the total number of labels per row. You also need to enter the spacing between the labels when multiple labels appear on each row.

As you enter the dimensions of the label, the Dimensions text box is automatically filled in with the dimensions you've entered. This dimension is displayed along with the Label Name whenever you choose a label in the Label Wizard or the Label Designer. If you'd like to override this information, check the Set check box to the right of the Dimensions text box. Now you can enter any description you want in the Dimensions text box. However, VFP attempts to parse out the string you enter into a *dimension,* so what you type may not be what ends up being displayed in the list of labels.

> *Standard label formats are stored in a VFP table called LABELS.DBF and custom label formats are stored in a VFP table called USERLBLS.DBF. These tables are stored in the tools/addlabel subdirectory of your VFP Home directory.*

Once you've chosen the label format you want from the Step 2 dialog, select the Next button to move on to the next step.

Step 3—Define Layout

The third step in creating labels is to tell the VFP Label Wizard what information to print on the label. The Define Layout dialog is designed with the basic concept of a mailing address in mind and assumes you want the information centered between the top and bottom edges of the label. To enter a typical mailing address (using the Customer table), follow these steps and when finished, the dialog should look like the one shown in **Figure 8**. As you add items to the Selected fields list box, the graphic image in the upper left changes to reflect how the label looks.

1. Either double-click the Company_Name field in the Available fields list box or highlight it and select the right arrow button to move it to the Selected fields list box.

2. Select the Carriage Return button (which looks like the Enter key on your keyboard) to indicate you're done with this line.

3. Select the Address field and move it to the Selected fields list box.

4. Select the Carriage Return button.

5. Select the City field and move it to the Selected fields list box.

6. Select the Comma button (,) to add a comma after the city.

7. Select the Space button (Space) to add a space after the comma.

8. Select the Region field and move it to the Selected fields list box.

9. Select the Space button to add a space after the region.

10. Select the Postal_code field and move it to the Selected fields list box.

11. Select the Carriage Return button twice.

12. Enter "Attn:" in the Text text box and then select the right arrow button to move it to the Selected fields list box.

13. Select the Space button.

14. Select the Contact_name field and move it to the Selected fields list box.

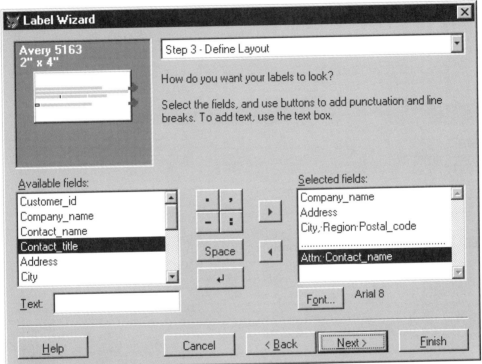

Figure 8*. Use Step 3 to tell the VFP Label Wizard what information to print on the label.*

As I have already mentioned, this dialog is definitely designed with the assumption that you're creating mailing labels. If you aren't, don't worry. Enter as much or as little information as possible here, and then when you're done creating the label with the wizard, use the Label Designer to fine-tune it.

When you're done with Step 3, select the Next button to move on to Step 4.

Step 4—Sort Records

The fourth step in the Label Wizard is to tell it how to sort the data. This dialog works the same way as the Report Wizard, so I'm not going to go into the specifics of how to set the sort order. You can review Chapter 2, "The Report Wizard," if you need more information.

Step 5—Finish

The final step can be used to preview the label by selecting the Preview button (see **Figure 9**). If the label doesn't look the way you intended it to, use the Back button to go back through the steps and make the necessary changes. Once you're satisfied with the label design, you have three options for saving it.

- **Save label for later use:** This option saves the label and closes the Label Wizard.

- **Save label and modify it in the Label Designer:** This option saves the label and then brings up the Label Designer so you can make changes to the label generated by the wizard.

- **Save and print labels:** This option saves the label and immediately prints them.

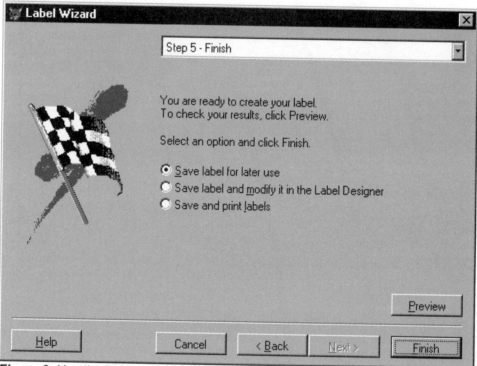

Figure 9. *Use the final step to preview the labels and save them.*

Once the labels are created with the Label Wizard, they can be modified with the Label Designer. And just as with reports created by the Report Wizard, once saved, labels are no different from any other label created with the Label Designer.

The Label Designer

Much of the Label Designer is the same or similar to the Report Designer; therefore, I won't explain every detail all over again. This chapter is only meant to describe the differences or idiosyncrasies of the Label Designer. Another point to make is that labels can be hacked just as reports can. The only thing different is that labels have an extension of LBX and LBT.

Invoking the VFP Label Designer can be done a number of different ways. If you're the type of person who prefers using menus, you can create a new label or modify an existing label through the main VFP Menu bar. If you're the type of person who prefers to do things through the Command Window, you're in luck too. You can create new labels and modify existing labels through the use of commands in the VFP Command Window.

Invoking the Label Designer via the Menu

To create a new label, select File | New... from the main VFP Menu bar. This invokes the New dialog, from which, you can select Label and then select the New file button. Prior to the Label Designer opening, you're first prompted with the New Label dialog (see **Figure 10**).

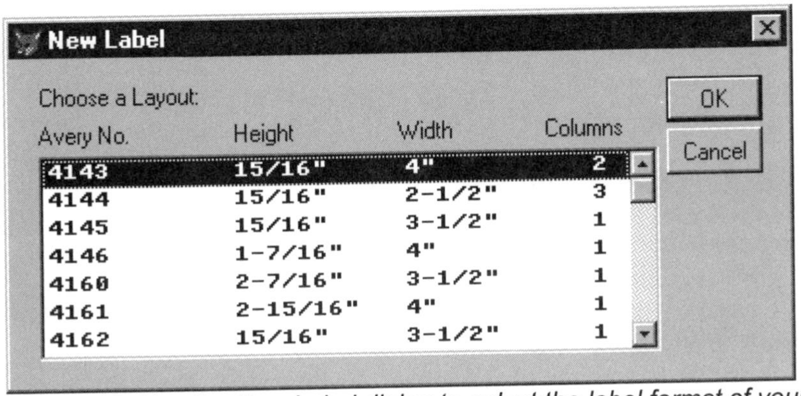

Figure 10. Use the New Label dialog to select the label format of your choice.

Select the label format of your choice and then select the OK button. Next, the Label Designer is invoked with the selected label format laid out and ready for you to create (see **Figure 11**).

To open the Label Designer and modify an *existing* label, select File | Open... from the main VFP Menu bar. This displays a standard Open dialog. Navigate to the directory that contains your label and make sure Label is in the Files of type drop-down combo box. Find the label you want to modify, select it, and click the OK button. This invokes the Label Designer with the selected label opened and ready for editing.

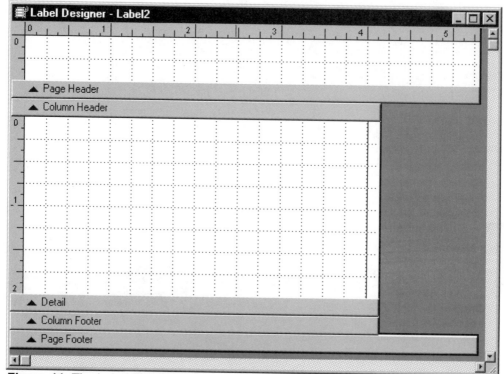

Figure 11. The Label Designer opens with your selected label format laid out for you.

Invoking the Label Designer via the Command Window

For those who prefer to use the Command Window (present company included), you can create new labels and edit existing labels very easily with the CREATE LABEL command and the MODIFY LABEL command, respectively. Unlike reports, there is no *Quick Label* option when dealing with labels.

Create a blank label

The following command is the simplest way to create a blank label.

```
CREATE LABEL
```

This creates the same unnamed blank label shown in Figure 11. If you prefer to name the new label as it's created, use either of the following commands.

```
*-- Create a new blank label called "MyLabel"
CREATE LABEL MyLabel

*-- Create a new blank label, prompting for a name
*-- (This allows you to navigate to the desired directory and enter a name)
CREATE LABEL ?
```

If you choose a name that already exists and you have SET SAFETY ON, you're prompted with a dialog that asks whether you want to overwrite the current one. If you don't have SET SAFETY ON, the existing label of the same name is opened so you can modify it.

Modify an existing label

Modifying an existing label through the Command Window is very simple as shown in the following code samples.

```
*-- Modify a label called "MyLabel"
MODIFY LABEL MyLabel

*-- Prompt for the name of the label to modify
MODIFY LABEL ?
```

Either of these commands invokes the Label Designer with the specified label loaded and ready for editing. If no label exists by the name you've specified, a new one is created just as if you had used the CREATE LABEL command and not the MODIFY LABEL command.

Both the CREATE LABEL and MODIFY LABEL commands have additional clauses that function the same as their respective REPORT commands, so I'm not going to repeat the explanations in this chapter. You can refer to Chapter 9, "Running Reports," for more information on these clauses.

Setting up the page

Now that you know several different ways to invoke the Label Designer, it's time to explore the intricacies of the Label Designer itself.

Paper size

The first, and very annoying, thing I need to point out is that when labels are first created, the default paper size is *not* a standard sheet of paper. It defaults to the *User-defined size* set up for the default printer, and who knows what that size is?

Select File | Page Setup… from the main VFP Menu bar to invoke the Page Setup dialog. From this dialog, select the Print Setup… button to invoke the Print Setup dialog. From this dialog, set the paper size to your desired choice. For example, when printing labels on laser and inkjet printers, labels are commonly printed on stock the same size as paper so choose your standard paper size.

Columns

Another annoying side effect of the Label Designer defaulting to the *User-defined size* is that it can affect the number of columns. Even though I chose a label format that is 2-up, the Label Designer doesn't think two labels can fit on the page, at least not according to the current user-defined paper size. Therefore, it reduces the number of columns to one. So besides changing the paper size, you may have to reset the number of columns on the Page Setup dialog.

Print area

 Bug Alert! *There's a bug in VFP that can cause some objects to be truncated when printed on labels due to the unprintable margins on the page. Changing the print area setting to either* Printable page *or* Whole page *makes no difference. Only certain label formats are affected by this bug as documented in Microsoft Knowledge Base Article #Q139215. The only workaround to the problem is to move the objects on the label to avoid truncation.*

Special issues
Printing continuous and sheet labels each have their own unique issue.

Continuous labels
When printing continuous labels on dot matrix printers, things get a bit trickier. Usually, the label format causes a page eject after each page of labels, which skews the alignment of the labels. Therefore, you have to take a different approach and use the Report Designer and *not* the Label Designer and then define a custom paper size. Microsoft Knowledge Base Article #Q125967 explains the exact steps involved to overcome this issue.

Sheet labels
With the introduction of laser printers, the use of continuous labels has declined in favor of using sheet labels. However, sheet labels have one drawback because they have the potential to waste a lot of labels when a batch only uses a portion of the sheet.

To overcome this situation, you need to pull a few tricks prior to printing the labels. Start by displaying a dialog with a spinner box that asks the user how many labels have already been used on the first sheet. Now that you know this number, you can add one blank record to the table or cursor for each *used* label on the sheet. Now, when you print the labels, the first *n* labels that print have no data and use those blank areas on the sheet.

Wrapping up
From here on out, using the Label Designer is the same as using the Report Designer. Objects are added the same way. Report Variables can be created the same way. Data Groupings can be created the same (although you should be sure to make the height of the Data Grouping the same height as the Detail band so you don't throw off the label alignment). You can use On Entry and On Exit expressions to pull the same kind of tricks you do with reports. Everything you learned about reports, you can apply to labels.

Chapter 13
Beyond the VFP Report Writer

This is the last time I'm going to say it, "The Visual FoxPro Report Writer is a very powerful tool." I truly believe this with all my heart. However, I also realize that there are times when the *Fox* needs a little help. This chapter is dedicated to exposing you to a variety of other tools and utilities to extend your report-writing arsenal.

When the Visual FoxPro Report Writer isn't capable of doing what you want, you may have to resort to other utilities or tools. In this chapter, I describe some common tools and utilities for working with Visual FoxPro tables. This chapter won't be a detailed instruction manual on each tool, but rather a general description about what each tool does and where you can go to get more information. I want to expose you to other possibilities and let you make the decision about whether any of these tools or utilities benefit your situation.

Within Visual FoxPro

The VFP Report Writer is a great tool for printing or previewing reports within Visual FoxPro; however, it's not the only way. There are four native commands within Visual FoxPro that can be used to view reports on the screen or print reports to a printer. The @...SAY command and the three variations of the ? command can all be used to accomplish this task.

@...SAY

The @...SAY command sends output to the current device, as determined by the SET DEVICE TO command. One of the valid devices for this command is a printer, and therefore, you can combine these commands to send output to a printer as shown in the following sample code.

```
SET DEVICE TO PRINTER
@ 1,1 SAY "Hello World"
@ 3,11 SAY "Fox Rocks!"
@ 5,21 SAY "Visual FoxPro"
EJECT
SET DEVICE TO SCREEN
```

The first number following the @ symbol represents the row and the second number represents the column. The EJECT command tells the printer to advance the page. In fact, had I omitted the EJECT command, the output would have stayed in the print buffer until I exited FoxPro.

When sending output to the printer with the @...SAY command, you cannot jump around the page. You have to send the output in top to bottom order. As soon as you send output to a row number that is less than the previous row number, a page eject is automatically sent to the printer prior to printing the new row.

Contrary to what you might think, the output goes to the *Windows* default printer and not the *Visual FoxPro* default printer. This means you cannot use the SYS(1037) function to let the user select which printer to send the output to. Another common misconception is that the optional PROMPT clause available on the SET DEVICE TO command allows the user to choose a printer. This is not correct as the PROMPT clause allows the user to set certain settings, such as the number of copies and a range of page numbers, that is, if the default printer driver allows these settings to be changed (some do not).

Another important point to make about using this method is that you're still printing through the Windows Print Manager. This means you cannot send printer control codes directly to the printer using this method.

? and ?? commands

The ? and ?? commands send output to the current active window or the printer or both, depending on some settings. If SET CONSOLE is ON, output is sent to the window. If SET PRINTER is ON, output is sent to the printer. If both settings are ON, output is sent to both devices.

The ? command sends a carriage return / line feed prior to sending the specified expression. In other words, whatever expression follows the ? is displayed or printed on the *next* line. This means you have to remember that the last line you print is still sitting in the buffer until you send another carriage return / line feed or a page eject. The ?? command sends the specified expression without preceding it with a carriage return / life feed. The following code and sample output demonstrates the difference between the ? and ?? commands.

```
*-----------------
* Here's the code
*-----------------

*-- Turn on the printer
SET CONSOLE OFF
SET PRINTER ON

*-- Print with ?
? 'Line 1 - Hello World'
? 'Line 2 - Fox Rocks!'
?

*-- Print with ??
?? 'Line 3 - Hello World'
?? 'Line 4 - Fox Rocks!'

*-- Eject the paper
EJECT

*-- Turn off the printer
SET PRINTER OFF
SET CONSOLE ON

*-------------------
* Here's the output
*-------------------

Line 1 - Hello World
Line 2 - Fox Rocks!
Line 3 - Hello WorldLine 4 - Fox Rocks!
```

Pay particular attention to the last line of the output and notice that when I used the ?? command, the output of both lines 3 and 4 was streamed together on the same line. This is because the ?? command does not issue any carriage returns or line feeds. You should also notice that there is no blank line between line 2 and line 3, even though a ? command was executed after printing line 2. The reason is that the ? sends the line feed first, then the print head stays on that line waiting to print. When the ?? command was issued to print line 3, it printed at the current print head position, which was the line immediately following line 2.

The ? and ?? commands have additional clauses that make it easy to control the appearance and position of the text.

PICTURE and FUNCTION
The PICTURE and FUNCTION clauses can be used to format the output. You can use the same codes available in the Format Property and InputMask Property (see the VFP Help for details about these properties).

VnWidth
You can use the V as a special FUNCTION option to force word-wrap within a specified width. For example, the following code and sample output shows how word-wrap intelligently wraps text between words when possible. Keep in mind, however, that the text is not wrapped at every tenth character. Instead, the wrapping occurs at the point where 10 characters of *average* width for the current font would occur. So depending on your font, you may see different results than shown below.

```
? "This will wrap about every 10 characters" FUNCTION "V10"


*-------
* OUTPUT
*-------
This will
wrap
about
every 10
character
s
```

AT nColumn
The AT clause lets you specify a certain column position for printing. You can combine multiple AT clauses on the same line as shown in the following example.

```
? "Hello" AT 10, "Goodbye" AT 20, "Fox Rocks" AT 40


*-------
* OUTPUT
*-------
         Hello     Goodbye              Fox Rocks
```

FONT cFontName [, nFontSize]

The FONT clause lets you specify a particular font. If the font size is not given, a 10-point font is used.

STYLE cFontStyle

The STYLE clause lets you specify characteristics such as Bold, Italic, and so on.

??? command

The ??? command sends output directly to the printer, bypassing the printer driver. You can use it to send plain text as well as special printer control codes. For example, the following code sends three lines of text, each formatted differently, to my Panasonic dot matrix printer.

```
SET Console OFF
SET Printer on
??? CHR(27) + 'P' + "Line 1 - PICA" + CHR(13) + CHR(10)
??? CHR(27) + 'M' + "Line 2 - ELITE" + CHR(13) + CHR(10)
??? CHR(27) + 'g' + "Line 3 - MICRON" + CHR(13) + CHR(10)
SET Printer off
SET Console ON
```

Unfortunately, what also happens is an EJECT gets sent to the printer as soon as the first ??? command is executed. Some of the utilities described later in the next section, "Freeware utilities," can be used to overcome the limitations of using the ?, ??, ???, and @...SAY commands.

Freeware utilities

The FoxPro community is one of the best—and most unique—development communities I've seen in my 20 years of developing software. The members of this community are always willing to share ideas and dedicate their time to helping others. Many developers even go so far as to give away their code for free. It's not often you see developers put hours and hours of their time into a project and then give it away (or trade it for a beer at a local pub or a case of Mountain Dew at a conference).

This section is dedicated to these special people who have done just that. The next time you see these guys at a conference, be sure to buy them a drink and say thanks!

FRX2Word by John Koziol

The FRX2Word utility is a class that lets you specify an existing Visual FoxPro report definition (FRX) and output it to Word, an RTF file, or an HTML file. This is an excellent means for e-mailing your existing Visual FoxPro reports. It's also an excellent tool to use when you need to manipulate or tweak a report. Use FRX2Word to send it to Word and then use Automation to manipulate the Word document.

Be advised, though, that an exact duplicate of your report is not created, so it shouldn't be used when you need perfect alignment of each and every object. Because of the differences between Word and VFP Reports there's no way to create a pixel-by-pixel, exact representation. However, the output in Word is very similar, and certainly the intent and content of the report is well represented in the Word document.

FRX2Word can be downloaded from the Universal Thread using ID 1226 (www.universalthread.com).

Visual GenRepoX by Markus Egger

Visual GenRepoX is a utility that extends the native Visual FoxPro Report Writer. Some of the most important features of this utility are as follows:

- **Object-based reports:** Reports can be treated as objects, which can be subclassed or dropped on any other container object.

- **Contained classes:** You can create classes for each object you want to use on a report.

- **Embedded functions, methods, and events:** This allows you to code functions and methods directly in the report. It also supports events such as GotFocus(), LostFocus(), and Error().

- **Enhanced layout:** You can dynamically change layout features such as font, color, and many other layout properties.

- **Multiple Detail bands:** The *Detail Extender* allows you to create multiple Detail bands, which are simple subreports.

- **Field Sorter:** The user can select which fields to print and in which order.

- **Top-Level previews:** The optional top-level preview overcomes the tricky antics you have to do in VFP when viewing reports in top-level forms.

- **New Driver Model:** You can easily write drivers and add-ons with Visual GenRepoX.

Visual GenRepoX can be downloaded from EPS's website at www.eps-software.com.

RAS PrintFRX by Rick Schummer

The Report Code Lister provides a printout of the details inside of the Report Form metadata file. First, you're prompted for an FRX (report metadata table), and then the program evaluates the different objects. The listing presents the code (methods in the Data Environment or fields on the report) and attributes for each object as well as some other details stored inside the metadata. The objects are listed in the order they appear on the report from left to right and top to bottom.

This tool was designed to allow teams to review code developed by other developers on their team. The output is presented in a report preview so the developer can check it out before printing the report to the printer. There is no tool in Visual FoxPro that lists code stored in the report form, so this utility is a must-have.

RAS PrintFRX can be downloaded from the Geeks and Gurus Web site at www.geeksandgurus.com.

VBPrinter by John Koziol

VBPrinter is an ActiveX control that allows precision control over printers not afforded by the native VFP functions. It allows the programmatic selection of paper bins, orientation, copies, paper size, and much more.

VBPrinter can be downloaded from the Universal Thread using ID 1103 (www.universalthread.com).

Direct Print by Ed Rauh

The Direct Print class writes streams directly to the Windows spooler, completely bypassing the GDI interface. It does not use the VFP printer assignment nor does it force normal Windows printer behaviors such as page resets and blank pages between jobs. It also provides for direct, uninterpreted spooling of files.

This class is available for download from the Universal Thread using ID 1498 (www.universalthread.com).

wwPDF by Rick Strahl

This class is a wrapper to the Adobe PDFWriter software. It allows the unattended creation of rich Adobe Acrobat documents that can be used over the Web. You can print VFP reports on the server, output to PDF, and send the results to a browser.

wwPDF can be downloaded from the West Wind Technologies Web site (www.west-wind.com). As with everything Rick offers, he has provided excellent documentation for this utility.

Epson POS Demo by Mark McCasland

Printing on receipt printers is not always easy. Mark has struggled through this difficulty and made his hard work available for the rest of us. He put together a class as an example of how to print receipts on an Epson receipt printer and integrate it with a cash drawer.

This POS Demo can be downloaded from the Universal Thread using ID 1494 (www.universalthread.com).

WinFax Demo by John Henn

Sending output to a fax server is not always easy, even with documentation and manuals. John has put together a short demo that sends any report to the WinFax printer. It allows you to specify all items such as fax number, company, person, and so on. It includes options for sending with or without a cover page as well as being able to specify the quality of the fax.

The WinFax demo can be downloaded form the Universal Thread using ID 1283 (www.universalthread.com).

Text Mode by Hilmar Zonneveld

This utility allows you to print in text mode for faster printing. You can create text files with the ? and ?? commands (or @...SAY) and then send printer codes along with the text file to the printer. This class emulates many features of the Visual FoxPro Report Writer.

This utility can be downloaded from the Universal Thread using ID 1533 (www.universalthread.com).

Raw Print by Ramon F. Jaquez

Raw Print is a class library that allows you to send data, including printer control codes, to a print queue in raw format. This utility provides an interface for printing from a file or memory variable. It also allows you to specify a document name to show in the print queue.

This utility is available for download from the Universal Thread using ID 1069 (www.universalthread.com).

Commercial Report Writers

Beside the Visual FoxPro Report Writer, there are several third-party reporting tools on the market that allow you to create reports from Visual FoxPro data. Some of these tools I've used personally and others I've just heard of through the VFP community. This section is not meant to evaluate each tool and give you a comparison or recommendation of which is the best tool. It's only meant to make you aware of what commercial reporting tools are currently out there.

Foxfire! Query and Report Writer

Foxfire!'s goal is to make queries and reporting a no-brainer for end users. A developer (this is you) can preload *Foxfire!*'s data dictionary and system tables with metadata from the application. Once loaded, creating queries, reports, spreadsheets, pivot tables, charts, and so on is ultra fast and doesn't require technical skills such as understanding joins, expressions, and group totals. The end users don't even have to lay out where the information goes on the report. *Foxfire!* does it all for them.

Contact Information

Micromega Systems
2 Fifer Ave, Ste. 120
Corte Madera, CA 94925
(415) 924-4700
www.micromegasystems.com

How *Foxfire!* works

Creating a report is as simple as picking which data items you want to see. *Foxfire!* figures out which tables the data resides in, figures out any joins necessary when multiple tables are involved, and systematically places the data items on the report. Of course, not all reports are this simple and *Foxfire!* has the ability to accommodate more complex reports, too.

Foxfire! presents a simple user interface that collects specifications for a report *Request* and then processes that *Request* when you click Run. It provides visual feedback throughout the specification process so users always know what to expect when they click Run. After specifying the report, *Foxfire!* generates a SQL statement, queries the tables (via Rushmore or ODBC), and stores the returned result set in a cursor or XML data stream. Next, it generates an FRX or an XSLT sheet from a template, and finally pumps the cursor or XML stream through the appropriate report-formatting engine to produce the results. Of course, this is a mild simplification—it can also create XLS and Pivot Tables, PDFs, *Web-readable* reports, and so on.

Extensible

Foxfire! was written with several hooks in place so it's extremely extensible. At each key phase of execution, the *Foxfire!* application calls FFCONFIG.PRG, passing a parameter indicating which phase it's at. This means you can put you own FoxPro code in FFCONFIG.PRG to alter the way it behaves. The FFCONFIG.PRG file is well documented and meticulously explains each of the variables you can alter to get different behavior. The whole concept of the FFCONFIG.PRG file is great because whenever *Foxfire!* releases a new version, you don't have redo your modifications. In fact, you don't even have to recompile their source code.

The FFCONFIG.PRG file has the following hooks in all versions of *Foxfire!*: Startup, Preference File Setup, Global Setup, Request Setup, Before SQL Generation, Before FRX Generation, After FRX Generation, Before Select, After Select, Before Report, After Output, Batch Builder Add, Batch Builder Run, and Cleanup.

In addition to the standard hooks, the Enterprise Edition offers the following hooks: Queue Job, New Server Record, Before Connection, After Connection, Before Disconnect, After Disconnect, and After User Login. And if all these hooks aren't enough, there are four more that are available for each individual request that is run: Before SQL Generation, Before Query, After Query, and After Output.

Future release

As of this writing, additional hooks for such features as Send Email, After Request Export, and Before Request Import are in the works and should be available by the time you read this. The last two refer to *Foxfire!*'s new ability to export report Requests and all related metadata to an XML data file, send that file to another machine (for example, at a remote user's site), and let them import the file so that a report you created can be passed to the end user.

As previously noted, *Foxfire!* is designed to be flexible. However, in its current form, it's not based on an object model or n-tier architecture. So you could say it implements state-of-the-art flexibility with a more *traditional* architecture. Since *Foxfire!* has been on the market nearly 10 years, the strength of this approach is that it's compatible with any version of FoxPro from 2.x, 3.0, 5.0, 6.0, and 7.0 and for all levels of developer, including those who haven't gotten a handle on dealing with COM components or who were scared off.

However, development never stops and by the time you read this, an object model and a COM component will be available that further extends *Foxfire!*. The *Foxfire!* object model allows users to register *add-ins* at specific time frames in a similar manner to the Class Browser. This extends *Foxfire!* further by allowing developers to enhance the interface, run additional validations and more, in combination with the existing hooks within FFCONFIG.PRG. The primary purpose of the object model and component is to enhance the non-visual interface to *Foxfire!* so developers can build reports behind the scenes. The existing hooks, accessible via the FFCONFIG, make it easy for developers to make changes, recompile the FFCONFIG, and then provide it to their end users.

The object model is designed so that developers can access virtually any piece of the *Foxfire!* metadata programmatically as well as create and run reports without the need to display an interface to the user.

Bottom line
Foxfire! is an excellent product to include in your application when you have end users who need to create their own reports—especially when the end users aren't technically savvy!

R&R Report Writer
The Xbase version of R&R Report Writer is a tool you can use to create reports from Visual FoxPro data. It uses the same *banded* concept as the Visual FoxPro Report Writer, but it has additional features. For example, R&R has *Scan Groups*, which allows you to create multiple Detail bands.

Contact Information

Liveware Publishing, Inc.
1406 Society Drive
Claymont, DE 19703
(800) 936-6202
www.livewarepub.com

Design-time features
R&R allows you to define relations between tables without having to know SQL. It even gives you more power by allowing you more flexibility when no matching records are found. You can also define relationships between non-normalized tables requiring multiple fields to find a match. It also has a *FlexLink* feature that lets you define an index that can be created on-the-fly.

R&R has Report Variables that can be used for calculated fields, total fields, user-defined fields, and parameter fields. The *Parameter* fields option is used to prompt the user for values in the report. These parameters can be used on the report as well as in the query conditions and other calculated fields. This feature offers a lot of flexibility to the user.

Output
R&R has several output options including previewing the report on the screen, printing it on the printer, and exporting the report to another format. The export options include Excel, HTML, text files, and other DBF files. You can also create a PDF file (without having Adobe Acrobat) or send the report via e-mail. When using the e-mail feature, you can use the *Burst* feature to distribute each group of a report to a different recipient (however, to use the *Burst* feature, the end user must have the R&R Report Designer).

Dictionary Editor
R&R has a Dictionary Editor you can use to create a table of *friendly* names for the end user. You can also hide certain fields from the users. While this makes life easier for the end user, because the Dictionary Editor does not access FoxPro's DBC you, as the developer, will have to spend a lot of time re-entering information.

Report Librarian
Users can manage reports easily with the Report Librarian tool. This tool handles keeping track of all the reports along with a description for each report. To run a report, the user chooses a report from the Catalog and the Report Librarian figures out where the report is and how it should be run. The Librarian can be used to define user security and determine which reports a particular user can run.

Rapid Runner
The Rapid Runner utility lets you define a batch of reports to run. The batch can be set to run at a specific time or can be run on demand. You can also define certain settings, such as the number of copies to print. And keep in mind, a batch can consist of one report or many reports.

Result Set Browser
The Result Set Browser feature allows the user to drill-down and see the data used to generate a report. The user can sort or group the data on any field on the screen. The look and feel of this feature is similar to VFP's browse command.

Bottom line
Finding a Report Writer that's extremely simple for non-technical end users, yet still maintains enough power to keep developers happy is not easy. R&R Report Writer does a great job at keeping both ends of the spectrum happy.

Crystal Reports
Crystal Reports is a powerful Report Writer that works with many software development languages, including Visual FoxPro. You can create simple reports as well as complex reports and provide a variety of output options to your users. However, it's not a Report Writer that can easily be learned by non-technical people, so it's not a feature that you can add to your application and expect most users to immediately use.

Contact Information

> Crystal Decisions
> (a division of Seagate Technology)
> (800) 877-2340
> www.crystaldecisions.com

Accessing the data
Crystal Reports can access the data a number of different ways. You can use ADO with an OLE DB provider. You can use ODBC, which gives you the ability to access data of numerous sources. This also gives you the ability to access VFP views defined in a database container via ODBC. You can also access FoxPro 2.x tables directly, which is by far the fastest method. When using Visual FoxPro, you can prepare a cursor and then use the COPY TO … FOX2X command to copy the data to a FoxPro 2.x table.

Feature-rich

Crystal Reports includes many features that are not available in the Visual FoxPro Report Writer. One of the most popular features is subreports, which allows you to embed reports inside of other reports. Another popular feature is Crystal's drill-down feature, which allows users to drill-down a particular piece of information into more detailed information when viewing on the screen. Crystal also offers graphing, hyperlinks, running totals, and much more with little effort on your part.

Output

Crystal Reports has many different forms of output. Besides the typical printing and viewing options, you can send output to Excel, Word, RTF, HTML, XML, DHTML, and PDF formats. You can also produce Web reports that can be called from ASP pages.

Leverage your Visual FoxPro code

The Report Designer Component of Crystal Reports is a COM-based tool that gives you great control over the report layout and formatting. You can use Visual FoxPro code to manipulate the report layout and the data as the report is being run. You can even alter the format, such as colors, fonts, and so on.

The Report Viewer is an object model that gives you complete control of how the Crystal Reports Viewer appears and functions. You can use Visual FoxPro code to access its properties and methods.

You can access your VFP functions directly from within Crystal Reports, which gives you the ability to use your existing library of code and business rules without having to duplicate them. And with VFP 7.0's Event Binding, you can tap into events that are exposed by Crystal Reports with little effort.

Bottom line

Crystal Reports is an excellent tool for creating reports when you need more power than is offered by the Visual FoxPro Report Writer. It's also very useful when you have end users who are technically savvy and want to create their own reports.

Virtual Print Engine

Virtual Print Engine (VPE) is a tool for creating reports in numerous development languages. It allows you to generate dynamic output by calling functions within your application. Information can be placed anywhere on the report and can include text, graphics, pictures, and even MICR bar codes. This tool is excellent for creating complex forms requiring exact positioning of information, as it's completely printer-independent.

Contact Information

> Ideal Software
> www.idealsoftware.com

How it works

Through code, you *build* the report on-the-fly. You scan through the data and place objects on the report by calling functions and passing the vertical and horizontal position, which is measured in millimeters with a resolution of up to 0.1mm. You don't feed any SQL queries or directly access the data with VFP—it's database-independent. You access the FoxPro data through FoxPro code, build a string, and call a function to *write* that string on the report.

With VPE you have complete control over the font, pen size, bolding, and other characteristics of each and every item you print on the report. This means you can dynamically change the characteristics as you print each item. And because you build the entire report before printing, you can jump around the page and even jump around between pages while building the report. Once you have built the entire report, you output it with a simple function call. Thousands of pages can be generated and printed with VPE and it's amazingly fast.

Output

VPE can send a report to the screen, the printer, and many other export options. A report can be exported to common image file formats as well as e-mail and Internet/intranet publishing of reports.

Reports created by VPE can include drawings, graphs, charts, images, and diagrams. Images of all the common types can be imported. You can even print bar codes, Rich Text Format, and MICR codes.

Leverage your FoxPro knowledge

With some Report Writers, you need to learn *their* language for formatting. With VPE, you use a language you're familiar with, such as Visual FoxPro. There's no need to learn a new way to deal with if/else/then structures, calculations, string manipulation, and so on. Just use Visual FoxPro to build the strings you want, format them the way you want, and simply call a method to write the string on the page.

You have total control over the layout of the document at all times. You're not tied down to static layouts and banding technologies. You can even change the layout at will.

Bottom line

Virtual Print Engine is an outstanding tool when you need complete and finite control over building an entire report. You can virtually build a report exactly as you want it and are not locked into *bands* or other constraints of many Report Writers. This, however, is not a tool to be used by end users.

Other forms of output

In today's *electronic* society, people expect more than just printed reports. End users want to be able to e-mail documents back and forth, download documents from the Web, and all kinds of other options. This usually involves one or more third-party products.

PDF

The term PDF stands for *Portable Document Format* and refers to a generic standard widely used to transmit reports and documents. A PDF file retains all the formatting, graphics, fonts, and so on in the PDF file and is completely self-contained. A PDF file can be electronically transmitted, e-mailed, posted on the Web, and passed around among many different people. The person who creates the PDF file needs to have a full-blown application capable of creating the correctly formatted file. The person receiving and viewing the document only needs to have a *reader* version of the application, which is usually available free of charge from many sites on the Internet.

There are several different PDF applications available and they vary greatly in price and features. You need to evaluate your situation to determine which PDF application is right for you. Some products require full-blown licenses for every user who creates PDF files and other products offer site licensing. Three of the commonly used PDF applications are Adobe Acrobat, Amyuni, and ActivePDF.

Adobe Acrobat

It's probably a fair statement to say that Adobe Acrobat is the most popular application used to create PDF files. When the full-blown version is installed on your machine, it installs a special printer driver that creates the PDF file. All your application needs to do is select the Adobe PDF Printer Driver as the printer and that's it. The printer driver captures your output and creates the PDF file that anyone can read with the appropriate reader utility. Of course, I've oversimplified this because there are many additional options and features available.

One drawback to using Adobe Acrobat is that it does not come cheap. It's one of the more expensive PDF applications available. Each user who needs to create PDF files must have a licensed copy of Adobe Acrobat.

Contact Information

Adobe Systems, Inc.
www.adobe.com

Amyuni

The Amyuni product is often a much more reasonably priced option, especially for commercial applications or situations where many people need to create PDF files. There are several different versions available, each with different abilities. Check out their Web site for more information.

Contact Information

AMYUNI Technologies
www.amyuni.com

ActivePDF

ActivePDF Server is the first and only product available for Windows NT/2000/XP engineered to run concurrent, simultaneous jobs under stress. With tuning parameters for both single and multiprocessor machines, ActivePDF Server is licensed per server, so you can harness the power of large multi-CPU machines without paying a premium.

Contact Information

ActivePDF
www.activepdf.com

Automation (Word and Excel)

Word processors and spreadsheets are great for presenting information and, in some cases, these tools do a much better job than the VFP Report Writer. Automation is a way to programmatically *drive* these tools right from Visual FoxPro. If you've had the pleasure to see a demonstration of JFast, you know exactly what I'm talking about. JFast is a logistics application developed for the U.S. Department of Defense and it uses Automation to spew out tons of Word documents, PowerPoint slides, and so on—all with the touch of a button.

Another advantage to using Microsoft Word or Excel is that these software applications are very commonplace. This means you can create a Word document, e-mail it to a co-worker across the country, and let them modify it and then e-mail it back to you. It also means you can save huge printing costs if you use Word or Excel to create large documents, distribute the documents through e-mail or as downloadable files on your Web site, and let the recipient be the one to print the document.

Explaining how to implement Automation from within Visual FoxPro is way beyond the scope of this book. However, I highly recommend that you read *Microsoft Office Automation with Visual FoxPro* by Tamar E. Granor and Della Martin, edited by Ted Roche (Hentzenwerke Publishing). This book explains how to automate the most common Microsoft Office products, such as Word, Excel, PowerPoint, and Outlook. It's a *must-have* for anyone learning Automation.

The end!

I hate to say goodbye, but it's that time. I've enjoyed writing this book and I'm very glad to have had the opportunity to give back to the Fox Community. I truly hope you learned a lot from this book and found it worthwhile. I also hope that you'll come away from this book with a greater passion for writing reports of the highest caliber for all your applications.

Fox Rocks!

Index